W9-BKR-157

Academic Labor Markets and Careers

The Stanford Series on Education and Public Policy

General Editor: Professor Henry M. Levin, School of Education, Stanford University

The purpose of this series is to address major issues of educational policy as they affect and are affected by political, social and economic issues. It focusses on both the consequences of education for economic, political and social outcomes as well as the influences of the economics, political and social climate on education. It is particularly concerned with addressing major educational issues and challenges within this framework, and a special effort is made to evaluate the various educational alternatives on the policy agenda or to develop new ones that might address the educational challenges before us. All of the volumes are to be based upon original research and/or competent syntheses of the available research on a topic.

School Days, Rule Days: The Legalization and Regulation of Education *Edited by David L. Kirp, University of California, Berkeley, and Donald N. Jensen, Stanford University.*

The Incompetent Teacher: The Challenge and the Response *Edwin M. Bridges, Stanford University.*

The Future Impact of Technology on Work and Education *Edited by Gerald Burke, Monash University, Australia and Russ W. Rumberger, University of California, Santa Barbara.*

Comparing Public and Private Schools: Volume 1 Institutions and Organizations *Edited by Thomas James, Brown University and Henry M. Levin, Stanford University.*

Comparing Public and Private Schools: Volume 2 School Achievement *Edited by Edward H. Haertel, Stanford University, Thomas James, Brown University and Henry M. Levin, Stanford University.*

Managing Educational Excellence *Thomas B. Timar, Harvard Graduate School of Education and David L. Kirp, University of California, Berkeley.*

The Changing Idea of a Teachers' Union *Charles T. Kerchner, Claremont Graduate School, California and Douglas Mitchell, University of Calfornia.*

Academic Labor Markets and Careers *Edited by David W. Breneman, Kalamazoo College and Ted I.K. Youn, State University of New York at Albany.*

Academic Labor Markets and Careers

Edited by

David W. Breneman
Kalamazoo College

and

Ted I. K. Youn
State University of New York at Albany

 The Falmer Press
(A member of the Taylor & Francis Group)
New York · Philadelphia · London

UK   The Falmer Press, Falmer House, Barcombe, Lewes,
      East Sussex, BN8 5DL

USA   The Falmer Press, Taylor & Francis Inc., 242 Cherry Street,
      Philadelphia, PA 19106-1906

First published 1988

British Library Cataloguing in Publication Data

Academic labor markets and careers
  1. United States. Academic personnel.
Careers
I. Breneman, David W. II. Youn, Ted I. K.
331.11'91378111'0973
  ISBN 1-85000-414-5
  ISBN 1-85000-415-3 Pbk

Jacket design by Caroline Archer

Typeset in 11/13 Bembo by
David John Services Ltd, Slough, Berkshire

Printed and bound in Great Britain by
Redwood Burn Limited, Trowbridge, Wiltshire

Contents

Dedicated to the Memory of Allan M. Cartter

Acknowledgements

We are grateful for the ideas and insights of many leading scholars who shed light on complex problems of higher education. They include the late Allan M. Cartter, Burton R. Clark, Howard Bowen, Clark Kerr, Stephen P. Dresch and Richard B. Freeman.

Maribel Gray patiently typed and re-typed our chapters over many months. Fran Lewis carefully edited the entire manuscript. We want to express our thanks to Christine Cox, the Falmer Press editor for shepherding the manuscript through the publishing process. Finally, we thank Henry M. Levin, General Editor of the Stanford Series on Education and Public Policy for his continuing encouragement and support.

Introduction

David W. Breneman and Ted I. K. Youn

The chapters in this volume examine academic careers and academic labor markets in American higher education from a perspective based on both economic reasoning and sociological analysis. Considering the substantial overlap in subject matter – labor mobility and labor turnover problems, for example – we are struck with the impoverished level of interchange between economics and sociology. This book, therefore, in the larger context, draws upon research common to both fields.

In social science, two traditions dominate recent research on careers and labor markets: status attainment research in sociology and human capital theory in economics. The sociological literature on status attainment, marked by Blau and Duncan's *American Occupational Structure* (1967) and the substantial body of literature that followed, examines careers as individual achievements measured by education, occupation and income. Careers are studied in the context of the socio-economic life cycle and successive linkages among family background, ability, school performance, and occupational attainment.

Meanwhile, the economic theory of human capital (Becker, 1964; Mincer, 1971; Rees and Shultz, 1970) demonstrates how endowments such as ability and schooling translate into returns in the market place, and how an individual's attributes and background generate educational, occupational, and economic attainment at different points in the life course. Typical examples of economic analyses of academic markets can be seen in work by Freeman (1971, 1976, 1980), Scott (1979), Hansen *et al.* (1978) and Ashenfelter and Mooney (1968).

These traditions are similar in their exclusive attention to the individual as the unit of analysis and in their neglect of social structure and institutional arrangements which might affect careers and labor markets. Career outcomes are explained by personal factors; institutional and structural aspects of organizations and work are largely ignored.

During the 1970s, however, challenges to these dominant perspectives emerged among a group of institutional theorists in economics (Doeringer and Piore, 1971; Alchian and Demsetz, 1972; Reich, Gordon, and Edwards, 1973; Williamson, 1975) and sociological researchers whose central concern is the broader problem of social organization of labor markets (Stolzenberg, 1975; Spilerman, 1977; Kalleberg and Sorensen, 1970; Berg, 1981).

These researchers argue that labor markets are characterized by complexities that go beyond simple supply and demand schedules. Instead, supply and demand depend on a variety of institutional and structural arrangements. There is not a single labor market but many overlapping ones, so that one worker's prospects depend on the behavior of participants in related markets. The concept of 'internal labor market' is developed as an administrative unit that can occur within a single organization or can span establishments such as trade unions and professional associations. Administrative rules and procedures determine the price and allocation of labor for jobs. 'Internal labor markets' contain good jobs, stable employment, and promotional hierarchies. 'External labor markets', on the other hand, price and allocate labor on the basis of direct economic relationship such as competition.

In sociology, both organizational and career theories are well-developed, but often neither of these theories relates to labor markets. Careers occur within an organization or over a population of organizations, and organizations do form internal labor markets. In economics, the theory of the firm is used to explain the nature of markets and uncertainty associated with markets. The idea of organizational structure that may affect careers and mobility in conjunction with the firm, however, is largely ignored. Exchanges between the two groups – the institutionalists in economics and the structuralist sociologists whose research relates to the social organization of labor markets – have opened up some useful insights about research problems in academic labor markets.

The essays included in this book, therefore, argue that the nature of labor market outcomes may be explained by the nature of academic organizations. They find the basic problems of academic markets are largely rooted in the structure of American higher education. Economic incentives for academic careers are embedded in the structure of academic organizations. Individual positions in the organization and the nature of the organization affect incentives and

career mobility. Thus, organizations cause both labor market stratification and segmentation.

The American higher education system consists of differentiated
sets of academic organizations. Large research and graduate-training
institutions are in the market for different kinds of services than are
institutions that emphasize undergraduate teaching. Institutions that
provide only two years of college training look for still another range
of skills in their prospective employees. Even among undergraduate
teaching colleges a wide range of variations exists, depending upon
whether the institutions are small or large, public or private, secular
or religious, regional or national.

The relative emphasis on the two major organizational tasks –
educating students and advancing knowledge through research and
training – differs widely among academic organizations as well.
Universities that stress research tend to place less emphasis on
teaching, while colleges that emphasize teaching tend to require
greater teaching loads. Even though these are not independent
phenomena, organizations with an emphasis on research offer a
distinctively different form of reward. Different organizations, therefore, impinge differentially on academic career outcomes.

Because it is a critical review of several dominant perspectives in
academic careers and markets among social science studies, the review
essay by Youn (chapter 1) is a natural extension of this section. The
chapter suggests that broader threads from studies over the past
several decades may be traced and, further, may be generalized.

The study by McGinnis and Long (chapter 2) focuses on entrance
into academic careers. After examining a national sample of biochemists in America, they conclude that, as a structural property of
the mobility system, institutional prestige (or its correlates, such as
sponsorship or mentorship) determines entrance into academic
careers. Other factors such as predoctoral productivity or even
pecuniary incentives play a less significant role, particularly among
academic scientists. Stratification in science or academia is an
important force that affects not only entry into careers but also future
scholarly productivity.

McGinnis and Long unravel their argument that stratification in
science or in the academic system, at best, works contrary to the
principle of universalism. Young scientists in academic markets are
allocated according to pedigrees, such as the prestige of doctoral
institution and mentorship. The rewards of academic positions are
better explained by the prestige of doctoral institution than by
predoctoral productivity.

This study, indeed, raises a number of broader questions about the nature of the academic organizations that foster science and new knowledge. Even though the notion of academic markets *per se* is not introduced, the effects of competition among Ph.D. institutions, as well as location, on career mobility are measured and analyzed. These factors, together with other variables such as race and sex, contribute to segmentation of markets for academic scientists.

If the relationship between the prestige of academic origin and the first job constitutes an entry to a career, how does this entry to the first job from doctoral training affect one's subsequent career mobility? This question follows naturally from the problem of entrance analyzed by McGinnis and Long (chapter 2) and Long *et al.* (1979).

The study by Youn and Zelterman (chapter 3) demonstrates the effects of doctoral prestige over one's career cycle. While the Youn-Zelterman paper supports the basic argument presented by McGinnis and Long, the picture it presents is more complex, particularly if one looks at academics from different fields employed by a wide range of institutions, unlike elite scientists in biochemistry who are often employed in university departments.

The American system of higher education consists of some 3,400 institutions with varying degrees of differentiation. The relative emphasis on two major tasks – educating students and advancing knowledge through research – differs widely among academic organizations. Each institution forms its own internal labor market, and individual career success depends on the workings of internal labor markets. Each organization's norms and requirements impinge on career outcomes of academics. Thus, the entry portal to either a research or a teaching career line does, in fact, matter to career outcomes.

While mobility operates within or among research organizations and from research to teaching positions, it is much less common for an academic to move from teaching to a research position. This study also demonstrates that academic career outcomes are a function of academic fields, with each field demonstrating distinctive allocative processes.

Further, the study by Rosenfeld and Jones (chapter 4) concludes that the employment structure of academia in different institutions is important in explaining labor mobility and labor turnover. The type of academic position held in the employment ladder, whether tenure track or non-tenure track, part-time or full-time, explains the propensity to move from academic careers to other types of employment. In other words, holding a tenure-track position decreases the rate of movement to other types of career, while holding a non-tenured position increases the propensity to move to non-academic positions. Mobility in general depends on the nature of labor markets – the primary market for tenure track positions, which is competitive, and the secondary market for non-tenure track positions, which is less competitive and often administratively determined.

While effects of the employment structure are analyzed by Rosenfeld and Jones, firm-specific or organization-specific labor markets often breed part-time employees. Tuckman and Pickerill (chapter 5) note that little has been written about part-time academics and their careers. Many economic and demographic characteristics of part-time academics are surprising. For example, the majority of part-timers are male academics, even though the growth rate for female part-timers in academia exceeds that for male part-timers. The authors propose an insightful taxonomy of part-timers in higher education, which is, indeed, more sociological in describing the motivations and psychosocial characteristics of this group. Part-timers are subject not only to a different career ladder and a different set of administrative allocative rules, but the social organization of part-time academics is distinct from full-time academics, as well. This paper raises a number of important institutional policy questions as well as public policy issues in a period of declining academic labor markets.

Almost every organization is concerned with rewarding quality performance by its employees. The practice of granting merit increases, however, may be difficult to understand. W. Lee Hansen's argument (chapter 6) begins with the recognition of differentiated missions among institutions of higher education. Here, the distinction between research and teaching becomes more salient. Different institutions do not evaluate their output in the same way. Thus, the issue of merit pay raises a complex problem regarding the sociology of wages in academia. To an extent, merit is viewed within the context of academic markets. Hansen implies that discretely structured labor markets work and that these different markets segment research and teaching roles among different institutions. Finally, merit plays a greater role in non-unionized institutions than those that engage in collective bargaining. Collective bargaining agreements may allocate only a small proportion of salary increases for merit.

How have academic salary differences between males and females changed over the recent period of increasingly slack labor markets? After controlling for differences in scholarly productivity, experience, academic field, and employing institution, Barbezat's study (chapter

7) suggests that the proportionate salary advantage of male academics, while declining, is still substantial.

After a decade of affirmative action in higher education, the proportion of the observed wage differences attributable to gender discrimination declined between 1968 and 1977. Women faculty, however, are still more likely to be employed at a college with a lower quality rating and are less likely to be associated with leading research universities.

Increased specialization in scientific experiments and increased demand by industry for expert knowledge have resulted in the emergence of a new form of entrepreneurship among faculty in universities. Based on interviews with twenty-eight scientists in a major private university, Maurice Richter examines how the careers of some scientists are affected by rewards that often conflict with the traditional norms of academic research (chapter 8). The growth of firms started by faculty suggests the intriguing notion that the entrepreneurial scientist will have a distinctively different academic career. The essay implies some important public policy questions regarding problems of the distinctive nature of experimental research in science and careers among scientists.

Michael McPherson and Gordon Winston (chapter 9) examine the institution of academic tenure, and argue that it is not simply a constraint imposed on universities to protect faculty jobs or to ensure academic freedom, but is an integral part of the way universities function. The tenure system is a response to the highly specialized nature of academic work and to the long training such work requires. The system is rooted in the basic nature of the higher education organization.

In the concluding essay (chapter 10), economist and college president David W. Breneman sets these essays into their historical and policy context, interprets their findings, and suggests new directions for future research by economists, sociologists, and others concerned with the development of higher education.

References

Alchian, A. and Demsetz, H. (1972). 'Production, information cost, and economic organization'. *American Economic Review*, 62, No. 5 Dec., 777–795.

Ashenfelter, O. and Mooney, D.L. (1968) 'Graduate education, ability and earnings'. *Review of Economics and Statistics*, Vol. 49, No. 1.

Becker, G.S. (1964) *Human Capital*, New York: Columbia University Press.

Berg, Ivar (Ed.) (1981) *Sociological Perspectives on Labor Markets*, New York: Academic Press.

Blau, P.M. and Duncan, O.D. (1967) *The American Occupational Structure*, New York: Wiley.

Doeringer, P. and Piore, M. (1971) *Internal Labor Markets and Manpower Analysis*, Lexington, Mass: Heath.

Freeman, R.B. (1971) *The Market for College-Trained Manpower: A Study in the Economics of Career Choice*. Cambridge: Harvard University Press.

Freeman, R.B. (1976) *The Overeducated American*, New York: Academic Press.

Freeman, R.B. (1980) 'The job market for college faculty', in M. McPherson (Ed.) *The Demand for New Faculty in Science and Engineering*, 85–134, Washington, D.C.: National Academy of Sciences.

Hansen, W.L., Weisbrod, B.A., and Strauss, R.P. (1978) 'Modeling the Earnings and Research Productivity of Academic Economists', *Journal of Political Economy*, 86, 729–741.

Kalleberg, A.L. and Sorensen, A.B. (1979) 'The Sociology of Labor Markets', *Annual Review of Sociology*, 5, 351–379.

Long, J.S., Allison, P.D., and McGinnis, R. (1979) 'Entrance into the Academic Career', *American Sociological Review*, 44, 889–908.

Mincer, J. (1979) *Schooling, Age and Earnings*, New York: National Bureau of Economics Research.

Rees, A. and Schultz, C. (1970) *Workers and Wages in an Urban Labor Market*, Chicago: University of Chicago Press.

Reich, M., Gordon, D.M., and Edwards, R.C. (1973) 'Dual Labor Markets: A Theory of Labor Market Segmentation', *American Economic Review*, 63, 359–365.

Scott, C.E. (1979) 'The Market for Ph.D. Economists: The Academic Sector', *American Economic Review*, 137–141.

Stolzenberg, R.M. (1975) 'Occupations, Labor Markets and the Process of Wage Attainments', *American Sociological Review*, 40, 645–665.

Williamson, O.E. (1975) *Markets and Hierarchies: Analysis and Anti-Trust Implications*, New York: Free Press.

1 Studies of Academic Markets and Careers: An Historical Review

Ted I. K. Youn

In the social sciences, studies of careers and labor markets are fragmented in the sense that the various disciplines have adopted different units of analysis and have employed different levels of generality and abstraction. Indeed, with few exceptions, social science research has not developed any explicit conceptualizations that relate careers, organizations, and labor markets. For example, studies by social psychologists have generally treated careers either with the trait-factor assumption (Super, 1957; Holland, 1973) or the notion of life-stage (Kohn and Schooler, 1973, 1978; Miller *et al.*, 1979). Psychological analyses of careers and life stages have been concerned only with elements of individual choice and personal development over life cycles. By themselves, these psychological perspectives do not help us understand the nature of interaction between academic careers and academic labor markets.

On the other hand, treatments of careers and markets in economics and sociology have been dominated by the economic theory of human capital and the theory of status attainment and stratification in sociology. Both explain careers and income attainments in terms of individual endowments, ability, and investments. These studies, however, have consistently ignored social structures and other institutional arrangements that shape job histories and workers' mobility. For the most part, these two traditions have treated careers as a matter of individual achievement. Positional inequality formed in careers generated by firms, organizations, industries, and sectors of the economy has been largely excluded in such studies.

Historically, research by social scientists on academic careers and academic labor markets is also fragmentary. Reviewing several major developments, we can organize these studies into five general categories:

1. Fixed-Coefficient Model
2. Human Capital Theory
3. Screening Model
4. Institutional Ascription Model
5. Structural Perspectives on Careers and Market

This chapter reviews these perspectives critically and offers several propositions that seem to govern labor markets and careers in academia.

To classify perspectives and traditions of thought may over-simplify reality, but classification aids exposition of the different lines of research. Our remarks on trends and preoccupations of recent work through these categories represents an organization of convenience. The classification does not necessarily imply mutually exclusive approaches to analysis.

1. Fixed-coefficient Model

One of the earliest comprehensive attempts to analyze trends in academic employment was carried out by Allan Cartter (1965, 1966, 1971, 1972, 1974, 1976). His studies were based on a demographic trend analysis, emphasizing the changing size of a national cohort of college-age students in predicting future doctoral outputs and require-ments for Ph.D.s in colleges and universities.

Cartter's approach relied on linear extrapolation from current enrollment levels in higher education. He established that both supply of, and demand for, Ph.D.s bulged in the 1960s when the baby boom population enrolled in universities and colleges (Cartter, 1974). For a decade, academic demand for Ph.D.s exceeded supply and wages rose accordingly. Expanding undergraduate enrollments generated demand for faculty, which in turn encouraged larger graduate enrollments.

Yet, the process is more complex. According to Cartter, while a relatively fixed portion of university-aged students will become Ph.D.s, they concentrate in certain fields in response to market trends. Cartter argued that graduate and professional students commonly continue their education beyond the B.A. only if they are interested in specific fields, and if there are jobs available in those fields. At advanced levels of education, the market-responsive model clears the market and, therefore, serves as a successful mechanism for balancing supply and demand.

As to factors that determine the level of demand for Ph.D.s, Cartter argued that demand for Ph.D.s is also generated by research and development (R&D) expenditures, but that greater demand comes from colleges and universities that need Ph.D.s to teach under-graduates, whose numbers are determined largely by demographic trends. The technology of education generates a coefficient that, when coupled with the size of undergraduate enrollments in a given period, determines the demand for Ph.D.s. Thus, Cartter's method is generally called a 'fixed-coefficient' model.

Cartter's approach deals with the total production of Ph.D.s, but not the number in a given field or set of institutions. Furthermore, his studies fail to present a systematic analysis of how the academic occupational structure works over time or how Ph.D.s move from one part of the system to another. Cartter describes the shifting relationship between supply and demand, but does not adequately explain mobility of Ph.D.s among different institutional groups.

Although not central to his work, some of Cartter's assumptions are relevant to our inquiry. In *Ph.D.s and the Academic Labor Market* (1976), Cartter hypothesized the following relationship between graduate schools and employing institutions:

> First, it is evident that Ph.D.s from any given class of graduate schools tend to spread themselves out through the job market, but principally in a downward direction. Second, regardless of the labor market tightness or looseness, institutions tend to hire from the same array of graduate schools. Hiring probably is influenced by school ties of present faculty and personal relationships built up over the years between graduate depart-ments and employing institutions.

Cartter then proposed that:

> One way of viewing the difference in market effects is to measure the proportion of doctorate recipients who take first teaching positions in institutions of superior, equal, or lower prestige than their Ph.D. granting school.

What Cartter refers to as 'market effects' on the production and employment of Ph.D.s in different institutional sectors raises the question of whether the rate of movement over time from Ph.D. producing to employing institutions is constant or changing.

What might be the relationship between 'market effects' and different academic careers? If institutions tend to hire from the same array of graduate schools, what are the consequences of such 'self-recruitment' processes? While Cártter's studies represent an attempt to generalize trends in academic employment, several fundamental questions related to academic careers and labor markets are not adequately treated in his work.

2. The Human Capital Theory

In economics, the theory of human capital explains how endowments such as ability and schooling translate into returns in the market place, and how an individual's attributes and background generate educational, occupational, and economic attainment at different points in the life course (Becker, 1964; Mincer, 1971; Rees and Schultz, 1970). Early economic studies of academic professionals examined effects of graduate education on earnings (Ashenfelter and Mooney, 1968; Hansen, 1967; Ashenfelter, 1969; Scott, 1979; Ault *et al.*, 1979) or the extent of relationships between scholarly productivity and earnings (Hansen *et al.*, 1978; Tuckman and Hagemann, 1976).

These economic analyses generally conclude that returns to graduate education are fairly substantial, even though there are differences among fields. Scholarly productivity does explain earnings among academics. While an additional unit of research productivity yields a substantial increase in annual earnings, such earnings tend to decline over the career cycle at an increased rate with the number of publications (Hansen *et al.*, 1978).

A more comprehensive economic analysis of academic markets is carried out by Richard Freeman (1971, 1975, 1976). Freeman explains post-war developments in the high-level manpower market on the basis of price. The theory of price, according to Freeman, explains the allocation of resources by means of wage differentials. In his analysis of research physicists (1975), Freeman treats the labor market as national, with a demand for physicists from universities, government, and private industry, and a supply consisting of young men and women, each choosing a particular career and committing to as many as ten years of university training. Labor markets for the highly educated differ from other job markets in the length of training time required. This training lag means that the supply of Ph.D.s cannot adjust quickly to changes in demand, which results in a 'boom and bust cobweb cycle phenomenon'. A shortage of graduates results in higher wages, which attracts an increased number of graduate students into the field. Five or more years later these students enter the market, driving wages downward and reducing the quality of placements, causing prospective students to shift into different fields. Enrollments drop, and five years later there is again a supply shortage, leading to a wage increase.

Empirically, Freeman (1971) demonstrates that, beginning in 1968, there was a student decline in the growth rate of first-year graduate enrollments in all fields. At that time, he writes, there was an unemployment rate of 5.4 per cent, out-mobility of 3.0 per cent for scientists under 30 years of age, and a drastic decline in the growth rate of starting salaries for Ph.D. scientists. Freeman argues that from 1964 to 1969, starting salaries for physicists showed an annual increase (controlling for inflation) of 11.7 per cent, and from 1969 to 1973 the physics labor market witnessed a significant fall in real wages. By 1970 physics earnings over male professional earnings dropped to the level of 1954, the pre-Sputnik era. Physics seems to have experienced the most dramatic decline in the science and engineering fields, but the pattern applies to all fields.

Changes in the academic labor market are described, therefore, in a recursive model that balances wages, enrollments, and Ph.D. outputs over time. Freeman's model assumes that changes in total science Ph.D. output are a function of changes in R&D expenditures, GNP, previous Ph.D. cohort size, starting salaries in alternative occupations, stipends, and the stock of available baccalaureates.

Freeman's approach is widely accepted by economists, although several methodological and conceptual arguments disputing his findings are raised by James P. Smith and Finis Welch (1978). Economic studies in the neo-classical tradition have long focused on the workings of the labor market and the interplay between supply and demand to determine individual earnings. Put another way, economic analysis of the labor market posits a marginal productivity theory of distribution which assumes perfect competition, complete knowledge, and rationality. Therefore, theory points to wage competition as the force driving the labor market. This particular theory also assumes that people come into the labor market with definite, pre-existing skills, or lack of skills, and that they compete against one another on the basis of wages. According to this theory, education and training are crucial because they generate the skills that people bring into the market. A highly skilled person raises his productivity and, thus, his earnings.

While there have been emerging criticisms of human capital models from radical and Marxist economic theorists who challenged this orthodox theory from the perspective of historically-rooted class based conflicts between workers and employers (Bowles and Gintis, 1975; Marglin, 1976), sociologists have challenged human capital models with different conclusions. While human capital theory posits that labor markets offer open opportunity and workers' wages are largely a function of ability, education, and training, sociologists regard wages as heavily constrained by institutional inflexibility rather than by the skills and merit of the worker. The prevailing economic analysis usually ignores institutional structures and occupation as intervening variables (Berg, 1981). For sociologists, occupations are the key to understanding earnings or other workings of the labor market. The forces that determine an individual's occupational attainment affect earnings (Granovetter, 1981). Structural properties such as rigid career ladders and early career attainments are imposed by the nature of the occupation.

The influence of occupational categories is most apparent in measuring career mobility between occupations. Occupational segmentation generates relatively impermeable barriers to mobility between different occupational boundaries (Tolbert, 1982).

In a way, occupational categories are analogous to an array of institutions that are differentially ranked in the academic system. In other words, the logic used to determine occupational segmentation between professional, managerial and manual work is similar to the logic that discretely separates academic research work at elite research institutions from teaching at two-year or technical institutions. Thus, there are relatively impermeable barriers between research and teaching sectors. While the rate of mobility between these sectors may be facilitated in early career periods, later career mobility among academics may be constrained by institutional barriers (Youn, 1981).

Sociological critics do not deny that an individual's ability, skills, and personal characteristics are important in determining one's success and failure. But they also argue that ideologies vary from one institutional setting to another, and institutional structures of occupation and work organizations contribute to the persistence of inequality among workers. The general idea of institutional sorting and the notion of occupational impediments to workers' mobility have led to an alternative perspective to human capital theory, the 'job-competition' model.

3. The Screening or 'Job Competition' Model

This approach is almost a direct antithesis to the theory of marginal productivity of distribution which is postulated by the theory of human capital. It argues that labor markets are rarely competitive and that institutional impediments create market imperfections (Reder, 1955; Berg, 1971). Contrary to the conventional theory of marginal productivity, alternative distributional mechanisms must be introduced, based on market imperfections that actually exist.

The institutional screening model or 'job competition' model has also been called 'credentialism' or 'queuing' theory, involving the idea of 'vestibules' in the labor market. The central idea is that a given degree or field is valuable because of the advantage it offers in a job market where training is differentiated in terms of 'quality' (Niland, 1972; Stiglitz, 1975).

Proponents of the screening model (Niland, 1972; Adkins, 1974; Moffat, 1976) argue that social factors, such as institutional prestige, or organizational location, induce higher aspirations in the college-going population and hence determine enrollment and outputs in graduate education.

Screening model advocates argue that jobs are also differentiated according to their quality and attractiveness, regardless of the current labor market situation. Change in the demand for higher education would lead to job-shifting among Ph.D.s – that is, some less-qualified Ph.D.s would be absorbed into new types of jobs, such as two-year college teaching. In effect this would upgrade the credentials required for certain occupations (Thurow, 1972, 1975, 1976). Since it emphasizes an upgrading of credentials, this approach can be characterized as 'job competition', in which Ph.D.s are placed in a queue based largely upon the quality of their education.

According to this approach, the prestige and resources of a field and a particular graduate department would determine its appeal to students, who believe that high-prestige degrees will help them obtain better jobs. A Ph.D. student with a high-prestige education would merely displace another student with less desirable institutional origins from a job for which the latter may be equally qualified (Niland, 1972).

Advocates of the 'job-competition' theory, in contrast to the orthodox 'wage-competition' theory, argue that: (1) the number and type of job slots are *technologically determined*; (2) the workers' skills and their wages are nearly irrelevant in determining the number and type of job positions actually filled; (3) wages are, in fact, claimed to be rigid, and 'queues' of workers at relatively fixed wages constitute the supply of labor; and (4) hiring employers use screening devices based on the attractiveness of individual workers.

Based on this theory, several relevant conclusions can be drawn on the general state of academic markets and higher education in America. First, the distribution of academic job opportunities is determined partly by the character of technological progress, which generates specific jobs in certain proportions. Society's demands for certain types of knowledge, as well as technical changes since World War II, have profoundly affected research-oriented personnel in univerisites. The post-Sputnik upsurge of scientific development and public policy changes brought a massive change in institutions of higher education.

Second, institutional habits and customs influence academic wage rates. Wages are generally inflexible in entry-level academic jobs. Thus, skills, ability, and other qualifications for a given job will have a minimal effect on wages. Academic jobs are segmented by a variety of institutional factors. Thus, academic workers, by and large, seem to operate in *labor markets* that offer different working conditions, different opportunities, and different institutional norms to govern incentives.

In the 'wage competition' model, according to Thurow, wages fluctuate in the short-run to clear the market, while in the long-run, wage changes precipitate shifts in supply and demand curves. In the case of the 'job competition' model, Thurow contends, changes in hiring standards and required training help to clear markets. Only after a substantial period of disequilibrium in relative wages, do changes occur. If we follow the 'job competition' model, the academic labor market can clear its disequilibrium by inducing more credential requirements (Ph.D. requirements) and additional (postdoctoral) training.

Finally, in Ph.D. labor markets, supply is constituted by the 'queue' of highly trained workers. An individual's job prospects are determined by his relative position in the academic labor queue (i.e., prestige of the Ph.D.-granting institution) or labeling of individuals (Stiglitz, 1975) and distribution of job opportunities in academic labor markets. As Thurow observes, the most preferred workers (Ph.D.s from the most prestigious institutions, in this case) get the best institutional offers. These preferred workers may receive wages that are not related to their productivity but to the rank order of their institutional positions (Lazear and Rosen, 1981). In this context, an academic job is best thought of as 'a lifetime sequence of jobs rather

than as a specific job with a specific employer with specific skills'
(Thurow, 1975), and the basic allocative process depends on institutional screening.

4. Institutional Ascription Model

Several sociological studies of scientists' careers in academic markets
analyze the relationship between scientific productivity and institutional prestige (departmental prestige). Although they differ in
research design, data, measures of scientific or scholarly productivity,
and measures of institutional prestige and location, these studies
consistently report a positive relationship between scientific productivity and departmental prestige (Caplow and McGee, 1958; Berelson,
1960; Crane, 1965, 1970; Hargens and Hagstrom, 1967; Hagstrom and
Hargens, 1968; Hargens, 1969; Cole and Cole, 1973).

In reviewing major studies in the field, we find two explanations
for the relationship between institutional position and productivity.
One suggests that more prestigious departments select more productive scientists for their faculties; that is to say, productivity is causally
prior to institutional position. The alternative proposes that being at a
more prestigious department or institution facilitates greater productivity.

The first argument is promulgated by Storer (1966) and Cole and
Cole (1973), whose studies are based on Merton's notion of the
normative structure of the social system of science. Merton argues
that science is governed by norms of universalism, according to which
careers are determined by scientific achievement (1973). Studies by
Hargens and Hagstrom (1967), Storer (1966), and Cole and Cole
(1973) show that a scientist's productivity has as strong an effect on
academic appointment as does the ranking of the scientist's doctoral
department.

Taking the second position, Diana Crane's study (1970) concludes that the prestige of one's doctorate has more influence on being
selected by a prestigious position than productivity does. 'Despite the
system's normative commitment to universalistic criteria', she argues,
'they are not utilized in practice', suggesting that ascriptive rules may
explain the academic reward system. Recent studies by J.S. Long
(1978), Long *et al.* (1979), Long and McGinnis (1981), and B. Reskin
(1979) support Crane's thesis. Long's careful analysis of careers in
biochemistry challenges the contention that academic positions are
allocated exclusively or largely on the basis of scientific productivity.
The study by Long and his colleagues (1979) finds that the effect of
departmental location on individual productivity is strong, while the

effect of productivity on the allocation of academic positions is weak. The prestige of a scientist's first teaching position is influenced by ascriptive processes or particularistic rules. Doctoral prestige has the strongest impact on the prestige of first position, even though it may have a smaller impact on future productivity. Pre-employment productivity among scientists has little impact on the prestige of the first position. Furthermore, the study finds that the effect of departmental prestige on productivity increases steadily over time.

As the debate over achievement vs. ascription goes on, Reskin (1979) introduces another source of ascriptive effects. Her work is concerned primarily with the influence of sponsorship on students' careers. She concludes that – in the academic stratification system – ascriptive rules play an important role. (The institutional versions of ascriptive rules are the prestige of doctoral origins and the first job, and the notion of sponsorship). Sponsorship by eminent scientists and scholars at the initial career stage furthers the later careers of academic scientists. Reskin concludes that institutional ascription, not achievement, explains successful careers.

Several points are employed by the institutional ascription model. First, studies in this vein conclude that academic or scientific career mobility does not resemble an open-opportunity model. The central argument is similar to the basic point made by advocates of 'the job competition model' that institutional factors screen workers. The point is different from the 'job competition' or 'screening model', where the initial screening is solely emphasized. Academic job seekers' decisions are constrained by social structural attributes such as doctoral prestige, the prestige of hiring department, the eminence of sponsorship, and the nature of the hiring organization. The academic stratification system does not promote a perfectly competitive system where individual members are valued on the basis of universalism. Social factors that determine career mobility in academia are more particularistic.

Secondly, the location of initial job has an important effect on future success. The prestige of first career position is determined largely by the prestige of the graduate institution. Even pre-employment productivity has little impact on the location of first job.

While these studies aid understanding of the theoretical problems of academic stratification, they are concerned only with elite academic scientists in particular fields. They ignore problems faced by academics who are recruited by teaching institutions or other organizations in the system of higher education. The ascription model presents an argument that institutional rules continue to breed inequality of opportunity in the system.

Does the extent of ascription increase as job market conditions change? In tighter markets, do ascriptive aspects of the allocative process predominate? As Reskin suggests (1979), these questions need to be further explored.

5. The Structural Perspective on Careers and Labor Markets

In the mid-1970s the growing interest among social scientists in problems of social inequality and poverty led to a radical perspective on the nature of labor markets (Gordon, 1972; Doeringer and Piore, 1971; Harrison, 1972; Reich *et al.*, 1973; Rumberger and Carnoy, 1980; Bluestone, 1968).

While the conventional status attainment theory and the neo-classical theory of human capital treat social inequality as evidence of differences among individuals in terms of endowments possessed and returns expected in the marketplace, the emerging structural perspective focuses on the larger structural and institutional mechanisms that might cause inequality among social positions (Kerr, 1954; Kalleberg and Sorensen, 1979; Tolbert *et al.*, 1980; Baron, 1984; Stolzenberg, 1975; Spilerman, 1977). One such structural mechanism is the organization, or firm, which relates to the complex nature of labor markets.

Jobs may fall in one of two discretely related labor markets – internal or external. Internal labor markets impose administrative rules and procedures which determine the allocation of labor for jobs, while external markets allocate labor to jobs on the basis of direct economic relationships, such as competition. Hence, the dual labor market hypothesis explains differences among individuals and social inequality in a social system.

The dual labor market hypothesis has led to useful exchanges between labor economics and sociological analyses of occupations. A career is no longer viewed as merely a matter of individual achievement. Depending on a person's location in the job ladder, career opportunities are set beyond personal control. The extent of labor market segmentation shapes career outcomes (Kalleberg and Sorensen, 1979). Hence, structurally-formed career lines are created and maintained by labor market complexities (Spilerman, 1977).

Important contributions arising from the exchanges between sociological studies and radical economic literature in the mid-1970s include the knowledge that social structure and institutional arrangements shape careers and an understanding of how labor markets interact with careers.

Yet, in social science research, substantial disagreements exist on the conceptualization and measurement of sectors and labor markets (see Baron and Bielby, 1980, for the debates). Some say that the structuralist perspective, and radical economic theory, ignore the role of personal factors and individual choice in careers and attainments (see Cain's discussion – Cain, 1976). Nevertheless, some basic propositions set out by structuralists and radical/institutional economists are useful in understanding the nature of academic careers and their relationship to academic labor markets. The individual choice model pursued by orthodox economic studies falls far short of explaining the more institutional and sectoral characteristics of academic labor markets, as well as complex interactions between academic organizations (firms) and labor markets.

Having thus reviewed a number of perspectives, we can make some generalizations regarding the nature of academic markets and careers. Even though they represent areas of controversy, these propositions should help us understand the nature of academic careers and labor markets.

Effects of Academic Organizations

Exchanges between structuralist sociologists and institutional/radical economists that explore social inequality have resulted in a shift in emphasis to organizations from the attributes of individual workers. To structuralists, the organization is the key explanatory variable. In explaining the nature of both markets and careers through the division of labor among different organizations in a social system, structuralists argue that organizations distribute different rewards and opportunities to employees. Each organization or firm generates its own internal labor market and imposes a bureaucratic mode of social control over employees, while external labor markets regulate competition among various organizations or firms.

An extension of this emphasis on organizations or firms may apply to the American higher educational system, which consists of more than 3,400 organizations (universities and colleges) of varying degrees of differentiation. American universities and colleges are differentiated on the basis of distinct, though not independent, tasks: educating students and advancing knowledge through research.

Rewards provided by organizations that emphasize research are distinctively different than those provided by teaching institutions.

While empirical studies of academic ascription represent the bulk of stratification literature, critics of the stratification literature argue that structural effects of organizations have been largely ignored. Much of the rich detail of academic organizations – universities and colleges – that explains division of labor, job ladders, and other hierarchies and forms of authority, has been omitted.

Colleges that emphasize teaching require heavier teaching loads than research universities. Thus, the institutions impinge on career outcomes and opportunities by generating inequality and stratification.

While Cartter's analysis fails to incorporate the nature of academic organizations into the fixed-coefficient model, orthodox economic studies typically argue that variables under investigation – income and prices, for example – are worth studying on their own merits. The model Freeman proposes assumes that either unmeasured variables, such as organizational or other institutional attributes, do not change, or that they change without affecting the expected values of the variables under investigation (see also Cain, 1976, for a similar argument). Indeed, this controversy renders the issue more empirical than theoretical.

The 'job-competition' model of the screening perspective recognizes that the types of job positions available affect labor market outcomes. Thus, an academic's location may affect his or her chance of being attractive in different types of markets. The screening model fails to indicate, however, that organizations impinge on labor market outcomes. Instead, emphasis is placed on the individual who competes in a queue for various academic jobs (Niland, 1972).

Studies by sociologists of science recognize the importance of institutional ascription, such as the prestige of the graduate department, and its effects on mobility and career success. These studies are often involved in case studies of elite scientists and, therefore, are unable to incorporate a more dynamic relationship between different organizations and their markets.

Structuralists argue – euphemistically referring to 'Bringing the Firm Back In' (Baron and Bielby, 1980) – that organizational structure and process should be incorporated into empirical analysis of economic segmentation and work. Yet, models for measuring structural effects on individual attainment or covariation among occupational industrial characteristics remain incomplete.

Effects of Labor Market Outcomes

The multiple nature of academic markets raises the possibility of multiple career outcomes. Multiple markets are likely to generate multiple careers among academics (Rosenfeld and Jones, 1987; Youn, 1981). Sectors that affect mobility and career success have distinct boundaries; an academic can presumably start out in a research career and either continue there or move to an academic teaching career (Rosenfeld, 1984; Youn and Zelterman, 1986), but may not be able to move from a teaching career to a research career at a major research institution (Parsons and Platt, 1973).

The differences in emphasis on organizational tasks – educating students and acquiring knowledge through research – illustrate how discretely different labor markets may be operating in higher education. Yet, the degree of differentiation among academic organizations (Clark, 1983) and the degree of differentiation among academic fields suggest a multiplicity of overlapping markets – markets for research and graduate training organizations, for undergraduate teaching, for two-year college teaching (Brown, 1967; Clark, 1966; Cohen and Brawer, 1977), and so on (Smelser and Content, 1980; Youn and Zelterman, 1986; Youn, 1981). The relatively impermeable barriers to mobility from teaching and research or vice versa seem to exist. Among academic fields, constraints for mobility may be even greater between and among academic fields.

Thus, one can empirically conclude that the persistence of inequality of opportunity among academics exists in the educational system and ask whether relative differences in the distribution of earnings may continue.

Generally, orthodox economists find little empirical support for the dual-market theories of status or mobility and most empirical analyses produce no support for immobility across the occupational boundaries (Leigh, 1976). Freeman's studies argue that there is evidence of interfield mobility as well as intersectoral mobility when the level of demand decreases, while no inter-organizational mobility has been suggested. The screening model suggests little or no evidence of immobility among jobs or sectors in academia.

Structuralists and institutional economists have long argued for generalization about outcomes of labor markets, namely evidence of immobility between different segments (Tolbert *et al.*, 1980; Bluestone, 1968; Osterman, 1975).

Effects of Entry Job on Career

Several studies (Long, 1978; Long *et al.*, 1979; Reskin, 1979) argue that in the academic stratification system, the prestige of an academic's first job depends a great deal on institutional ascription, such as doctoral prestige and doctoral sponsorship. Even pre-doctoral productivity matters little to career success. Even though the point was not stressed by Long *et al.* (1979) and Reskin (1979), an extension of this argument may raise the possibility that an initial position in an organization may be subject to internal labor markets. That is, entry jobs or entry portals lead into predetermined progression systems. Entering a research career may affect the option of continuing in research or moving to a teaching career, but entering a teaching career may not easily lead to a research career (Youn and Zelterman, 1986). There exists also the possibility of two career lines (Spilerman, 1977), which are age-specific and organization-specific. The research career line may be susceptible to the level of scholarly productivity and other institutionalized norms, while success in a teaching career line may be determined by organizational and bureaucratic rules.

Between research and teaching roles, organizations are ordered in terms of prestige. Institutions stressing research are the most prestigious, while two-year colleges have the least status.

The natural question is: if organizational prestige is subject to allocative rules, how much can career attainment depend on individual attainments and earnings?

Effects of Temporal Changes on Labor Markets and Careers

Expansion and slowdown in the growth of the educational system over time raise important questions regarding the nature of career mobility and structural changes in markets (Freeman, 1975; Smelser, 1974; Smelser and Content, 1980; Youn, 1981; Youn, 1984). When the level of demand changes substantially, a number of complex institutional changes may follow (Breneman, 1976; Smith and Karlesky, 1977). For instance, the change from a period of expansion to a period of decline may increase the effect of the institutional ascription and, thus, increase the probability of downward distribution. Change from one period to another may increase the degree of market rigidity, and with it the degree of career segmentation between research and teaching. The study by Smelser and Content (1980) points out that the social structural base of the academic profession that is created in a period of expansion of higher education becomes a source of inflexibility when the phase gives way to a period of reduced growth. The structural base that a growing system needed to perform to capacity then faces a problem of excess capacity. This problem, in turn, raises a number of other questions.

Does the change over time affect shifts in demand among disciplines? Does the temporal change widen salary differential among fields? These questions may not be answered by relying solely on either the structuralist model or the individual choice model. Individual earnings and career attainment in higher education may be explained by social and economic changes which explain the shift in demand and supply. There are a number of provocative research issues that remain.

Finally, the implications of temporal change in higher education introduce a number of intriguing research questions regarding the political dimension of the academic recruitment system and the role of political actors in making decisions in academic organizations (Smelser, 1974; Trow, 1974).

This chapter has reviewed the empirical corpus of literature on the subject matter and summarized several propositions that help to explain the relationship between academic labor markets and academic careers. Even though our basic intent is not to argue that one perspective or theory should replace the others, this chapter suggests that there is evidence of the shift toward more structural explanations in studies of academic careers and markets.

Our examination of the levels and units of analysis adopted by different approaches implies areas where different perspectives may overlap or diverge. This chapter argues that research on academic careers and markets would benefit by incorporating the organizational structure and process of higher education into empirical analyses of economic segmentation and work. Much of our problem, therefore, is rooted in ways in which higher education is organized and functions.

References

Adkins, D.L. (1974). 'The American educated labor force: An empirical look at theories of its formation and composition', in M. Gordon (Ed.), *Higher Education and the Labor Market*, New York: McGraw-Hill.

Ashenfelter, O. (1969). 'Some evidence on the private returns to graduate education', *Southern Economics Journal*, 30 (3).

Ashenfelter, O., and Mooney, D. (1968). 'Graduate education, ability and earnings', *Review of Economics and Statistics*, 49 (1).

Ault, D.E., Rutman, G., and Stevenson, T. (1979). 'Mobility in the labor market for academic economists', *American Economic Review*, 69: 148–153.

Baron, J.N. (1984). 'Organizational perspectives on stratification', *Annual Review of Sociology*, 10: 37–69.

Baron, J.N., and Bielby, W. (1980). 'Bringing the firms back in: Stratification, segmentation, and the organization of work', *American Sociological Review*, 45: 737–765.

Becker, S. (1964). *Human Capital*, New York: Columbia University Press.

Berg, I. (1971). *Education and Jobs: The Great Training Robbery*, Boston: Beacon Press.

Berg, I. (1981). *Sociological Perspectives on Labor Markets*, New York: Academic Press.

Berelson, B. (1960). *Graduate Education in US* New York: McGraw-Hill.

Bluestone, B. (1968). 'The tripartite economy: Labor markets and the working poor', *Poverty and Human Resources* (July/August), pp. 2–41.

Bowles, S., and Gintis, H. (1975). *Schooling in Capitalist America*, New York: Basic Books.

Breneman, D.W. (1977). 'Effects of recent trends in graduate education on university research capability in physics, chemistry, and mathematics', in B.L. Smith and J. Karlesky (Eds), *The State of Academic Science*, New York: Change Press.

Brown, D.G. (1967). *The Mobile Professors*, Washington, D.C.: American Council on Education.

Cain, G. (1976). 'The challenge of segmented labor market theories of orthodox theory: A survey', *Journal of Economic Literature* (December), 1215–1257.

Caplow, T., and McGee, R. (1958). *The Academic Marketplace*, Garden City: Doubleday.

Cartter, A.M. (1965). 'The supply and demand of college teachers', *American Statistical Association*, Social Statistics Proceedings, pp. 70–80.

Cartter, A.M. (1966). *An Assessment of Quality in Education*, Washington, D.C.: American Council on Education.

Cartter, A.M. (1971). 'Scientific manpower trends for 1970–1980', *Science*, 172: 132–140.

Cartter, A.M. (1972). 'Faculty needs and resources in American higher education', *Annals of the American Academy of Science*, 404: 71–87.

Cartter, A.M. (1974). 'The academic labor market', in M.S. Gordon (Ed.), *Higher Education and the Labor Market*, New York: McGraw-Hill.

Cartter, A.M. (1976). *Ph.D.s and the Academic Labor Market*, New York: McGraw-Hill.

Clark, B.R. (1966). 'The mass college', in Vollmer and Mills (Eds), *Professionalization*, New York: Prentice-Hall.

Clark, B.R. (1983) *The Higher Education System: Academic Organization in Cross-National Perspective*, Berkeley: University of California Press.

Cohen, A., and Brawer, F. (1977). *A Two-Year College Instructor Today*, New York: Praeger Press.

Cole, J.R., and Cole, S. (1973). *Social Stratification in Science*, Chicago: University of Chicago Press.

Cole, S. and Cole, J.R. (1967). 'Scientific output and recognition: A study in the operation of the reward system in science', *American Sociological Review*, 32: 377–390.

Crane, D. (1965). 'Scientists at major and minor universities: A study in productivity and recognition', *American Sociological Review*, 30: 699–714.

Crane, D. (1970). 'The academic marketplace revisited', *American Journal of Sociology*, 7: 953–964.

Doeringer, P.B., and Piore, M.J. (1971). *Internal Labor Markets and Manpower Analysis*, Lexington, MA: Heath Lexington Books.

Freeman, R.B. (1971). *The Market for College-Trained Manpower: A Study in the Economics of Career Choice*, Cambridge: Harvard University Press.

Freeman, R.B. (1975). 'Supply and salary adjustments to the changing science manpower market: Physics, 1948–73', *American Economic Review*, 65: 27–39.

Freeman, R.B. (1976). *The Overeducated American*, New York: Academic Press.

Gordon, D.M. (1972). *Theories of Poverty and Unemployment: Orthodox, Radical and Dual Labor Market Perspectives*, Lexington, MA: Heath Lexington Books.

Granovetter, M. (1981). 'Toward a sociological theory of income differences', in I. Berg (Ed.), *Sociological Perspectives on Labor Markets*, New York: Academic Press.

Hagstrom, W.O., and Hargens, L.L. (1968). 'Mobility theory in the sociology of science', paper presented at the Cornell Conference on Human Mobility, Ithaca 9.68.

Hansen, W.L. (1967). 'The economics of scientific and engineering manpower', *Journal of Human Resources*, II (Spring, 1967), 191–215.

Hansen, W.L., Weisbrod, B.A., and Strauss, R.P. (1978). 'Modeling the earnings and research productivity of academic economists', *Journal of Political Economy*, 86: 729–741.

Hargens, L.L. (1969). 'Patterns of mobility of new Ph.D.s among American academic institutions', *Sociology of Education*, 42: 18–37.

Hargens, L.L., and Hagstrom, W.O. (1967). 'Sponsored and contest mobility of American academic scientists', *Sociology of Education*, 40: 24–38.

Harrison, B. (1972). *Education, Training and the Urban Ghetto*, Baltimore: Johns Hopkins University Press.

Holland, J.L. (1973). *Making Vocational Choices: A Theory of Careers*. Englewood Cliffs, NJ: Prentice-Hall.

Kalleberg, A.L., and Sorensen, A.B. (1979). 'The sociology of labor markets', in *Annual Review of Sociology*, Vol. 5, Alex Inkeles *et al.* (Eds), Palo Alto, CA.

Kerr, C. (1954). 'The Balkanization of labor markets', in E. Wright Bakke *et al.* (Eds), *Labor Mobility and Economic Opportunity*, Cambridge, MA: M.I.T. Press.

Kohn, M.L., and Schooler, C. (1973). 'Occupational experience and psychological functioning: An assessment of reciprocal effects', *American Sociological Review*, 38: 97–118.

Kohn, M.L., and Schooler, C. (1978). 'The reciprocal effects of substantive complexity of work and intellectual flexibility: A longitudinal assessment', *American Journal of Sociology*, 84: 24–52.

Lazear, E.P., and Rosen, S. (1981). 'Rank-order tournaments as optimum labor contracts', *Journal of Political Economy*, 89: 135–148.

Leigh, D.E. (1976). 'Occupational advancement in the late 1960s: An indirect test of the dual labor market hypothesis', *Journal of Human Resources* (Spring), 11: 155–171.

Long, J.S. (1978). 'Productivity and academic position in the scientific career', *American Sociological Review*, 43: 889–908.

Long, J.S., Allison, P.D., and McGinnis, R. (1979). 'Entrance into the academic career', *American Sociological Review*, 44: 816–830.

Long J.S., and McGinnis, R. (1981). 'Organizational context and scientific productivity', *American Sociological Review*, 46: 422–442.

Marglin, S.A. (1976). 'What do bosses do? The origins and functions of hierarchy in capitalist production', *Review of Radical Political Economy* (Summer) 60–112.

Merton, R.K. (1973). *The Sociology of Science*, Chicago: University of Chicago Press.

Miller, J., Schooler, C., Kohn, M., and Miller, K. (1979). 'Women and work: The psychological effects of occupational conditions', *American Journal of Sociology*, 85: 66–94.

Mincer, J. (1971). *Schooling, Age, and Earnings*, New York: National Bureau of Economic Research.

Moffat, L. 'Departmental prestige and doctoral production: An analysis of the structure of graduate education in physics from 1964 to 1972', unpublished doctoral dissertation, Cornell University, Ithaca.

National Board of Graduate Education (1975). *Outlook and Opportunities for Graduate Education*, Washington, D.C.

Niland, J.R. (1971). 'Allocation of Ph.D. manpower in the academic labor market', *Industrial Relations*, 2: 141–156.

Osterman, P. (1975). 'An empirical study of labor market segmentation', *Industrial Labor Relations review*, 28: 508–523.

Parsons, T., and Platt, G.M. (1973). *The American University*, Cambridge: Harvard University Press.

Reder, M.W. (1955). 'The theory of occupational wage differentials', *American Economic Review* (December), 45: 833–852.

Rees, A., and Shultz, G. (1970). *Workers and Wages in an Urban Labor Market*, Chicago: University of Chicago Press.

Reich, M. *et al.* (1973). 'A theory of labor market segmentation', *American Economic Review* (May), 62 (2): 359–365.

Reskin, B. (1979). 'Academic sponsorship and scientist careers', *Sociology of Education*, 52: 129–146.

Rosenfeld, R.A., and Jones, J.A. (1987). 'Institutional mobility among academics', *Sociology of Education*, 59: 212–226.

Rosenfeld, R.A. (1984). 'Academic career mobility for women and men psychologists', in V. Haas and C. Peiruci. (Eds). *Scientific and Engineering Professions*, Ann Arbor: University of Michigan Press.

Rumberger, R.W., and Carnoy, M. (1980). 'Segmentation in the US labor markets: Its effects on mobility and earnings of whites and blacks', *Cambridge Journal of Economics*, 4: 117–132.

Scott, C.D. (1979). 'The market for Ph.D. economists: The academic sector', *American Economic Review*, 69: 137–141.

Smelser, N.J. (1974). 'Growth, structural change, and conflict in California public higher education, 1950–70', in Smelser and Almond (Eds), *Public Higher Education in California*, Berkeley: University of California Press.

Smelser, N.J., and Content, R. (1980). *The Changing Academic Market: General Trends and a Berkeley Case Study*, Berkeley: University of California Press.

Smith, B.L.R., and Karlesky, J.J. (1977). *The State of Academic Science: The Universities in the Nation's Research Effort*, New York: Change Magazine Press.

Smith, J.P., and Welch, F. (1978). 'Overeducated American?'. Proceedings of the National Academy of Education, Volume 5, 49–83.

Spilerman, S. (1977). 'Careers, labor market structure and socioeconomic achievement', *American Journal of Sociology*, 83: 551–593.

Stiglitz, J.R. (1975). 'The theory of screening, education and the distribution of income', *American Economic Review*, 65: 315–342.

Stolzenberg, R.M. (1975). 'Occupations, labor markets and the process of wage attainments', *American Sociological Review*, 40: 645–665.

Storer, N.W. (1966). *The Social System of Science*, New York: Holt Rinehart and Winston.

Super, D.E. (1957). *The Psychology of Careers*. New York: Harper and Row.

Thurow, L.C. (1975). *Generating Inequality*, New York: Basic Books.

Thurow, L.C. (1976). 'Education and economic equality', *The Public Interest*, 28: 66–81.

Thurow, L.C., and Lucas, R.E.B. (1972). *The American Distribution of Income: A Structural Problem*, Joint Economic Committee Print, 92nd Congress, 2nd Session.

Tolbert, C.M. (1982). 'Industrial segmentation and mens' career mobility', *American Sociological Review*, 47: 457–476.

Tolbert, C.M. Patrick, M., and Beck, E.M. (1980). 'The structure of economic segmentation: A dual economy approach', *American Journal of Sociology*, 80: 1–10.

Trow, M. (1974). 'Problems in the transition from elite to mass higher education', *Policies for Higher Education*, Organization for Economic Cooperation and Development.

Tuckman, H., and Hagemann, R. (1976). 'An analysis of reward structure in two disciplines', *Journal of Higher Education*, 26–39.

Youn, T.I.K. (1981). 'The careers of young Ph.D.s: Temporal change and institutional effects', unpublished Ph.D. dissertation, Yale University.

Youn, T.I.K. (1984). 'Changing academic markets: Effects of the expansion and contraction of higher education', paper presented at the Annual Meeting of the American Sociological Association.

Youn, T.I.K., and Zelterman, D. (1986). 'Academic career mobility in multiple labor markets', Paper presented at the Annual Meeting of the American Sociological Association.

2 Entry into Academia: Effects of Stratification, Geography and Ecology

Robert McGinnis and J. Scott Long

Introduction

This paper has two purposes. First, it provides a brief summary of selected results of our research over the past decade into patterns of institutional stratification and their effects on the careers of scientists who are affiliated with the institutions. Our research strategy involves two distinct but interacting units of analysis: individual scientists and organizations.

Our second purpose is to present for the first time preliminary results of what may prove to be an important extension of our research. In it, we extend the concepts and measures of stratification to include those of geographic and ecological differentiation. In this way we are able to investigate the consequences of location not only in a vertical system of stratification, but also in a horizontal system that contains components such as distance, centrality, and isolation. We must emphasize the tentative and preliminary nature of the second set of results and the need for a great deal more refinement of both concepts and measures. Even so, the results seem to us to suggest a promising new line of analysis in the sociology of science.

Overview of the Academic Career

The Matthew Effect argues that unto those that have shall be given, and from those that have not shall be taken away (Merton, 1973 [1968]:445). The institutional version of the Matthew Effect argues that in systems of stratification it is easier for those who have resources to obtain additional resources than it is for those who do not (Merton, 1973 [1968]:457; Price, 1965). The application of this principle of cumulative advantage to the academic career implies that the success of a scientist in securing an initial tenure track position may be one of the most important factors determining the success of the scientist. Obtaining a position in a prestigious university is associated with receiving three resources that are valuable for a successful research career: time, money and knowledge (Zuckerman, 1970:246).

Time is gained with lighter teaching loads and more able support staffs. Money is in effect gained with the availability of better equipment and facilities. Knowledge is gained from the availability of stimulating colleagues. To the extent that these resources can be transformed into scientific productivity, that productivity can be used to secure even more resources to facilitate further scientific productivity. The significance of departmental location, independent of other factors, on later productivity has been demonstrated by Long (1978). In short, it is found that the advantages of one's initial job placement accumulate over the career. Given the lasting impact of auspicious beginnings, it is important to understand the process by which scientists are allocated to jobs in the stratification system of science.

The process of allocating scientists to positions is also of interest for examining the normative structure of science, and in particular, the extent to which the hiring process is based on universalistic criteria. If the institutionally sanctioned goal of science is the extension of certified knowledge (Merton, 1973 [1942]:267–85), and if jobs in more prestigious institutions are a form of reward or at least a scarce resource to be sought, the allocation of Ph.D.s to positions should be based on their scientific productivity.

This would be seen in the effects of a scientist's productivity prior to obtaining a job on the success of obtaining one that is prestigious. It can also be argued that prestigious departments hire those candidates who demonstrate the most potential, where potential would be assessed on the basis of the student's training. Scientists with eminent mentors and from prestigious departments could be considered better trained, and hence potentially more productive. Alternatively, positions could be allocated on the basis of particularistic influences operating through social ties. For example, Caplow and McGee (1958:110) argue that departments often choose candidates on the basis of their social ties to the hiring department. The effects of the mentor and the Ph.D. department may then be seen not as indications of a student's potential, but of who they know who knows influential people in prestigious departments.

There is evidence that all of these factors operate in the allocation of academic positions. While it is impossible to unambiguously assign the effect of the mentor and/or Ph.D. department as a universalistic effect operating through the better training and increased potential of the student or as a particularistic effect operating through the influence of social ties, it is possible to consider the new Ph.D.'s productivity as an indicator of his or her productivity. The failure of predoctoral productivity to influence the allocation of positions relative to the influence of less clearly universalistic factors suggests the operation of particularistic factors in science. Given the importance of the initial position on later productivity, this potential inequality is likely to be magnified as the career develops.

The specific process of determining the prestige of the first position and the effects on the later career is complex. In a series of earlier papers (Long, 1978; Long, Allison and McGinnis, 1979; Long and McGinnis, 1981; McGinnis, Allison and Long, 1982; Long and McGinnis, 1985) various aspects of this process have been analyzed in detail. These will be reviewed before presenting the extensions to those analyses that are new to this paper. The first process is that determining which scientists pursue postdoctoral study, generally in the form of a fellowship. Scientists who are not in an agricultural area, who are young and unmarried upon receipt of the Ph.D., and who come from prestigious departments studying under prestigious mentors are most likely to obtain fellowships. The predoctoral productivity of the scientist has no effect on obtaining a postdoctoral fellowship position.[1] The competition for a permanent position begins after the fellowship for those seeking additional training, and immediately upon the receipt of the degree for those who do not. The allocation of scientists among the organizational contexts including faculty position in a research university (the focus of this paper), teaching positions in non-research universities, industrial research positions, non-industrial research positions and administrative positions has a lasting impact on the career of the scientist. The most interesting findings for the purposes of this paper concern the determinants of faculty positions in research universities. The two strongest effects are having a postdoctoral fellowship and obtaining a degree from a non-agricultural department. The number of pre-doctoral publications and citations does not significantly differentiate faculty in research departments from any other organizational context. For those who become faculty in research departments, the factors determining the prestige of the department are reviewed in the beginning of the results section.

Factors influencing career productivity, as measured by publications and citations to them, can be classified into three types: the reinforcing effects of prior productivity, contextual effects, and effects of training. While the prestige of the doctoral or postdoctoral department or the eminence of the mentor, which might be considered effects of training, have the most significant effect on determining the context of employment (whether among organizational contexts or to the prestige of a given department), they have only minor effects on productivity later in the career. Thus, while characteristics of the mentor and Ph.D. department are significantly correlated with later productivity, these effects disappear after controlling for organizational or departmental context and earlier productivity. Conversely, the effects of predoctoral productivity, which were negligible on determining position, are the strongest factors influencing later productivity. The best predictor of a scientist's later productivity is his productivity during graduate training.[2] Finally, organizational context and departmental prestige have strong and statistically significant effects on later productivity.

Thus, understanding the factors determining the employment of an academic scientist are important for understanding his future success. To further this understanding, we have extended our analysis of the social processes that influence entry into research universities to include geographic and ecological aspects of the process.

Effects of Geography and Ecology on Entry into Academia

We have argued that a number of factors in the educational background of biochemists strongly influenced the paths that they took into their careers. We now suggest that yet another cluster of factors, those of geography and ecology, have similar influences on their career paths. By 'geography' we refer to one's location on north–south and east–west axes at a particular point in one's career. By 'ecology' we refer to that location relative to the location of other relevant objects such as employment opportunities.

The idea that one's spatial and relative locations have a bearing on subsequent career paths is not new. Perhaps the best studied of such effects is that of physical location at a point in the career on location at a subsequent point, with the move itself being referred to as geographic mobility. It is well known that there is friction in distance. If a move is observed it is more likely to be short than long. Thus, where one ends up in a geographic move is strongly influenced by where one starts. But it is also known that both the probability of making a move and its length are positively associated with level of education (Ladinsky, 1967; Lichter, 1982).

One might extrapolate from the observed association between education and geographic mobility to conclude that, among the most highly educated – doctoral scientists in particular – such mobility should be approximately perfect, that location of destination should be nearly independent of location of origin. Such, however, is not the case. Hargens (1969), for example, in a study of career moves of a set of scientists, showed that inter-regional moves were far fewer than would have been expected under the assumption of perfect mobility. Thus, the friction of distance is a force that influences the geographic mobility of doctoral scientists as well as of most others.

For this reason, we introduce geography in the form of latitude and longitude into our analysis. The measurements are for the institutions from which our scientists received their baccalaureate or doctoral degrees, at which they did postdoctoral study, and where they were employed as faculty members. These measures permit us to derive the distance travelled in various career moves, as from the place of final professional training to that of first faculty employment. These geographic measures, in turn, permit us to examine the hypothesis that the location of the origin of a career move influences the location of its destination.

Closely related to the geography of academia is the concept of academic ecology.[3] The ideas developed here – especially those of academic centrality and competition – are rooted in the perspective of organizational ecology as developed by Hannan and Freeman (1977). For a recent statement that more fully develops the concept of organizational competition, see Hannan (1986). We must note, however, that our static analyses of academic organizations bear little resemblance to the differential equation models that characterize this perspective. Moreover, our motivation in this paper is not to examine academic organizations as a population *per se*, but rather as a set of environments in which some scientists conduct their careers. To get a better sense of this idea, consider two scientists emerging from their training and onto the job market. Suppose that one has just finished her postdoctoral training at Harvard and the other his doctoral degree at the University of Alabama in Tuscaloosa. We have argued that differences in their academic backgrounds will strongly differentiate their first steps into careers.[4] But heretofore we have not considered another difference that could be equally important: their relative distances from resources such as employment opportunities and personal contacts with potential employers. On the face of it, the one emerging from Cambridge is far more central to opportunities than is the one from Tuscaloosa. It is not difficult to imagine that this difference in centrality could differentiate their career paths quite aside from their personal and academic differences. But there is another side to this coin: coupled with the force of centrality is that of competition. Just as there are more academic employment opportunities for scientists in the Boston metropolitan area than there are in all of Alabama, there are also far more competitors for the resources. We will take account of both the concepts of centrality (which we will call 'potential' for reasons discussed in the following section) and competition in an analysis of ecological influences on entry into academia and on several aspects of academia itself.

Data and Measurement

The sample consists of 239 male biochemists who received their Ph.D.s from US universities in fiscal years 1957, 1958, 1962 and 1963 and whose first non-fellowship job was a faculty position in a department rated by Roose and Andersen (1970). Career histories were obtained from *American Men and Women of Science* (10th, 11th and 12th Editions).

The prestige of the doctoral department was measured by the complete three-digit rating of faculty quality of biochemistry departments, a partial listing of which appeared in Cartter (1966). These scores ranged from 100 for the least-prestigious to 500 for the most-prestigious. The prestige of the first job was somewhat more difficult to measure since the biochemists worked in departments in several different fields. Accordingly, a prestige score for each university was constructed based on a weighted average of the Roose and Andersen (1970) ratings of the departments of biochemistry (1/2), chemistry (1/4), physiology (1/12), microbiology/bacteriology (1/12) and pharmacology (1/12); weights in parentheses were based on approximate numbers of biochemists employed in each type of department. These scores also ranged from 100 to 500.

For all but two of the sample, the name of the mentor was obtained from *Dissertation Abstracts, Directory of Graduate Research,* or a mail survey of graduate deans. A measure of the mentor's accomplishments was obtained by counting citations to his or her first-authored publications in the 1961 *Science Citation Index.* While these counts are interpreted as a measure of productivity, it should be kept in mind that they may reflect both the performance of a scientist and his or her standing in the scientific community.

Productivity of the sample members was measured using counts of both publications and citations to them. *Chemical Abstracts* (1955–1973) was used to locate the articles published by the sample members, whether or not they were the senior author. Citations to these articles were coded from *Science Citation Index* (1961, 1964, 1966, 1968, 1970, 1972, 1974). The name of the first author on multiple-authored papers where the cohort member was not the first author was used to locate citations to junior authored papers; thus downward bias in counts for scientists who were predominantly junior authors was avoided. For a given year in the scientist's career, the publication measure reflects publications in a three-year period ending in that year. The citation measure for that year is restricted to citations to papers published in that three-year period. Since coverage of *Science Citation Index* and *Chemical Abstracts* increased during the period covered by our analyses, counts were standardized within years of the Ph.D.

In addition to these key variables, Astin's (1971) measure of selectivity of the scientist's undergraduate institution was used. This index has values ranging from one to seven, with seven being the most selective category. This measure has been interpreted by some as a crude indicator of intelligence and by others as a measure of the quality of the undergraduate education.

Geographic and ecological coding was begun by recording the latitude and longitude of each of the 383 North American academic institutions with which any biochemist was affiliated. Distances between each of the 73,000 plus pairs of institutions were computed in statutory miles.[5] The distance of each career move was derived from our distance matrix. The matrix also was essential to the operationalization of the two ecological measures of centrality to resources and competition.

To measure institutional centrality we borrowed the concept of demographic potential from quantitative geographers who, in turn, borrowed it from the Newtonian concept of gravitational potential (Hammond and McCullough, 1970). By our construction for a given institution i, its centrality to a second institution j is given by the ratio $r(j)/d(i,j)**k$, where $r(j)$ is the volume of a specified resource at j and $d(i,j)**k$ is the distance between the two raised to power k. In gravitational theory the value of k is 2, but in our case it is estimated from fitting models using different values of k. The total potential of institution i with respect to a specific resource is the sum over all other institutions of this ratio. The fundamental notion behind the concept of demographic potential is that there is friction in distance. No matter how large the resource at location j, the farther it is from location i, the less available it is to i. Moreover, the larger the value of k, the exponent of distance, the more severe the friction of distance. Although k is taken to be a positive number, assume for a moment that it is zero. Then all positive distances become identically one and resources at any location become equally available to consumers at all other locations. Consequently, distance is rendered irrelevant and centrality to resources or isolation from them become irrelevant as the measure of demographic potential becomes a constant across locations.

Several potential measures were constructed for each institution. In the analyses described below we use a variable name PHDPOT2, which measures the centrality of each US doctoral program to our set of biochemists at the time when they received a North American baccalaureate degree. It measures the relative availability of those eligible for admission to doctoral degree candidacy to each doctoral degree program. For institution i, its PHDPOT2 is the sum over all other North American baccalaureate-granting institutions j of the number of baccalaureate degrees that they grant divided by their distance from graduate program i. The number 2 in PHDPOT2 indicates that distances was raised to the power 2.

We posit the existence of a second force that may mediate between an institution's potential for acquiring a resource and its level of success in acquiring it. This second force, which we call institutional competition, was suggested by a now classic theory of geographic mobility called intervening opportunities (Stouffer, 1960). The basic idea underlying the posited second force is this: whatever advantage an institution may have from its potential, it will be mitigated to the extent that it is surrounded by successful competitors for the same resources. The measure of institutional competition that we propose is identical to that of institutional potential except that each ratio's numerator is replaced by a measure of institution j's success at acquiring the resource in question. The measure that we use in the present analysis is called PHDCOM2. It is similar to PHDPOT2, but in the numerator for each institution j it substitues the size of its graduate program as measured by the total number of doctoral degrees produced between 1957 and 1966. Thus the larger the graduate program of j and the closer its location to i, the greater is its competition to i for potential graduate students.

Since the ecological concepts that are applied below may not be familiar, let us illustrate them as in Figure 1. We create a hypothetical system consisting of three four-year undergraduate colleges that produce 100 graduates who proceed immediately into graduate training at one of three available graduate schools. The three graduate institutions, none of which produces baccalaureate degrees, are indistinguishable in all characteristics except for the size of the specific graduate program under investigation (biochemistry, in our case) and geographic location. The institutions are separated by distances given in Figure 1. Note that distances among the undergraduate institutions are not reported since they are irrelevant in our model. The purpose of the exercise is to determine how the 100 graduates become distributed among the three graduate schools that compete for them.

Assume that prior research has shown: first, the optimum exponent of distance is 1.00 for both the potential and competition measures; and second, that the estimated regression coefficients are 1.00 for potential and -0.5 for competition in a regression model in which recruitment success is the dependent variable. Note that the algebraic signs of these two coefficients are critical to the validity of the model that we posit. The potential coefficient must be positive to indicate that the greater the potential the greater the success in recruitment; the competition coefficient must be negative to indicate that the greater the competition the less the success in recruitment.

Potential measures are computed for each graduate institution by summing over undergraduate institutions A, B and C the number of graduates (the values of the potential numerator PN in Figure 1) divided by its distance to the exponent 1.00. Thus, graduate school F has a considerably larger potential measure than either of the others, due largely to its adjacency to the largest undergraduate producer C. The competition measures are computed by summing the measures of size of graduate program of the two competitors (the competition numerator CN in Figure 1) divided by distance. Because of its centrality, graduate school E is seen to be in the poorest competitive position while F, because of its relatively greater size and isolation from the other two, occupies the most favorable competitive position.

Finally, using the estimated coefficients, the 'net' potential of each graduate school is computed (to the kth power). If recruitment is linearly related to this net measure, then we see that graduate school F gets the lion's share of the entering graduate students because of its ecological position within the system. The reader may wish to verify that if elements of the system were changed then the outcomes would also change, drastically under certain different circumstances. For

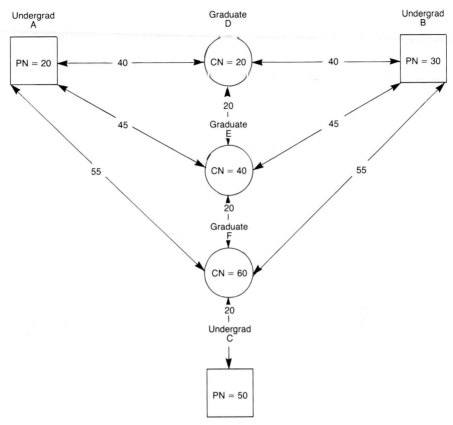

□: Undergraduate Institution (A, B, C) with PN: (Potential Numerator)
Size of Supply—Baccalaureate Degrees Awarded in Biochemistry.
○: Graduate Institution (D, E, F) with CN: (Competition Numerator)
Size of Competition—Doctorate Degrees Awarded in Biochemistry
← xx →: Interinstitution Distance.

Computation of Potential
Source of Supply

Consumer	A	B	C	Potential
D	20/40	30/40	50/60	2.083
E	20/40	30/45	50/60	2.361
F	20/55	30/55	50/20	3.409

Computation of Competition
Source of Competition

Competitor	D	E	F	Competition
D	0	40/20	60/40	3.50
E	20/20	0	60/20	4.00
F	20/40	40/20	0	2.50

Computation of Net Potential (= NP)
Where NP = Potential − 0.5*Competition

Net Potential Of:			Percent
D	2.083 − (.5)*(3.50)	=	0.333 11.7
E	2.361 − (.5)*(4.00)	=	0.361 12.7
F	3.409 − (.5)*(2.50)	=	2.159 75.6

Figure 1: Hypothetical System of Suppliers of Baccalaureate Scientists and Their Consumers by Graduate Program, With Computations of Potential and Competition.

instance, if the values of PN for schools A and C were reversed, the potential measures of the three graduate programs would become nearly constant.

While it is far simpler to think of these computations as resulting in unitless numbers, we argue that they have the same properties of relative units as, for example, miles per hour (MPH) or revolutions per minute (RPM). Where MPH represents units of distance per units of time, potential is just units of resources per unit of distance. Competition can be interpreted similarly, as units of competitors per unit of distance. The net competition measure is precisely what would result from a least squares estimate net of the effects of other variables entered.

Results

In our earlier papers noted above, detailed analyses were presented on the determinants of the prestige of academic positions obtained by our sample of male biochemists. The basic results are presented in Table 1. In the first equation all scientists who obtained positions in rated graduate programs either immediately upon completion of the Ph.D. or after a period of postdoctoral study are included. The prestige of the job is regressed on the prestige and size of the graduate program, the productivity of the mentor, the selectivity of the scientist's baccalaureate degree, and the scientist's predoctoral productivity as measured by their publications and citations. There are two findings of major importance.

First, predoctoral productivity has no significant effect on the prestige of the academic position. Thus, what other analyses have shown to be the most important factor predicting future productivity has no effect on the prestige of the job obtained. This finding has held up under a variety of extensions to the basic model presented in Equations 1 and 2. It could be argued that the scientists do not have enough publications for departments to assess the new Ph.D.s' work, or that students' publications are too closely linked with work of the mentor. In analyses controlling for collaboration with the mentor and examining productivity occurring during postdoctoral fellowships, it is found that the scientist's productivity at the time of applying for a faculty position still has no effect on the prestige of the job. Because the universalistic model of science posits a strong positive relation between productivity and the prestige of a position, many regression models were considered. In no instance, however, was an effect of

Table 1 Regressions Relating Pre-employment Statuses of Biochemists to
Prestige of First Position[a]

	Equation 1: All Biochemists			Equation 2: Inbred Biochemists Excluded		
	B	Beta	t	B	Beta	t
INTERCEP	130.535	–	5.364	160.742	–	5.604
PHD	0.343	0.401	4.783	0.271	0.326	3.303
ENROL	−0.463	−0.165	2.151	−0.672	−0.253	2.743
MENT	4.292	0.136	1.985	2.961	0.094	1.164
SEL	7.627	0.119	1.990	8.408	0.135	1.905
PUB	−2.741	−0.026	0.328	−5.127	−0.049	0.517
CIT	4.284	0.227	1.212	4.026	0.094	0.979
R^2–F		.240	12.175		.164	5.898
df			232			180

Note: Dependent variable is the Roose-Andersen bioscience prestige score of the first academic position. Item identifications are: PHD = Ph.D. prestige, Cartter prestige of the Ph.D. department; MENT = square root of five-year citation counts for mentor; SEL = selectivity of baccalaureate institution; PUB = publication level, square root of standardized levels of three-year publication counts ending in the first year of the first job; CIT = citation level, square roots of standardized values of citations to publications in the three-year period ending in the first year of the first job; ENRL = number of biochemistry graduate students enrolled in the doctoral department in 1961.

[a] Column Beta gives standardized regression coefficients; column B gives unstandardized regression coefficients; column t gives the t− statistics (with more than 120 degrees of freedom in the regression, critical values for a two-tailed test of significance at the .10, .05 and .01 levels are: 1.645, 1.960 and 2.576, respectively; for a one-tailed test the critical values are 1.282, 1.645 and 2.326 for significance levels .10, .05 and .01, respectively).

productivity prior to the job found to have an effect on the prestige of the job.

Second, the prestige of the Ph.D. institution positively affects prestige of employment, while the size of the Ph.D. program affects it negatively. The effect of Ph.D. prestige on job prestige may be an effect of inbred scientists, those who obtain jobs at the institutions where they obtained their degrees (Hagstrom and Hargens, 1968). Equation 2 demonstrates that excluding inbred scientists does not decrease the significance of the effect of Ph.D. prestige on job prestige. It could be argued that the effect of Ph.D. prestige is spurious, that it is simply a correlate of other more fundamental variables that have been excluded from the model. A large variety of other departmental and institutional characteristics have been examined, none of which diminished the importance of departmental prestige (although see the results on geographic and ecological factors given below). Or, departmental prestige may serve as a proxy for characteristics of the student's mentor. While Table 1 includes a single measure of the mentor's productivity, there may be additional characteristics that are important.

Long and McGinnis (1985) considered a variety of such possibilities, including rank of the mentor, awards received and interactions between having collaborated with the mentor and other characteristics of the mentor. It was found that the productivity of the mentor positively affects the prestige of the student's job, if the student collaborated with the mentor. The effects of Ph.D. prestige did not, however, diminish. The only case in which the prestige of the Ph.D. department is found to have an insignificant effect on the prestige of the job is when both prestige of the Ph.D. department and prestige of the fellowship department are included in the same regression for those who took postdoctoral fellowships. In this case, the prestige of the fellowship department replaces that of the Ph.D. department in determining the prestige of the first job. In short, it appears that the prestige of training, whether in a Ph.D. program or a postdoctoral fellowship, has the strongest effect on the prestige of the first job. The reputation of past institutional affiliations, more than characteristics of one's mentor or demonstrated productivity of the student, determines the prestige of the first job.

Three interpretations of the negative effect of size of the graduate program on the prestige of the first faculty position are possible. First, large graduate programs may reflect more lenient admissions policies and thus lower average ability of graduates. Second, large enrollments may reduce the effectiveness of graduate education. Finally, large enrollments produce large graduating cohorts and the increased competition for jobs may hurt all of the graduates of the department.

Geographic and Ecological Effects

We extended the analysis reported in Table 1 to include an investigation of the geographic location of the doctoral institution and of its centrality. We first examined whether graduates in a particular region of the country might have advantages in obtaining prestigious positions, independent of the variables included in Table 1. When longitude and latitude of the doctoral institution were added to the equations reported in Table 1, their effects were not significant (regressions not shown). As a further test of the effect of geographic location, an analysis of covariance was run allowing the effects of each independent variable to differ by region of the country and for each region to have an effect. Regions were coded in a variety of ways. The effects of region on prestige were found to be insignificant (regressions not shown). Thus, there is no evidence that geographic location has an effect on job prestige independently of measures of training and productivity.

Table 2   Extension of Regressions in Table 1 to Include Two Ecological Variables

| | Equation 1: All biochemists | | | Equation 2: Inbred Biochemists Excluded | | |
	B	Beta	t	B	Beta	t
INTERCEP	132.724	—	5.390	166.895	—	7.733
PHD	0.327	0.382	4.266	0.234	0.281	2.669
ENROL	−0.403	−0.144	1.708	−0.544	−0.205	2.037
MENT	4.304	0.136	1.988	2.913	0.092	1.146
SEL	7.418	0.116	1.925	7.917	0.127	1.788
PUB	−2.565	−0.024	0.306	−5.180	−0.049	−0.523
CIT	4.245	0.098	1.200	4.036	0.094	0.982
PHDCOM2	0.627	0.041	0.620	1.467	0.236	1.190
R^2−F		.241	10.463		.171	5.269
df			231			179

Note: PHDCOM2 is the competition measure of Ph.D. institution with distance squared (see text). See Table 1 for other definitions.

The ecological measure of competition for the Ph.D. institution (PHDCOM2) was then added to the model. A scientist with a large value of PHDCOM2 would come from an institution that was close to other large insititutions, while a scientist with a small value of PHDCOM2 would be from an institution that was not close to large, competing institutions. The results are presented in Table 2, where the top rows represent the same variables as those of Table 1. It was thought that graduating from an institution with large institutions nearby (i.e., having a large value of PHDCOM2) would be an advantage in that large employers would be relatively close. If this were the case, the effect of PHDCOM2 would be positive. Indeed the effect is positive, although weak and not quite significant at the .10 level for a one-tailed test. The non-significance of the effects suggests two possibilities. First, it could be argued that having large institutions nearby hurts the scientists by providing many other

Ph.D.s from those institutions competing for the same jobs, thus offsetting the advantage of having potential employers nearby. Or second, it may be that distance does not affect the job market, and consequently there is no advantage to being close to possible jobs. This leads us to consider the extent to which geographic origin affects the geographic destination of the scientist.

While geographic location was not found to have an effect on the prestige of the job obtained, this does not mean that geographic location does not have an effect on location of the first academic job. We expected to observe geographic effects to operate primarily in career moves through the hypothesized friction of distance. If the hypothesis is correct, then effects should be observed between longitudes of origin and destination and the same should be true of latitude pairs. To consider this possibility a series of regressions was run examining how location of the baccalaureate institution affected the location of the Ph.D. institution, and how the location of the baccalaureate and Ph.D. institutions affected the location of the fellowship and/or job institutions. It was consistently found that the longitude of a prior institution significantly affected the longitude of a later institution, and prior latitudes had similar, but weaker effects on later latitudes.

Table 3 Regressions Relating Location of Job Institution to Institutions of Baccalaureate, Last Fellowship and Ph.D. for Fellows Who Were Not Inbred to Fellowship Institutions

| | Equation 1: JOBLONG | | |
	B	Beta	t
INTERCEP	0.822	–	4.961
BALONG	0.041	0.050	0.444
PHDLONG	0.240	0.293	2.582
LFLONG	0.184	0.223	2.276
R^2–F		0.190	7.018
df			90

| | Equation 2: JOBLAT | | |
	B	Beta	t
INTERCEP	0.560	–	4.853
BALAT	−0.042	−0.371	0.298
PHDLAT	−0.023	−0.019	0.142
LFLAT	0.228	0.186	1.675
R^2–F		0.032	0.979
df			90

Note: JOBLONG, JOBLAT, BALONG, BALAT, LFLONG, LFLAT, PHDLONG and PHDLAT are the longitudes and latitudes in radians of the first academic job, the baccalaureate institution, the institution of last fellowship and the doctoral institution.

Table 3 presents two regressions that represent our findings. The regressions are based on those scientists who had postdoctoral fellowships and who did not receive their first academic jobs at the institution of their fellowship. Equation 1 shows that the longitude of both the Ph.D. institution and the fellowship institution have significant effects on the longitude of the job, with nearly 20 per cent of the variance being explained. Basically, we find that obtaining a Ph.D. and/or fellowship on the east coast significantly increases the chance of obtaining a job on the east coast; and so on for the midwest, the plains and the west coast. Much weaker effects are found for latitude, with only the latitude of the fellowship having a significant influence on the latitude of the job. Thus, while those in the east tend to remain in the east, they are more likely to move from north to south.

Our findings at this point are more suggestive than definitive. Future work will refine our measures of competition by refining measures of size, experimenting with the power to which distance is taken in computing competition, and adding other demographic and ecological variables such as size of the surrounding academic and nonacademic communities.

Results for Academic Institutions

To this point our units of analysis have been individual recipients of doctoral degrees in biochemistry. However, the results reported in Tables 2 and 3 strongly suggested to us that the prestige of an institution – and quite possibly other of its salient characteristics – are determined in part by forces of geography and/or ecology. In a regression not shown here the equations in Table 2 were extended to include the competition of the job (JOBCOM2) as a factor explaining the prestige of the job. The effect was found to be large, positive and statistically significant. However, the model is not sensible at the analytic level of the individual scientist. The ecology of destination can hardly be equated with background characteristics of individual scientists. What we seem to be seeing is a consequence of the ecology of institutions on other of their characteristics. Institutional centrality/ isolation may represent a force that influences other institutional characteristics.

In the remainder of this section we illustrate some of the ways in which these forces operate. We begin, naturally enough, with an analysis of the rated prestige of the 75 departments that awarded the

Ph.D. degree to at least one of our sample and that received a rating in the Cartter report. We began with a straightforward structural analysis of the hypothesis that a department's prestige is a reflection of the volume and visibility of the faculty's research. Thus, the primary analytic variables entered were the median citations received in 1961 by the members of the faculty who served as mentors of our sample and total NIH obligations to the institution obligated in FY 1964. Ownership (public versus private) was entered because of the belief that the private research universities may be more highly regarded than the publicly-owned institutions. Finally, size of faculty was included under the hypothesis that it represented both a measure of 'critical mass' and national visibility. Results of this analysis are reported in Equation 1 of Table 4. Despite the fact that only two of the four variables entered in the equation proved to be significant, the model proved to be effective, explaining nearly half of the variance in departmental prestige.

Table 4   Regressions Relating Prestige of Biochemistry at US Doctoral Institutions to Structural, Geographic and Ecological Factors

	Equation 1: Structural Factors Only			Equation 2: Geographic and Ecological Factors Added		
	B	Beta	t	B	Beta	t
INTERCEP	182.627	0.000	6.766	−57.201	0.000	−0.592
MDNMENT	0.702	0.327	3.426	0.583	0.271	2.966
NIH64	0.010	0.548	4.566	0.008	0.470	4.038
PUBPR	3.783	0.020	0.214	12.061	0.065	0.668
FAC	0.032	0.002	0.021	−0.546	−0.042	−0.367
PHDLAT				205.005	0.171	1.993
PHDLONG				60.935	0.178	1.992
PHDPOT2				2.799	0.197	2.133
R^2−F		.491	16.895		.570	12.710
df			74			74

Note: MDMENT is median citations to publications of faculty who served as mentors of the biochemists. See preceding tables for other definitions.

The two locational variables, latitude and longitude, were then added to the model along with one ecological variable, departmental centrality with respect to departments that produce B.S. degrees in biochemistry.[6] Again we reasoned that prestige may be centered in the major institutions of the midwest and east, that the north contains more highly-regarded research departments than the south and that being toward the center of activity should promote visibility and, when coupled with high levels of research, promote departmental reputations. As can be seen in Equation 2 of Table 4, each of the three added variables made at least a marginally significant addition to the model, together increasing the per cent of explained variance by eight points. The major surprise in these results was the positive sign of the coefficient estimate for longitude, suggesting that, among bio-chemistry departments, location in the west is an asset to reputation. We interpret these results to indicate that traditional structural analyses of academic stratification may be supplemented profitably by extension to less traditional geographic and ecological investigation. Once again, we must emphasize the tentative nature of this interpreta-tion. The results, especially for latitude and longitude, are only of marginal statistical significance and the measures of ecology clearly need further refinement.

Next, we present parallel evidence concerning the size of the graduate degree programs in biochemistry. We measure program size simply by using counts of the number of earned doctorate degrees that were awarded in biochemistry during the period from 1957 to 1966 by each institution. We have added the Cartter ratings of biochemistry to the other structural variables reported in Table 4. The results are reported as Equation 1 of Table 5. Two facts emerge clearly from this model: prestige rating, public ownership (as represented by the negative sign of the coefficient) and sheer size of faculty appear to be dominant factors in determining the size of graduate programs in biochemistry. Second, and surprisingly, the level of research activity in a department, as measured by size of NIH research obligations and mentors' citations have no significant bearing on the size of graduate programs.

When we turn to Equation 2 of Table 5, however, it becomes clear that Equation 1 was badly mis-specified. When geographic and ecological measures are added, the per cent of explained variance increases by nearly 22 points and the structural measures lose their statistical significance. The geographic axes turn out to be trivial, but the ecological measures of potential and competition, both of which are entered in this case (see footnote 6), are seen to be of overwhelming importance and operating exactly as hypothesized. That is, despite the fact that the two ecological variables are positively and rather highly correlated, when entered jointly in a multivariate model, they have opposite effects on program size as hypothesized. The greater a department's centrality to the supply of eligible graduates in biochemistry, the larger the graduate program. But, net of potential, the more central a department is to competing graduate programs, the smaller the number of entering graduates it recruits.

Table 5 *Regressions Relating Size of Graduate Program in Biochemistry at US Doctoral Institutions to Structural, Geographic and Ecological Factors*

	Equation 1: Structural Factors Only			Equation 2: Geographic and Ecological Factors Added		
	B	Beta	t	B	Beta	t
INTERCEP	−2.174	0.000	−0.206	−5.623	0.000	−0.216
PHD	0.112	0.406	3.077	0.061	0.220	1.831
MDNM6	−0.060	−0.101	−0.890	−0.031	−0.052	−0.547
PUBPR	−12.282	−0.036	−0.236	−0.000	−0.038	−0.298
FAC	1.388	0.389	2.954	0.362	0.101	0.847
PHDLAT				8.303	0.025	0.292
PHDLONG				−0.354	−0.004	−0.042
PHDPOT2				4.096	1.045	5.832
PHDCOM2				−4.789	−0.927	−5.504
R^2−F		.390	8.808		.606	11.124
df			74			74

Note: Size of graduate program is measured as number of Ph.D. degrees awarded by the institution between 1957 and 1966 inclusive. See preceding tables for other definitions.

Finally, we examine the process of recruiting and maintaining a faculty. We had hoped to use the numbers of our sample of biochemists recruited to colleges as the dependent variable. The distribution, however, was unsuitable since the modal number of hires by an institution was one with a small number hiring nine or ten. Thus, we turn instead to the number of biochemists that each department employed in 1963 according to American Chemical Society counts. Equation 1 of Table 6 provides a model derived from conventional wisdom in the academic community. In it we assumed that the reputation of an academic department and the resources that it brings should have a bearing on the size of faculty that the department can recruit. We also assumed that faculty size is heavily influenced by undergraduate course loads. Here our best available indicator was the number of B.S. degrees awarded to our larger sample of biochemists. The analysis produced reasonably good results with about a quarter of the variance in faculty size being explained. Somewhat surprisingly, NIH 1964 research funds and the indicator of undergraduate enrollments failed to achieve statistical significance. Better measures of research support and undergraduate teaching load might change this result.

We were troubled about whether the process of recruiting a faculty was more like that of recruiting graduate students or that of earning a reputation – whether or not competition should be taken into account. In our ignorance, we chose the former model. We had

Table 6 Regressions Relating Size of Faculty in 1962 in Biochemistry at US Doctoral Institutions to Structural, Geographic and Ecological Factors

	Equation 1: Structural Factors Only			Equation 2: Geographic and Ecological Factors Added		
	B	Beta	t	B	Beta	t
INTERCEP	0.340	0.000	0.168	2.389	0.000	0.376
PRST	0.033	0.359	4.063	0.000	0.005	0.051
NIH64	0.000	0.154	1.796	0.001	0.503	4.772
BACTOT	0.408	0.131	1.748	−0.987	−0.463	−2.688
LAT				8.301	0.089	1.075
LONG				−1.361	−0.051	−0.635
PCOM200				−1.543	−1.066	−4.008
PPOT200				1.370	1.247	4.015
R^2-F		.237	15.974		.613	15.189
df			145			74

computed measures of potential and competition at the level of employment, but problems of severe multi-collinearity forced us to fall back on the two measures at the Ph.D. level. Since these measures are available only for the institutions that produced at least one doctoral degree among our sample, we suffered a drop in degrees of freedom available. Nonetheless, the results are interesting.

When the measures of geographic and ecological location are added, as shown in Equation 2 of Table 6, some dramatic changes from the results of Equation 1 occur. Departmental prestige loses statistical significance altogether while the two remaining variables become strongly significant. The coefficient of BACTOT, the number of undergraduate degrees awarded, is reversed. Both potential and competition are highly significant and in the hypothesized directions, although geographic location plays a trivial role. The model provides a good fit, with the proportion of variance accounted for being more than double that of Equation 1. What emerges is a picture of departments that are highly active in research, avoid heavy undergraduate activities, that are central but not too close to the competition as being the departments that successfully recruit and maintain large faculties.

Conclusions

We reached our initial conclusion more than seven years ago and can find no reason to change it whether as a result of our own subsequent investigations or those of others with which we are familiar. Stratification in science is an important force that influences not only entry into careers – in other sectors as well as academia – but also subsequent outcomes, especially productivity. Our second and more important conclusion is that as stratification appears to operate in the United States it is at best independent of and at worst quite contrary to the principle of meritocracy. To over-simplify a bit, young scientists seem to be arrayed into hierarchies either in terms of pedigree, such as the prestige of doctoral institution and the visibility of mentor, or in terms of early indicators of productivity, especially predoctoral publications and citations to them. To the extent that pedigree is a poorer predictor than early productivity of later productivity – as is decisively the case in our results – then pedigree must be equated with particularism. Since, as we have shown, the rewards of prestigious academic positions are much better correlated with measures of pedigree than of productivity we conclude that the stratification system in science is out of kilter.

We hope that our third conclusion will be of some interest to our fellow researchers in the social science of science. It is that an increased emphasis on organizations that produce science in addition to that on individual scientists, with the introduction of geographic and ecological analyses may well add to our understandig of the social system of science. Although the results presented above are extremely preliminary, we think that they are of sufficient strength to support this conclusion.

Policy Implications

Our contention that the stratification system of science fails to support the principle of meritocracy may, of course, be quite wrong. Further research is needed in several areas: to determine the best early predictors of later scientific productivity, to better establish what it is about organizations that make them conducive to high levels of output, and to understand how individuals are matched – or mismatched — with appropriate organizations. Suppose such research further supports our contention, then what? Then policies should be established that improve the match between the most promising young scientists and organizations with the richest contexts for productivity. Such policies might well involve early career awards that benefit both the research of young scientists and the organizations that employ them. We recognize that any policy designed to support merit rather than equity creates political and ethical problems. These we gladly leave to the policy-makers.

Our final conclusion, if accepted, contains an obvious implication for policy-makers in agencies that support social research which, if stated, could only appear to be self-seeking. But there is a final observation to be made. If there are strong locational effects on the careers of scientists and on the organizations that train or employ them, as our evidence suggests, the fact can be of little interest to academic or science policy-makers. Location simply cannot be changed by acts of policy. There is a question, however, answers to which could be of intense interest: if centrality does indeed give an edge of advantage to individuals or organizations, what are the components that make it so? If it turns out that the advantages of Boston or Cambridge as against Tuscaloosa are merely those of prestige and extra-career delights, then little is to be done. If, however, it turns out that the advantages of centrality are made up of opportunities that can be passed on to those in more isolated locales, then the fact should be considered seriously by policy-makers. Suppose, for example, that the opportunities for intense face-to-face communication among those doing similar research proves to be an important component giving centrality its advantage. Then much could be done to provide possibly effective substitutes, such as improved electronic communication including video-networked seminars and workshops.[7] What we are suggesting is, in effect, a program of research that focuses on the friction of distance and how to eliminate it, that examines the exponent of distance in our potential and competition models and isolates the conditions by which it might be made to approach zero.

Notes

1. See Long and McGinnis (1985) for considerations of collaboration with the mentor in predoctoral productivity.
2. Throughout the remainder of this paper we will refer to scientists as males, since our results are based on a study of male scientists. A study comparing the careers of male and female scientists is currently being conducted by the junior author.
3. For a thorough discussion of organizational ecology, see Hannan and Freeman (1977) and Hannan (1986).
4. Others have shown that their gender difference is also extremely important in this regard. See Reskin (1976) and Rosenfeld and Jones (1985).

5. Latitude and longitude were coded in degrees, minutes and seconds. The measures were converted to radians and movement distances were calculated from the formula $D(P1,P2) = K^{\star}\arcsin(((1-A)/2)^{\star\star}.5)$, where $D(P1,P2) = $ distance between points P1 at location [lat1, long1] and P2 at [lat2, long2] on a sphere; $K = $ diameter of the sphere (7900 miles for the earth); and, $A = \cos(long1 - long2)^{\star}\cos(lat1)^{\star}\cos(lat2) + \sin(lat1)^{\star}\sin(lat2)$.

6. We did not enter PCOM2 in this equation because we would not be able to interpret how the two centrality measures would operate differentially in influencing the rated prestige of a graduate program. Unlike competition for limited resources, the establishment of a reputation does not appear to represent a zero-sum game.

7. We note in this regard that this paper was written by two co-authors who were separated by about 2000 miles. Despite the distance, the paper was the result of frequent and intense interaction between the authors by means of an international network that links the two computers on which we work.

References

Astin, A.W. (1971) *Predicting Academic Performance in College*, New York: The Free Press.

Caplow, T. and McGee, R. (1958) *The Academic Marketplace*, Garden City: Doubleday.

Cartter, A.M. (1966) *An Assessment of Quality in Graduate Education*, Washington: American Council on Education.

Hagstrom, W.O. and Lowell L. (1968) *Mobility theory in the sociology of science*, paper presented at the Cornell Conference on Human Mobility, Ithaca, NY, October 31, 1968.

Hammond, R. and McCullagh, P. (1970) *Quantitative Techniques in Geography*, Oxford: Clarendon Press.

Hannan, M.T. (1986) *A Model of Competitive and Institutional Processes in Organizational Ecology*, Technical Report 86-13, Dept. of Sociology, Cornell University.

Hannan, M.T. and Freeman, J.H. (1979) 'The Population Ecology of Organizations', *American Journal of Sociology*: 82, 929–964.

Hargens, L.L. (1969) 'Patterns of mobility of new Ph.D.s among American academic institutions', *Sociology of Education* 42: 247–256.

Ladinsky, J. (1967) 'Sources of geographic mobility among professional workers: A multivariate analysis', *Demography* 4: 293–309.

Lichter, D.T. (1982) 'The migration of dual-worker families: Does the wife's job matter?', *Social Science Quarterly* 63: 48–57.

Long, J.S. (1978) 'Productivity and academic position in the scientific career', *American Sociological Review* 43: 889–908.

Long, J.S. and McGinnis, R. (1981) 'Organizational context and scientific productivity', *American Sociological Review* 1981, Vol. 46 (August: 422–442).

Long, J.S. and McGinnis, R. (1985) 'Effects of the mentor on the academic career', *Scientometrics*, Vol. 7, Nos. 3–6, pg 255–280.

Long, J.S. Allison, P.D. and McGinnis, R. (1979) 'Entrance into the academic career', reprinted from *American Sociological Review*, Vol. 44, No. 5, Oct 1979.

McGinnis, R., Allison, P.D. and Long, J.S. (1982) 'Postdoctoral training in bioscience: Allocation and outcomes', *Social Forces*, Vol. 60: No. 3 March.

Merton, R.K. (1968) 'The Matthew effect in science', *Science* 159 (No. 3810): 56–63. Reprinted in *The Sociology of Science*, Ch. 20, pp. 439–459.

Merton, R.K. [1942] (1973) 'Science and technology in a democratic order', *Journal of Legal and Political Sociology* 1: 115–126. Reprinted in *The Sociology of Science*, Ch. 13, pp. 267–278.

Price, D.K. (1965) *The Scientific Estate*, Cambridge: Belknap.

Reskin, B.F. (1976) 'Sex and status attainment in science', *American Sociological Review* 41: 597–612.

Reskin, B.F. (1977) 'Scientific productivity and the reward structure of science', *American Sociological Review* 42: 491–504.

Roose, K.D. and Andersen, C.J. (1970) *A Rating of Graduate Programs*, Washington: American Council on Education.

Rosenfeld, R.A. and Jones, J.A. (1985) 'Patterns and effects of geographic mobility for academic women and men', *Journal of Higher Education*, Vol. 58, No. 5, 493–515.

Stouffer, S.A. (1960) 'Intervening Opportunities and Competing Migrants', *Journal of Regional Science*, Vol. 2, No. 1, Spring 1960, pp. 1–26.

Zuckerman, H. (1970) 'Stratification in American science', pp. 235–257 in Laumann, E.O. (Ed.), *Social Stratification*, Indianapolis: Bobbs-Merrill.

3   *Institutional Career Mobility in Academia**

Ted I. K. Youn and Daniel Zelterman

Introduction

Recent social science research in the American academic system has come to recognize the importance of institutional differentiation among academic organizations (Jencks and Riesman, 1969; Ben-David, 1972; Smelser, 1974; Clark, 1983). As the higher education system becomes loaded with more activities, the process of institutional differentiation becomes increasingly important. Evidence has also demonstrated that institutional attributes are significant determinants of rewards and opportunities of academics who are employed among a wide range of institutions (Youn, 1981; Smelser and Content, 1980).

Over 3,400 institutions that make up the American system differ widely in their emphasis on two major activities – educating students and advancing knowledge through research. Institutions that stress research tend to place relatively less emphasis on teaching; those that emphasize teaching, on the other hand, tend to assign greater teaching loads to academics. Although these are not independent phenomena, academic institutions with an emphasis on research provide a distinctive form of rewards (Fulton and Trow, 1974; Blau, 1973), while institutions with an emphasis on teaching are subject to bureaucratically controlled rewards.

The American academic system, in varying degrees, has its activities separated into different types of institutions. These institutions are arranged hierarchically (Youn, 1981; Clark, 1983). At the

* A version of this paper was presented at the Annual Meeting of the American Sociological Association (1986) in Washington, D.C.

top of the hierarchy, leading research universities command prestige and promote a more universalistic orientation toward rewards (Parsons and Platt, 1973), while on the lower rung of the academic status ladder, two-year colleges place a greater emphasis on localized and particularistic rewards for successful teaching (Cohen and Brawer, 1977). This hierarchy of institutions, partly based on level of task and partly on prestige, becomes increasingly important, particularly as it is related to formal organizations and careers.

This chapter is concerned with how organizational attributes affect patterns of academic career mobility in the academic system. How does career origin at a research university affect subsequent career developments? How does this differ from the effect of career origin at a college where teaching is the dominant organizational task? Does the institutional environment encompassing an academic's career origins shape opportunity structures and thereby constrain certain career outcomes?

In the recent literature on academic careers, the substantial effect of doctoral origin on the prestige of the institution that employs an academic has been demonstrated (Caplow and McGee, 1958; Berelson, 1960; Crane, 1965; Hargens and Hagstrom, 1967; Hagstrom and Hargens, 1968). The study by Long, Allison and McGinnis (1979) further concluded that the effect of doctoral prestige is even more important to first jobs than predoctoral publications. Although the work by Long *et al.* (1979) includes only a single academic field, it does suggest the importance of career origins to academic career outcomes. How, then, does the entry to the first job after doctoral training affect one's subsequent career mobility? What explains career mobility over the first, the second, and the third job? Finally, does the effect of career origin on subsequent mobility differ among academic fields? How do patterns of mobility differ among academic fields?

Data and Models

The data used are taken from the *Survey of the American Professoriate* conducted by Ladd and Lipset in 1975. It employed a sample size of 3,400 academics from 2,406 higher educational institutions.

The major source for the survey sampling was the American Council on Education's *Institutional Characteristics File*. Weighting was done by type of institution, academic rank, and discipline group. Fifty-two per cent of 3,400 faculty members responded. In type, the Research University group is slightly over-represented. Among ranks, Assistant Professors were slightly over-represented, while

Professors are represented by 36 per cent. In fields, social sciences are slightly over-represented with 45 per cent of the responses.

The survey asked for information concerning job transition in higher educational institutions. Respondents were asked about doctoral origins, doctoral discipline, and first, second, and current job institutions. Based on the American Council on Education's rating of graduate programs (Cartter, 1966; Roose and Andersen, 1970) and *Classification of Institutions of Higher Education* (1979), published by the Carnegie Commission on Higher Education, the study considers four categories of institutions: (1) Leading Research University; (2) Research and Doctoral-Granting University; (3) Four-Year College; and (4) Two-Year College.

The Leading Research University represents 20 prestigious universities where basic research is the dominant activity. The Research and Doctoral-Granting University includes those institutions which devote themselves to some research as well as graduate education. Obviously some teaching activities are expected, though research is emphasized. In terms of prestige and resources available for research, these institutions rank below the Leading Research University. The Four-Year College represents a wide variety of undergraduate colleges, among them some elite liberal arts colleges such as Amherst, Swarthmore, and Carlton. The Four-Year College strongly emphasizes undergraduate education even though, in many cases, its faculty members are engaged in basic research. The Two-Year College group stands opposite the Leading Research University. This group includes two-year community and junior colleges and other professional and special institutes offering associate (AA) degrees. Teaching is the predominant organizational task among two-year colleges, and bureaucratic norms are imposed on, and organizational loyalty is expected from, employees. In sum, the first two categories emphasize research, the second two emphasize teaching, and there is a hierarchical ordering within both categories.

The log-linear model is useful in the analysis of categorical data such as that examined in this paper. For a discussion in greater depth, the reader is referred to the texts by Goodman (1978), and Bishop, Fienberg, and Holland (1975).

The count x_{ij} is an observation on a random variable with mean m_{ij}. The indices $i = 1,..4$ and $j = 1,..4$ refer to decreasing orders of prestige among the Ph.D.-granting and -employing institutions, respectively, of a group of individuals. For example, x_{12} is the number of individuals sampled who obtained their Ph.D.s at one of the leading research universities and were employed subsequently by a research and doctoral-granting university.

Log-linear models are those which are linear in the logs of the means m_{ij}. The *model of independence* is described by

$$\log m_{ij} = \mu + \alpha_i + \beta_j$$

The interpretation of the parameters is as follows: μ describes the overall number of individuals in the survey; α_i and β_j take into account the differing ratios or marginal sum of Ph.D.s granted and employed, respectively, at the various types of institutions. Under the model of independence individuals are employed, seemingly at random, without regard to the institutions at which they did their graduate work.

A second log-linear model used in this article is that of *independence with a diagonal effect* (IDE)[1] described by

$$\log m_{ij} = \mu + \alpha_i + \beta_j + \gamma I(i=j)$$

$$\text{where } I\ (i=j) = \begin{cases} 0 & \text{if } i \neq j \\ 1 & \text{if } i = j \end{cases}$$

The interpretations of μ, α_i and β_j are the same as the model of independence. As before, α_i and β_j model the row sums and the column sums. Thus, both models take marginals into account. The parameter γ describes the tendency of individuals to remain in or leave the type of institution from which they obtained their Ph.D.s. The IDE model says that when $\gamma > 0$, individuals tend to be employed by the types of universities from which they obtained their degrees. When they leave for institutions with different levels of prestige, however, they appear to move at random, independently of where they did their graduate work.

These two log-linear models prove to be adequate in explaining most of the data analyzed in this chapter. Models which describe the propensity of individuals to move to more (or less) prestigious institutions are examined, as are the mobility models of Haberman (1974, ch. 6) but these additional models did not provide a more accurate indication of the trends in the data.[2]

The log-linear models were fitted using the Deming-Stephen iterative proportional fitting algorithm and the coordinate free approach of Haberman (1974). The necessary FORTRAN software is described in Zelterman, *et al.* (1984).

Let $\hat{m}_{ij}$ denote the fitted means for a given model with observations x_{ij}. The goodness-of-fit measure G^2 defined by

$$G^2 = 2 \sum x_{ij} \log [x_{ij} / \hat{m}_{ij}]$$

is used to indicate how well the model describes the data. If the model is correct, G^2 usually behaves as a chi-square random variable with degrees of freedom (D.F.) appropriate to the model. The difference between the G^2 statistics on the model of independence and the IDE model behaves approximately as chi-square with 1 d.f. when $\gamma = 0$ and is a measure of the importance of the γ parameter.

The data are examined by four individual areas of discipline (humanities, natural sciences and mathematics, biological and medical sciences, and social sciences) as well as all disciplines pooled. We examined the data with respect to the extent to which the prestige of the Ph.D.-producing institution may have influenced the prestige of the institution of the first, second, or third academic positions. Similarly, the effects of the first position on subsequent academic employment were studied as well.

Problems with the cross-sectional survey data should be recognized in contrast to the panel data analysis. The nature of survey data anticipates some limitations, while a panel data analysis would have had the added advantage of showing the precise patterns of persistence and change in mobility.

The Effects of Doctoral Origins on the First Job

In an early study of the academic labor market, Caplow and McGee (1958) claim that academics' Ph.D. origins 'indelibly mark their careers' and that the 'handling of individual identification with a department of low prestige is hardly ever overcome'. Hiring decisions, according to Caplow and McGee, are not based on actual evaluation of the applicant's work, but instead on the prestige of the candidate's graduate department and the eminence of his or her sponsors. The importance of the prestige that a young graduate obtains from his or her affiliation with a doctoral institution is demonstrated by many studies (Wilson, 1942; Berelson, 1960; Crane, 1965; Hargens and Hagstrom, 1967; Cole and Cole, 1973; Long, 1978; Long *et al.*, 1979).

Others modify the point made by Caplow and McGee and argue that these institutional effects, if any, may decline over an academic's lifetime (Hargens and Hagstrom, 1967).

Recent empirical studies by Reskin (1979) and Long *et al.* (1979) state that the prestige of the doctoral-granting institution has the greatest influence on the prestige of the institution in which the academic has his/her first job. According to these studies, their doctoral origins play an important role in determining first jobs, because: (1) relatively little objective evidence exists to judge the merits of new Ph.D.s in their early career stage (Reskin, 1979); (2) no established productivity measures among new Ph.D.s are available; and finally (3) pre-employment productivity has little or no effect on the first job (Long *et al.*, Reskin, 1979), even though it may be the best predictor of future productivity.

At first, our survey data show that a substantial number of academics hold only their first job and never move anywhere else (Table 1). Of those who stay in the first job, 53.5 per cent stay longer than seven years (Table 2). Academics often face their tenure reviews in the sixth year of their first job. The figure 53.5 suggests that over one half of them obtained their tenure status and stayed on at their first job institution. Referring to the mover-stayer models in stratification research (White, 1970; Mayer, 1972) we find more stayers and fewer movers in their first job. Or, using Spilerman's concept of the 'holding power of career lines' (Spilerman, 1977), which refers to the probability of people continuing in the line once they have entered a career, academics seem to demonstrate a greater 'holding power' by staying on their first jobs longer.

Table 1   Number and Per Cent of Academics That Held First, Second and Third Jobs (Full-time Only)

Jobs	N	Per cent	Mean age	SD (Age)
First job only (not second and third jobs)	1,855	56.8%	41	10.08
First and second (at least two jobs but not third)	887	27.1%	44	9.96
First, second and third jobs (at least three jobs)	525	16.0%	48	9.64
No answer	269			
Total	3,536	100.0%		

Table 2   Years in First, Second and Third Jobs (All Fields) (Full-time only)

	First job		Second job		Third job	
1–6 years	46.5%		47.4%		43.4%	
7–15 years	34.4%		35.0%		38.2%	
16–39 years	18.6%	53.5	16.8%	52.5	17.5%	56.5
40+ years	0.5%		0.7%		0.8%	
N	1,855		887		525	

It also seems clear (Table 3) that academics who have taken their first jobs at leading research universities tend to stay longer in those jobs, thereby suggesting the possibility of greater 'holding power' in research career lines. On the other hand, more mobility is demonstrated by academics whose first jobs are with two-year colleges, four-year undergraduate colleges, and doctoral-granting institutions where basic research may not be greatly emphasized. A greater 'holding power' on the first job also might mean one is likely locked into a particular career line – whether predominantly research or predominantly teaching.

Table 3 Mean Years at First Job by Institutional Type* (All Fields)

	Mean Years	Standard error of means	N
Research University	12	0.37	547
Doctoral Granting University	10	0.45	439
Four Year College	7.4	0.29	622
Two Year College	5	0.31	247
All Institutions	9	0.19	1,855

* Full-time only
Note: SEM = $6/\sqrt{N}$

The importance of the first job in academic careers is also stressed by recent studies. For example, Allison and Stewart (1974) point out that the type of first job indicates one's access to resources that are essential for future performance. Reskin's study (1979) supports this conclusion by adding that the effect of sponsorship by eminent scholars during the first job is important to the later careers of young Ph.D.s. The eminence of sponsorship is, however, often correlated with the caliber of doctoral institutions.

How important is the prestige of the Ph.D.-granting institution in determining the prestige of the first job? As can be seen from Table 4, the prestige of the Ph.D.-granting institution has the greatest influence on the prestige of the first job. Furthermore, this argument holds even among selective academic fields, as shown in Table 5. The high G^2 value for the independence model demonstrates this point.

Table 4   Effects of Doctoral Origins on First, Second, and Third Jobs (All Fields, Full-time Faculty)

Model	Effects of Ph.D. Granting Institution on First Job*	Effects of Ph.D. Granting Institution on Second Job*	Effects of Ph.D. Granting Institution on Third Job*
(1) Independence Model (9df)	193.5 (10^{-5})	31.83 (10^{-4})	27.57 (10^{-3})
(2) IDE Model (8df)	16.15 (0.04)	7.57 (0.5)	8.74 (0.4)
(3) G^2 for γ (1df)	177.3 (10^{-6})	24.26 (10^{-6})	18.83 (10^{-5})
(4) Estimated γ	0.83	0.48	0.67
(5) Estimated Standard Error of $(\hat{\gamma})$	.04	.03	.06

* Institutions are categorized into 4 types: the Leading Research University, the Doctoral Granting University, the Four Year College and the Two Year College. Approximate chi-square tail areas are given in parentheses. Mobility of gravity – second and third does not include intervening position.

(γ) represents the propensity of Ph.D's to stay in the same type of institution in which they received their degrees.

Mobility from doctoral granting institutions to the first, the second, and the third job institutions does not include the intervening position.

Table 5   Effects of Doctoral Origins on First, Second, and Third Jobs (Selective Fields, Full-time Faculty)

I. Humanities	Effects of Ph.D. Granting Institution on First Job*	Effects of Ph.D. Granting Institution on Second Job*	Effects of Ph.D. Granting Institution on Third Job*
(1) Independence Model (9df)	23.57 (0.005)	7.03 (0.63)	14.38 (0.11)
(2) IDE Model (8df)	11.86 (0.16)	5.23 (0.73)	7.36 (0.50)
(3) G^2 for γ (1df)	11.71 (10^{-3})	1.80 (0.18)	7.02 (0.01)
(4) Estimated γ	0.56	0.31	0.90
(5) Estimated SE of $(\hat{\gamma})$	0.05	0.04	0.16

II. Natural Sciences and Mathematics	Effects of Ph.D. Granting Institution on First Job*	Effects of Ph.D. Granting Institution on Second Job*	Effects of Ph.D. Granting Institution on Third Job*
(1) Independence Model (9df)	30.16 (10^{-3})	13.10 (0.16)	10.42 (0.32)
(2) IDE Model (8df)	13.90 (0.08)	12.24 (0.14)	10.21 (0.25)
(3) G^2 for γ (1df)	16.26 (10^{-4})	0.86 (0.35)	0.21 (0.65)
(4) Estimated γ	0.72	0.26	−0.27
(5) Estimated SE of $(\hat{\gamma})$	0.07	0.04	0.09

* Institutions are categorized into four types.
Approximate chi-square tail areas are given in parentheses.

(γ) represents the propensity of Ph.D's to stay in the same type of institution as they received their degree.

Table 5 contd

III. Biological and Medical Sciences	Effects of Ph.D. Granting Institution on First Job*	Effects of Ph.D. Granting Institution on Second Job*	Effects of Ph.D. Granting Institution on Third Job*
(1) Independence Model (9df)	30.94 (10^{-3})	8.27 (0.51)	4.43 (0.88)
(2) IDE Model (8df)	8.72 (0.4)	7.05 (0.53)	3.28 (0.92)
(3) G^2 for γ (1df)	22.22 (10^{-5})	1.22 (0.27)	1.15 (0.28)
(4) Estimated γ	0.99	0.42	0.81
(5) Estimated SE of $(\hat{\gamma})$	0.101	0.07	0.33

IV. Social Sciences	Effects of Ph.D. Granting Institution on First Job*	Effects of Ph.D. Granting Institution on Second Job*	Effects of Ph.D. Granting Institution on Third Job*
(1) Independence Model (9df)	51.19 (10^{-4})	13.63 (0.14)	11.40 (0.25)
(2) IDE Model (8df)	15.21 (0.06)	9.12 (0.33)	10.84 (0.21)
(3) G^2 for γ (1df)	35.98 (10^{-6})	4.51 (0.03)	0.56 (0.45)
(4) Estimated γ	0.89	0.43	0.25
(5) Estimated SE of $(\hat{\gamma})$	0.07	0.05	0.05

* Institutions are categorized into four types.

Approximate chi-square tail areas are given in parentheses.

Note: The significance of the (γ)'s can be approximated by comparing the standard errors of estimates.

The estimators are approximately normally distributed.

Mobility from doctoral institutions to first, second and third job institutions does not include the intervening position.

While the model of independence shows a satisfactory fit, the degree of dependence on the prestige of the doctoral institution decreases substantially at the second job, and thus, individuals move more randomly subsequent to the first job. The influence of (γ) decreases over later academic positions, indicating a decreased likelihood of staying within the same type of institution. Opportunities for upward and downward mobility in academic environments appear in the second position held after a Ph.D. is attained. Similarly, it appears that the third position is independent of the first. Table 5 shows that the influence of (γ) decreases over later positions in each discipline.

At the first academic position in the individual disciplines, the model of independence does not fit well, whereas the IDE model fits moderately well. Adding the single degree of freedom, parameter γ to the model of independence, produces a model that explains the data adequately and provides a reasonable interpretation of the observed phenomenon. The decreasing G^2 for γ over subsequent academic positions indicates that individuals become less dependent on the prestige of the institution at which their graduate work was performed. Perhaps by the second job, then, career mobility is more a function of accomplishments after graduate school than a function of the graduate school's prestige.

Allison and Stewart (1974) demonstrate a strong relationship between career age and productivity inequality among academic scientists. The increased inequality in productivity is associated with a changing distribution of time spent on research over the course of one's career. If the Allison and Stewart thesis is correct, it may be quite plausible that, as academics move from first to second to third jobs, one would expect greater productivity inequality. Highly productive academics who are located in research universities maintain or increase their productivity, while others who are located in teaching-oriented insitutions spend less time in research and are likely to publish less; thus, inequality persists in the system (see a similar argument made by Long and McGinnis, 1981). Opportunities for a more productive research career appear to start with an academic's first job.

By comparing G^2s for the independence model in Table 5, the social sciences show the greater influence of doctoral origin on the first teaching job, and, therefore, have the least mobility from the prestige of graduate training, meaning that among Ph.D.s there is a greater tendency to stay in the type of institution where they received their degrees. As far as the first academic position is concerned, the humanities have the greatest mobility. While natural sciences and mathematics appear to have modest mobility, biological scientists are more dependent on the prestige of their graduate departments, and, therefore, have a tendency to demonstrate less mobility. An emphasis on individual creativity, and the associated competition, may explain the fact that the humanities allow greater mobility from doctoral origins. Academics in the humanities are less lkely to depend on the prestige of their graduate training.

According to studies by Hagstrom (1964), Hargens (1975), and Gaston (1978), consensus about the validity of theories and research methodologies is markedly greater in physics and mathematics than in the social sciences. Although they do not involve any direct measures of consensus, these studies do rely on the consequences of the degree of consensus, through analyzing journal rejection rates and dissertation lengths. Previous studies (Lodahl and Gordon, 1972; Allison and Stewart, 1974; Pantin, 1968; Cole *et al.*, 1978) characterize the biological sciences as having lower levels of consensus than either physics or mathematics, and report, further, a greater dispersion in theory among social scientists.

In fields with higher consensus, academics will be more likely to make evaluations on the basis of scholarly accomplishments and less likely to rely on ascriptive characteristics (Pfeffer, Leong, and Strehl, 1977; Hargens and Hagstrom, 1982). Therefore, having higher consensus on theory and methodology tends to foster more 'competition for priority in reporting research findings and recency in the focus of published work' (Hargens and Hagstrom, 1983). One would expect less dependence on ascriptive rules such as the prestige of the graduate institution. This consensus hypothesis seems to support our analysis of the differences among fields shown in Table 5. G^2 for (γ) shown in the social sciences and the biological sciences are higher than the natural sciences and mathematics. The humanities shows the lower G^2 for (γ). This could mean a greater tendency to emphasize individual creativity while the humanities field exhibits less consensus in its paradigms.

Productivity and Academic Career Mobility

For the past few decades, two competing theories have influenced sociological studies of academic mobility and stratification. The first theory group argues that the inter-relationship between research productivity and location in the stratification system may be explained by the institutional goal of science (Merton, 1942). Rewards in the scientific community are allocated on the basis of an individual's contribution to scientific knowledge. Recruitment to prestigious positions in the hierarchy of academic departments is allocated according to a scientist's productivity (Cole and Cole, 1973). In sum, a scientist's achievements have a substantial effect on academic appointment.

In the late 1960s, several studies (Hargens and Hagstrom, 1967; Crane, 1970) began to question the hypothesis set out by the first group, although empirically these studies did not modify the prevailing theory. It was not until the late 1970s that several persuasive analyses presented by Long and his colleagues challenged the first theory.

Long's studies present an empirically-based argument stating that productivity is essentially a function of location in the academic stratification system. Among academic scientists, pre-employment productivity (as a measure of scholarly productivity) has little or no impact on the prestige of the first position, even though pre-employment productivity may be the best predictor of future productivity. Doctoral prestige has the strongest effect on the prestige of the first job. Thus, the career outcomes of academic scientists are most likely influenced by the ascriptive process.

One should note, however, that most empirical studies conducted by the sociologists of science were concerned only with elite scientists, those who are usually located in leading research universities. Our analysis, on the other hand, is based on survey data which includes academics in a wide range of institutions, including two-year colleges where the relationship between research productivity and location in the stratification system may not hold.

Despite the importance of research publication to science and scholarship, American academics across all fields demonstrate surprisingly low levels of research productivity. As Table 6 shows, over 52 per cent of the full-time academics have never written or edited any publication; more than one-third have neither written nor edited since receiving their Ph.D.s. J. Cole's study (1979) also supports this general pattern of skewed research productivity among academics. One or two years after obtaining a doctorate, according to Cole, 53 per cent have failed to publish a single paper and 34 per cent have published only one. In most years, three-quarters publish nothing.

Table 6   Research Productivity of Recent Years: 'How many of your professional writings have been published or accepted for publication?'

Research Productivity	Leading Research University	Doctoral-Granting University	Four-Year Colleges	Two-Year Colleges	All
1) None	24.7	41.9	64.8	83.8	52.9
2) 1–2	29.1	29.5	23.1	12.5	24.2
3) 3–4	22.4 } 40.2	16.0 } 26.1	8.2 } 11.0	1.7 } 3.3	12.3 } 20.4
4) 5–10	17.8	10.1	2.8	1.6	8.1
More than 10	6.0	2.5	1.2	0.4	2.5
	100.0	100.0	100.0	100.0	100.0

Particularly, the analysis of Tables 4 and 5 indicates that the effects of doctoral origin on the first position is significant, as IDE models in all fields fit uniformly well. As we concluded, for the second job, the effect of doctoral origin decreases dramatically. For the third job, there is even less effect. Even though no measures of research and scholarly productivity are employed in our models, we are able to hypothesize that, subsequent to the first position, academic mobility may be a function of achievements, research productivity among them. In the absence of productivity measures in our models, we can only speculate that academic mobility to second and third jobs may be partly explained by research productivity, even though the effects of research productivity are not uniform among different institutions.

The Contiguous Influences of Jobs on Career Outcomes

Career mobility in organizations refers to the flow of individuals along sequences of jobs. Rosenbaum (1979) argues that the career-trajectory hypothesis operates in organizations. Early attainments, net of personal attributes, have strong effects in setting the career trajectories of entering employees. Spilerman (1977) identifies the concept of a career line, which he defines as structurally-formed and age-graded sequences of jobs through which workers move. Spilerman asks how career lines are formed by larger social structures and institutional arrangements.

Referring to Tables 4 and 5, we argue that the entrance to a career, either in research or in teaching, shapes one's later career outcomes. Thus, it is the entry-level organization that leads to differences in opportunity, because different academic organizations offer different rewards to their members and set different performance standards. The effect of doctoral origin on the first job is consistently large. To what extent, then, does the prestige of the second job depend on the prestige of the first job? Similarly, does the prestige of the third job depend on the prestige of the second job?

The Markov model assumes a stochastic process where the outcome at time t, given all previous history, is only a function of the outcome at time $t-1$ and of nothing that occurred at any earlier time. Thus, the Markov process is referred to as a *one-step dependency process* (Ross, 1972), which implies a contiguous movement in sequence.

Table 7 shows that the one-step dependency process seems to work in describing mobility from the first to the second job. The effect of the prestige of the first job does not carry beyond the second job.[3] As shown from the table, the lack of dependence in mobility from the first to the third job suggests that the third job is more likely to be influenced by the prestige of the second job. We were unable to

test this hypothesis satisfactorily because there are very few observations of mobility from the second to the third job.

Table 7 *Effects of the Prestige of the First Job on the Second and Third Jobs:*
Computed G^2 on Fitted Table (All Fields — Full-time Academics)

Model	Effects of first job on second job	Effects of first job on third job
(1) Independence Model (9df)	145.06 (10^{-5})	36.81 (10^{-4})
(2) IDE (8df)	22.01 (0.005)	10.26 (0.25)
(3) G^2 for γ (1df)	123.05 (10^{-6})	26.55 (10^{-6})
(4) Estimated (γ)	0.68	0.53
(5) Estimated standard error of $(\hat{\gamma})$	0.04	0.07

Approximate chi-square tail areas are given in parenthesis.

From Table 8, we see a degree of variation among fields. While
the social sciences and biomedical sciences are less dependent on the
prestige of the prior job, in the natural sciences, mathematics, and in
the humanities the opposite trend seems to exist. Again, referring to
Hargens and Hagstrom (1982), the degree of consensus on theory and
methodology may help us to speculate about the mobility process.
Having a higher consensus tends to foster more competition among
individuals, while having a low consensus may mean a greater degree
of ascriptive processes in the initial placement. After the initial
academic placement, the fields that hold a higher degree of consensus
demonstrate a greater dependence on the prestige of the prior
academic positions than those which lack that degree of consensus.

The Effect of Multiple Markets on Career Outcomes

'Markets for academic services', as Smelser and Content argue
(1980:2), 'are multiple and overlapping'. Among employers, large
research institutions are in the market for a different kind of academic
than are institutions which specialize in undergraduate teaching alone.
Two-year colleges place a greater emphasis on teaching and tend to
look for yet another range of skills among their prospective
employees. Employing institutions can be subdivided even further,
according to whether they are large or small, public or private, and
secular or religious. At the general level, we can distinguish one

Academic Labor Markets and Careers

Table 8 Effects of the Prestige of the First Job on the Second and Third Jobs: Computed G^2 on Fitted Table (Full-time)

I. Humanities

Model	Effects of First Job on Second Job	Effects of First Job on Third Job
(1) Independence Model (9df)	30.65 (10^{-4})	13.81 (0.13)
(2) IDE (8df)	9.72 (0.29)	12.26 (0.14)
(3) G^2 for γ (1df)	20.93 (10^{-5})	1.55 (0.21)
(4) Estimated (γ)	0.66	0.30
(5) Estimated standard error of ($\hat{\gamma}$)	0.09	0.154

II. Natural Sciences and Mathematics

Model	Effects of First Job on Second Job	Effects of First Job on Third Job
(1) Independence Model (9df)	21.20 (0.01)	17.16 (0.05)
(2) IDE (8df)	5.68 (0.68)	12.55 (0.13)
(3) G^2 for γ (1df)	15.42 (10^{-4})	4.61 (0.03)
(4) Estimated (γ)	0.72	0.73
(5) Estimated standard error of ($\hat{\gamma}$)	0.12	0.22

Approximate chi-square tail areas are given in parenthesis.

III. Biological and Medical Sciences

Model	Effects of First Job on Second Job	Effects of First Job on Third Job
(1) Independence Model (9df)	15.50 (0.08)	11.73 (0.23)
(2) IDE (8df)	6.40 (0158)	5.72 (0.68)
(3) G^2 for γ (1df)	8.86 (0.003)	6.01 (0.01)
(4) Estimated (γ)	0.72	1.16
(5) Estimated standard error of ($\hat{\gamma}$)	0.17	0.284

IV. Social Sciences

Model	Effects of First Job on Second Job	Effects of First Job on Third Job
(1) Independence Model (9df)	16.95 (0.05)	7.72 (0.56)
(2) IDE Model (8df)	9.24 (0.32)	6.32 (0.61)
(3) G^2 for γ (1df)	7.71 (0.01)	1.40 (0.24)
(4) Estimated (γ)	0.42	0.29
(5) Estimated standard error of ($\hat{\gamma}$)	0.11	0.18

Approximate chi-square tail areas are given in parenthesis.

Note: The significance of the (γ)'s can be approximated by comparing the standard errors of estimates. The estimators are approximately normally distributed.

market for people who will do research and train graduate students and another market for people who will teach at the undergraduate level alone. Often, these markets overlap, but they are in fact separate and governed by distinct sets of internal allocative rules. Academic career outcomes depend on labor market structures. Different markets operate under distinct institutionalized rules (Reich, Gordon, and Edwards, 1973; Spenner *et al.*, 1982) based on consensus about the criteria employers use to assess excellence and promise. Yet, partly because of different normative expectations for organizations, there are enormous variations in consensus when it comes to rules in higher education.

The variability also exists because of disciplinary differences. Therefore, career outcomes largely depend on the nature of the discipline. Academics are differentiated by special fields of competence, and the extent of that differentiation prevents an interchangeability of fields. It is extremely rare for one academic discipline to recruit outside its own field (Brown, 1967). Further, each discipline is divided into many subspecialties and, therefore, into more segmented markets. Even though we observe more aggregated fields (such as the humanities, the social sciences, the natural sciences, and biological sciences), our analyses clearly demonstrate the extent of variability among fields.

Our paper suggests that the choice of the first job is an important decision for many academics. Entering a research career leads to subsequent mobility along the research career line, even though some academics may later move toward a teaching career. For others, the movement to teaching from research might occur as early as the second job. Because of the sequential influence of the second job on the third, the probability of staying on the teaching career line might increase subsequent to the second job.

On the other hand, the propensity for upward movement from a teaching institution to a research institution at the seond job or the third job could exist, given the progressive decline of the size of γ in all IDE models; productivity and other achievements could affect this upward movement. The probability of moving from a teaching career to a research career might be less than vice versa, although career mobility from a two-year college to a four-year college could take place. Mobility from the less prestigious doctoral-granting institution to the leading research university might also occur.

Dichotomizing entrants into either research or teaching may permit only a limited representation of Spilerman's argument (1977) concerning entry ports, mobility clusters, and career lines. Yet, the availability of two distinct ports of entry seems to have a profound influence on academic career outcomes.

Among all fields, the effect of doctoral origin on the first job seems pronounced. This influence diminishes greatly by the second job, however, and exhibits increasing randomness thereafter.

One may speculate that competition for the second position relies more on talent and achievements than on institutional prestige. This hypothesis seems to hold in the humanities, as well as in the natural sciences and mathematics.

The propensity for mobility (from either a teaching to a research career or a research to a teaching career) may increase between the second and the third jobs (Table 7). The contiguous influence of the previous job seems to increase in the humanities and the natural sciences and mathematics, although the effect appears modest in the social and biological sciences.

Summary and Discussion

In the late 1970s, stimulated in part by the dual labor market hypothesis demonstrated by Doeringer and Piore (1971), a growing literature in sociology attempted to understand the structure of labor markets and their effects on career outcomes (Spilerman, 1977; Stolzenberg, 1975; Baron and Bielby, 1980; Kalleberg and Sorensen, 1979; Baron, 1984; Rosenbaum, 1979). These studies recognized that organizations differ systematically in both recruitment processes and allocation of rewards to employees. Organizations both generate internal labor markets and provide procedures that match employees to jobs (Granovetter, 1981). In short, organizations in a social system cause inequality and affect career outcomes.

Career outcomes, we argue, are more than a matter of personal choices or achievements. Academic career outcomes depend largely on institutional arrangements and on the division of labor among academic organizations. There is a substantial relationship between the prestige of doctoral origin and the prestige of an academic's employing institution. This point has been made consistently by previous studies, which are cited in the text.

The choice of the first job after graduate school, while not entirely a matter of individual choice, has significant consequences for the young academic. Even though the effect of the entry portal declines after the second job, it continues to play an important role in career mobility. As Long *et al*'s. (1979) study suggests, the first job is not a good case for observing universalism in science; particularistic factors are likely to creep in. Information about young academics is relatively poor at the time of their initial appointment, for example. Therefore, according to Long, *et al.*, hiring departments virtually ignore the written work of new Ph.D.s, whether published or unpublished, in favor of doctoral origin and sponsorship. Although our analysis is not able to take later productivity into account, we can observe that academics who enter research careers tend to continue along the research career line. While some academics move down to a teaching career line from a research career line, opportunities to move from teaching to research institutions would likely decrease at the second and the third job.

We observed that two discrete markets, one for research and one for teaching, operate at the entry-level portal in academic careers, and entry is affected by doctoral prestige. The question is whether the influence of doctoral prestige persists in the second and the third job. Our models demonstrate that the level of influence declines. In fact, as one moves to the second job, the effect of the first job's prestige appears more significant than the effect of doctoral prestige. Similarly, the third job seems to depend much more on the second job than on the first.

Our analysis found that patterns of mobility differ among academic fields. Social sciences show the greatest influence of the doctoral origin on the first job, while the humanities shows the least dependence on the doctoral origin. While academics in the natural sciences and mathematics appear to have some mobility, biological scientists are more dependent on the prestige of their graduate departments.

A degree of variability in mobility over successive jobs among fields exists. The effect of the previous job seems to increase in the humanities and natural sciences. The effect appears to be modest in the social and biological sciences.

Notes

1. The details of the IDE model are derived here.
   If the observed counts x_{ij} ($i,j = 1,2,3,4$) are distributed as Poisson with respective means m_{ij} which satisfy

   $$\log m_{ij} = \mu + \alpha_i + \beta_j + \gamma I \ (i=j)$$

   (where $\Sigma\alpha_i = \Sigma\beta_j = 0$ for identifiability) then the log likelihood is given by

$$\log f = -\sum_{ij} m_{ij} + \sum_{ij} x_{ij} \cdot \log m_{ij} - \sum_{ij} \log x_{ij}!$$

The Fisher information for γ is

$$-\varepsilon \frac{\delta^2}{\delta \gamma^2} \log f = \sum_i m_{ii}$$

which is approximately the reciprocal of the variance of $\hat{\gamma}$. Birch's conditions (Bishop, Fienberg, and Holland, 1975, p. 69) assert that

$$\sum_i m_{ii} = \sum x_{ii}$$

The standard error of $(\hat{\gamma})$ is approximately $(1/\Sigma x_{ii})^{1/2}$. The estimated $(\hat{\gamma})$ is approximately normal in its distribution. [i]

2. Drawbacks to the Markovian process models described in Ross (1972) are appropriate. The process here does not assume stationality. See Chapter 4 of Ross' *Introduction to Probability Models* concerning the *ergodic* nature of the Markovian models.

3. When pooled, the magnitude of G^2 is much more significant, but this problem is not uncommon. See Diaconis and Efron (1985).

References

Allison, P., and Stewart, J.A.(1974) 'Productivity differences among scientists: Evidence for accumulative advantage', *American Sociological Review, 39*, 596–606.

Baron, J.N. (1984) 'Organizational perspectives on stratification', *Annual Review of Sociology, 10*, 37–69.

Baron, J.N. and Bielby, W.T. (1980) 'Bringing the firms back in: Stratification, segmentation, and the organization of work', *American Sociological Review, 45*, 737–765.

Ben-David, J. (1972) *American Higher Education*, New York: McGraw-Hill.

Berelson, B. (1960) *Graduate education in the United States*, New York: McGraw-Hill.

Bishop, Y.M.M., Fienberg, S.E., and Holland, P.W. (1975) *Discrete multivariate analysis*, Cambridge: M.I.T. Press.

Blau, P.M. (1973) *The organization of academic work* New York: John Wiley and Sons.

Brown, D.G. (1967) *The mobile professors* Washington, D.C.: American Council on Education.

Caplow, T., and McGee, R. (1958) *The academic marketplace*, Garden City: Doubleday.

Carnegie Commission on Higher Education (1979) *Classification of institutions of higher education*, New York: McGraw-Hill.

Cartter, A. (1966) *An assessment of quality in graduate education*, Washington, D.C.: American Council on Education.

Clark, B.R. (1983) *The higher education system: Academic organizations in cross-national perspective*, Berkeley: University of California Press.

Cohen, A., and Brawer, F. (1977) *A two-year college instructor today*, New York: Praeger Press.

Cole, J.R. (1979) *Fair science: Women in scientific community*, New York: Free Press.

Cole, J.R., and Cole, S. (1973) *Social stratification in science* Chicago: University of Chicago Press.

Cole, S., Cole, J.R., and Dietrich, L. (1978) 'Measuring the cognitive state of scientific disciplines', in Elkana, Y., Lederberg, J. *et al.* (Eds), *Toward a metric of science*, New York: Wiley and Sons.

Crane, D. (1965) 'Scientists at major and minor universities: A study in productivity and recognition', *American Sociological Review, 30*, 699–714.

Crane, D. (1970) 'The academic market place revisited', *American Journal of Sociology, 75*, 953–964.

Diaconis, P. and Efron, B. (1985) 'Testing for independence in a two-way table: New interpretations of the chi-square statistic', *Annals of Statistics, 13*(3), 845–874.

Doeringer, P.B. and Piore, M.J. (1971) *Internal labor markets and manpower analysis*, Lexington, MA: Lexington Books, D.C. Heath.

Fulton, O. and Trow, M. (1974) 'Research activity in American higher education', *Sociology of Education, 47*, 29–73..

Gaston, J. (1978) *The reward system in British and American science*, New York: John Wiley and Sons.

Goodman, L. (1978) *Analyzing quantitative/categorical data*, Cambridge: Abt Books.

Granovetter, M. (1981) 'Toward a sociological theory of income differences', in Berg, I. (Ed.), *Sociological perspectives on labor markets*, New York: Academic Press.

Haberman, S.J. (1974) *The analysis of frequency data*, Chicago: University of Chicago Press.

Hagstrom, W.O. (1964) 'Anomy in scientific communities', *Social Problems*, (Fall) : 186–194.

Hagstrom, W.O. (1976, August) 'The production of culture in science', *American Behavioral Scientist*, 753–768.

Hagstrom, W.O. and Hargens, L.L. (1968, September) 'Mobility theory in the sociology of science', paper presented at the Cornell Conference on Human Mobility, Ithaca, NY.

Hargens, L.L. (1975) *Patterns of scientific research: A comparative analysis of research in three fields*, Washington, D.C.: American Sociological Association.

Hargens, L.L. and Hagstrom, W.O. (1967) 'Sponsored and contest mobility of American academic scientists', *Sociology of Education, 40*, 24–38.

Hargens, L.L. and Hagstrom, W.O. (1982) 'Scientific consensus and academic status attainment patterns, *Sociology of Education, 55*, 183–196.

Jencks, C. and Riesman, D. (1968) *The academic revolution*, Garden City, NY: Doubleday.

Kalleberg, A.L. and Sorensen, A.B. (1979) 'The sociology of labor markets', *Annual Review of Sociology, 5*, 351–379.

Ladd, E.C. and Lipset, S.M. (1975) *1975 Survey of the American Professoriate* (Tech. Rep.). Storrs, CT: University of Connecticut, Social Science Data Center.

Lodahl, J.B. and Gordon, G. (1972) 'The structure of scientific fields and the functioning of university graduate departments', *American Sociological Review, 37,* 57–72.

Long, J.S. (1978) 'Productivity and academic position in the scientific career', *American Sociological Review, 43,* 889–908.

Long, J.S., Allison, P.D. and McGinnis, R. (1979) 'Entrance into the academic career', *American Sociological Review, 44,* 816–830.

Long, J.S. and McGinnis, R. (1981) 'Organizational context and scientific productivity', *American Sociological Review, 46,* 422–442.

Mayer, T. (1972) 'Models in intergenerational mobility', in Berger, J., Zald, M. and Anderson, B. (Eds), *Sociological theories in progress* (Vol. 2, pp. 308–357), Boston: Houghton Mifflin.

Merton, R.K. (1942) 'Science and technology in a democratic order', *Journal of Legal and Political Sociology, 1,* 115–126.

Pantin, C.F.A. (1968) *The relations between the sciences,* London: Cambridge University Press.

Parsons, T. and Platt, G. (1973) *The American University,* Cambridge, MA: Harvard University Press.

Pfeffer, J., Leong, A. and Strehl, K. (1977) 'Publication and prestige mobility of university departments in three scientific disciplines', *Sociology of Education, 49,* 212–218.

Reich, M., Gordon, D.M. and Edwards, R.C. (1973) 'Dual labor markets: A theory of labor market segmentation', *American Economic Review, 63,* 359–365.

Reskin, B. (1979) 'Academic sponsorship and scientist careers', *Sociology of Education, 52,* 129–146.

Roose, K.D. and Andersen, C.J. (1970) *A Rating of Graduate Programs,* Washington, DC: American Council on Education.

Ross, S.M. (1972) *Introduction to probability models,* New York: Academic Pres.

Rosenbaum, J.E. (1979) 'Tournament mobility: Career patterns in a corporation', *Administrative Science Quarterly, 24,* 220–241.

Smelser, N.J. (1974) 'Growth, structural change, and conflict in California public higher education, 1950–1970', in *Public Higher Education in California,* edited by Neil Smelser and Gabriel Almond, Berkeley: University of California Press.

Smelser, N.J. and Content, R. (1980) *The changing academic market: General trends and a Berkeley case study,* Berkeley: University of California Press.

Spenner, K.I., Otto, L.B. and Call, V.R.A. (1982) *Career lines and careers,* Lexington: D.C. Heath.

Spilerman, S. (1977) 'Careers, labor market structure and socioeconomic achievement', *American Journal of Sociology, 83,* 551–593.

Stolzenberg, R.M. (1975) 'Occupations, labor markets and the process of wage attainments', *American Sociological Review, 40,* 645–665.

White, H. (1970) 'Stayers and movers', *American Journal of Sociology, 76,* 307–324.

Wilson, L. (1942) *The academic man,* New York: Oxford University Press.

Youn, T.I.K. (1982) 'Segmented academic markets and segmented academic careers', paper presented at the Annual Meeting of the American Sociological Association.

Youn, T.I.K. (1981) *The careers of young Ph.D.s: Temporal change and institutional effects*, unpublished doctoral dissertation, Yale University, New Haven, CT.

Zelterman, D., Bonsignore, D. and Danziger, A. (1984) 'Analysis of large sparse tables of discrete data', *Proceedings of the Statistical Computing Section, 1984*, Washington, D.C.: American Statistical Association.

4 Exit and Re-entry in Higher Education

Rachel A. Rosenfeld and Jo Ann Jones

Introduction

In this chapter we look at exit from and re-entry into higher education. More new Ph.D.s are beginning their careers outside higher education even when they would prefer to be in academe because of the shortage of posts in colleges and universities (Bowen, 1981). Other people are forced out of academia into non-academic employment when they fail to obtain tenure or promotion and are unable to find other college or university jobs. Despite efforts of various disciplinary associations to deal with the special circumstances and problems of their members outside the academy, there has been little research on the process by which people leave or re-enter university and college work.

Much of what we know about the careers of Ph.D.s comes from sociology of science research on the careers of those with academic appointments. Such research reflects the assumption that scientific careers, with high value placed on creativity, free inquiry, and non-material rewards, are best carried out within universities. In most disciplines, academic employment, especially at large research universities, has more prestige than non-academic employment. Further, academic employment often gives more opportunity to publish, which in turn leads to higher prestige for the scholar. (See Hagstrom, 1965; Zuckerman, 1970.) Such prestige and the more autonomous working conditions of academia compensate for the often lower salaries paid there as compared with industry and government (Marsh and Stafford, 1967). In part because of these differences in academic and non-academic employment, market pressures forcing people out of academia are seen as problematic.

From the description above, one would expect two factors to affect movement out of academia: general market conditions, with people more likely to leave higher education when there are relatively few academic positions open; and scholarly success, with those publishing less and in less prestigious academic positions more likely to leave. Some of the information on who leaves academia is consistent with these hypotheses. Looking at full-time faculty members laid off from the City University of New York during the 1976 fiscal crisis, Kapsis and Murtha (1985) found that those who were less qualified and in fields with declining enrollments were most likely to have non-academic employment a year afterwards. Palmer and Patton (1981), using data from the 1977 Ladd-Lipset Survey of the American Professoriate, report that those who published less and rated themselves as less successful were more likely than other faculty members to have seriously considered in the previous two years leaving academia permanently. Smith (1983), looking at vacancy chains for coaches of intercollegiate sports, who often hold faculty rank, found that movement in the 'periphery' of the coaches' market tended to be out of college coaching. On the other hand, while Long and McGinnis (1981) found some tendency for those who published to get jobs in research-oriented settings, they found stronger effects of organizational setting on productivity. Those who changed type of employer over time adjusted their productivity to the norm for that setting.

One needs to guard against seeing only pushes out of academia, failing to consider the pulls. The style of non-academic work; reduced emphasis on publishing; not to mention higher income, may all make non-academic employment attractive to some Ph.D.s. One needs to be careful in interpreting effects of 'success' in academia on exit from academe: such lack of success can indicate lack of interest in such achievements rather than inability to succeed. Therefore, one needs to include career interests as a third factor affecting mobility out of academia.

If relatively little is known about exit from academia, even less is known about re-entry. In general, exit from academia is seen as an irreversible career move (e.g., Harmon, 1968). Much non-academic employment does not reward the sorts of activity that are important in academia (Chubin *et al.*, 1981), and as Long and McGinnis (1981) report, people tend to respond by publishing less. While teaching generally does not bring as much prestige within higher education as research, it is still an important activity for a faculty member. Those without academic employment usually have not had a chance to demonstrate that they can teach. Those without a record of teaching might have difficulty in returning to academia even if they have published. Still, Crowley and Chubin (1976) found considerable movement back to academic positions from non-academic ones for relatively young Ph.D.s in the 1960s, a period when academic employment was expanding. When the market is contracting, it might be more difficult to return to academia, not just because the number of positions is smaller but also because the standards for promotion and tenure become higher (Perrucci *et al.*, 1983). Thus, in looking at re-entry, we would expect to see the same general sets of factors at work: (1) career interests; (2) preparation for success in academia; and (3) general market conditions.

In this chapter, we use a sample of psychology Ph.D.s to examine (1) the extent of mobility between academic and non-academic employers and (2) how interests, performance, and time period affect such mobility.

Data

To test our hypotheses, we used data from a sample of academic psychologists selected frm the 1981 *Directory of the American Psychological Association* (APA). The APA is the major professional organization of psychologists in the United States, and its directory is one of the few that contains extensive biographical information about the members. Members submit information on degrees, birth date, jobs held, and interest within psychology to the APA. The APA questionnaire has a response rate of about 80 per cent, which compares favorably with an average return rate of 50 per cent for a typical mailed survey (see also Heinsler and Rosenfeld, 1987).[1]

The availability of career histories in the APA directories determined our decision to study psychologists. Various characteristics of the field, though, make this a good choice. Psychologists have more career options outside higher education (e.g., market research and private practice) than most social scientists, humanists, and even some natural scientists (Chubin *et al.*, 1981: Table 1). Russo *et al.* (1981: Table 8), for example, show that in 1978 only 43 per cent of full-time employed doctorate members of the APA had academic employment. Jones *et al.* (1982: 20) report that 47 per cent of 1975–79 psychology doctorates had made commitments to non-academic employment. We try to control for this phenomenon by selecting those with early academic employment, but also see these options as making this group more interesting to study. Other social scientists are trying to expand non-academic opportunities, and discussions of mid-life career changes out of academia (e.g., Palmer and Patton, 1981) are not limited to specific disciplines. What we find for psychologists might foretell the future for other disciplines. Further, even within academic careers there is considerable heterogeneity in psychologists' style of work. While some are concerned with the physical basis of behavior, others function more like social scientists, while still others do work that resembles philosophy. This heterogeneity makes psychology more representative of academia as a whole than would be true of many other disciplines.

Because we used career histories rather than cross-sectional data, we did not have an unambiguous definition of academic employment. Further, we had to decide when the career began. Given that a doctorate is often a requirement for holding better academic jobs and that early employment choices to some extent condition the nature of later ones, we defined the receipt of the Ph.D. (or in a few cases an Ed.D., though we will use the term Ph.D. for all doctorates) as the beginning of a career and selected only those whose first jobs (or first jobs following postdoctoral fellowships) were in academic institutions. After the first job, however, we put no restrictions on location of employment. Although some members of our sample had careers before they received their doctorates, we took the first post-Ph.D. job as the start of the career, because for some people the degree was a way to change fields and for others it changed the conditions of an existing career.

We chose our sample by making a random start and then selecting the first woman on every fourth page of the 1981 APA Directory who had both (1) received her Ph.D. between 1965 and 1974 and (2) held a first job (or job subsequent to postdoctoral training) in an academic institution. This procedure created a sample of 311 women. A sample with an equal number of men was then generated by including the first man who met the criteria above of degree year and first position following each selected woman. Sex was identified by first names.[2]

Our sample somewhat over-represents women. This imbalance is not as great as it would be in many other disciplines: psychology doctorates include a fairly high proportion of women, and women doctorates in general are more likely to have academic employment than men (National Academy of Sciences, 1979). We did not weight the data in any way to correct for the sex ratio.

The job histories were recreated for the sample from the biographical information given in the 1981 APA directory. Consistency of reporting and missing information were checked through comparison of the 1981 information with the preceeding seven APA directories. Each job was coded as tenure track, non-tenure track, or non-academic, with each of these groups further subdivided into more detailed job categories. We defined a job as a given rank or title at a given workplace. If a person held two or more jobs concurrently, the academic job (if any) was considered the main job.

We retrieved a history of each sample member's published articles from the Dialog Computer Search of the Social Science Citation Index, the Social Science Citation Index, and the Science Citation Index for the years 1962–81. Articles were assigned to jobs by comparing publication dates with the re-created job history dates.[3]

We thus have information on nearly all career changes, as well as on the sort of information that appears on curriculum vitae, which is supposed to be the basis for advancement within academia. We do not have information on personal situation (e.g., marital status or number of children) that might further constrain career choices.[4]

Variables and Hypotheses

Outcomes

When using type of employing institution as an outcome, we distinguish all non-academic employers from academic ones. As we discuss below, our analysis is in two parts: of where people are at a particular stage in their careers; and of rates of mobility out of and into academe. Our dependent variable is thus either the chance of being in an academic rather than non-academic institution or the rate of moving between type of institutions.

Academic Institutions

When we look at the determinants of re-entering academia, we do not differentiate among types of non-academic employers which people are leaving. (See Long and McGinnis, 1981, for an example of how non-academic jobs can be further classified by opportunity for research.) When we look at exits from academia, however, we do make distinctions among the types of employers which people leave.

From the several ratings and rankings of universities and psychology departments that exist, we draw on the Carnegie Commision (1971) rating of universities and colleges, done at the time when most of our respondents were beginning their post-Ph.D. careers.[5] Quality I institutions represent the top locations, the large research universities where one is likely to have the facilities, students, and money to do research. Quality II and III institutions were combined as the 'other' university category, distinguished from the category formed by IV, V, and VI institutions (four-year colleges), where teaching is more important. Quality VII institutions (junior and technical colleges) and 'unrated' (often smaller, less well-known universities and colleges) were kept as separate categories. This distinction between universities and colleges is similar to that Long and McGinnis (1981) and Reskin (1977) make.[6]

To the extent that an institution's prestige accrues to the individual, one would expect Smith's results (1983) for coaches to hold for faculty more generally. Holding overall market conditions and publication records constant, one would predict that those from lower rated universities or predominantly teaching institutions would be more likely to leave academia. On the other hand, it is often more difficult to get tenure at the more prestigious institutions and, therefore, perhaps more likely that a person denied tenure would feel a failure in academia and decide to leave. Further, there are more non-tenure track positions at the large research universities. Thus, being in a top research university, *ceteris paribus*, could represent a less secure future with perhaps greater incentive to leave academia. It is thus not clear that, controlling for type of academic position, Smith's results would hold for our sample. Because we control for period, publications, and rank within the institution, our expectation is that type of institution will not affect the probability of leaving academia.

Positions

We classify positions as assistant professor, associate professor, full professor, non-tenure track, and non-academic. The first three positions are generally considered the main promotional ladder in academia. Some of the positions we include in the non-tenure track category might in some institutions be part of this ladder, in particular the position of instructor (Howard, 1978). Instructor tends to be either the rank held until the Ph.D. is actually granted, however, or designates a temporary job. Some non-tenure track positions, such as dean, might be considered desirable and even promotions beyond tenure track. For many people in our sample, such appointments were held simultaneously with a tenure track position, and the main position would be coded as the latter rather than the former. Only nineteen of our 622 psychologists, for example, were coded as holding academic administrative positions at the end of their observed histories. Other non-tenure track positions listed in the APA directories were temporary positions, e.g., visiting professor, or ones where the main activity was not 'academic', e.g., counselor. Since it was difficult to tell when these positions reflected leaves rather than being limited appointments (see Roemer and Schnitz, 1982), we put them in the non-tenure track category. In general, putting all non-tenure track positions together does not seem to do an injustice to these careers. Also, we do not have enough cases to subdivide this category further. To the extent that higher rank indicates both success and desire to succeed in academia, we predict that full professors would be most likely to remain in academia and those off tenure track least likely.

In looking at those outside academia and predicting who would return, we use the history of academic positions to measure teaching experience. We do not have a direct measure of the activities in which people engage in a given job, but assume that tenure track positions usually involve at least some teaching. Therefore, we hypothesize that those outside academia with a greater number of previous tenure track positions will be more likely to return to academia.

When we analyze movement back to academia, we further characterize the non-academic positions held as consulting, research, clinical (for some employer), administrative, private practice, or a residual category. To the extent that it is easier to move back to academia when a person has been involved in activities resembling those of an academic, we predict that those with non-academic research jobs will be those most likely to return to academia and those in clinical positions least likely.

Productivity

A variable that we expect to be important in explaining employment positions and mobility patterns is productivity. To predict employment location, we include a cumulative number of articles published by the beginning of the job held at that career stage. Those who have a history of more publication are expected to be more likely to be within academia. In the analysis of mobility we calculate cumulative number of articles published by the beginning of each job and the rate of publication per year while in that job. Those who have published more and who publish at a higher rate should be those with the inclination and ability to stay in or move to academia.

Clinical Experience or Preparation

At least some members of our sample were involved in clinical practice. These people may have different career trajectories, expectations, requirements, and opportunities than other psychologists. To see the effect of a clinical or counseling orientation, we added to our models a variable that summarized the person's training and career: those who had a degree in counseling or clinical psychology, listed these areas as speciality interests, or did clinical or counseling psychology at some time during their careers were classified in a category different from those without these characteristics. For convenience, we call this group the clinical psychologists, although strictly speaking they are not all 'clinical psychologists'. We predict those who have clinical and counseling interests and training to be most likely to leave and remain out of academia. In addition, we suggest that the whole process of mobility differs for clinical as compared with non-clinical psychologists, with indicators of academic success being weaker predictors of mobility patterns for the clinical group. These would be the people for whom the pull of non-academic careers (something we cannot include directly in our models) could be a major motivation to leave academia. Those without clinical training and experience would be individuals for whom the push out of academia would be more important.

Period

We measure tightness of the academic labor market by a variable indicating whether the year a job began was before 1972. Around 1970, the number of new Ph.D.s equalled the number of junior faculty openings. Thereafter, the number of earned doctorates surpassed the number of openings (Bowen, 1981). By 1972, *The American Psychologist*, the journal of the American Psychological Association, had a special issue on 'Psychology's Manpower', focused in part on adjusting to the new academic market conditions (e.g.,

Boneau, 1972; Perloff, 1972). We expect that those who took jobs after 1971 would be more likely to end up in non-academic employment and less likely to return to academia.[7]

Other Variables

In looking at mobility patterns and outcomes, we also include ranking of psychology doctorate department (Roose and Andersen, 1970: ranging from 1 = institution with highest ranked graduate faculty to 62.5 = adequate, with 90 = unranked, following Cox and Catt, 1977), age at completion of the Ph.D., sex, and the number of previous institutional moves. A great deal of literature (e.g., Caplow and McGee, 1958; Long *et al.*, 1979) stresses the importance of academic origins for success, especially early in one's career. Age is also a factor. Being relatively young at any career stage is an asset in academia (Cole, 1979). Further, the young are more geographically mobile than those who are older (e.g., Sandefur and Scott, 1981). Thus, those who start their careers at younger ages might be more successful within academia, but also more likely to make career changes. Sex is included because the careers of women and men differ. Women might be more constrained than men by family and personal circumstances in following their careers. Further, women have not always been rewarded within academia with prestige and good positions (Rosenfeld, 1984). Women might be especially likely to leave academia because they would be unable to change jobs in a way to maximize their career returns (see Rosenfeld and Jones, 1986, 1987).[8] Previous mobility could also be an important variable to include. Previously mobile individuals might either be less mobile in the future or, conversely, be perennial movers. Further, too much mobility could be a liability if viewed as an indicator of instability.

Method of Analysis

We begin our analysis by examining the kinds of jobs (academic or non-academic) our sample members hold six years after receiving their doctorates. We have at least six years in most of our career histories, and by this time there has been at least some opportunity for promotion to associate professor with tenure for those who remained on tenure track. We use logistic regression (Harrell, 1980) to see how career beginnings, publications, period, and other variables predict type of sixth-year employment.

In looking at what has happened by the sixth year, we are treating our data as though they were from a panel study. This analysis can be viewed as looking at movement out of academia over a six-year period, given that we chose the sample to have academic first jobs. Using only the first- and sixth-year career locations, we cannot look at the process of re-entry to academia. Further, we lose information on moves made before and after the sixth year. Some people never change location, while others move among types of employment several times. To take advantage of having career histories of up to fifteen years, rather than only information on where people are at specific times, we also use a method to describe mobility that conceptualizes it as a continuous time, discrete state process. Models are of the form

$$r_{ij} = \exp\,(XB),$$

where X is a row vector of independent variables; B is a column vector of coefficients; and r is the instantaneous transition rate,

$$r_{ij} = \lim_{d \to 0} \frac{P_{ij}(t,t+d)}{d}$$

i.e., the limit of the probability (P) of making a move from state i to state j over some time period t to t+d per unit time (see Carroll, 1983; Tuma *et al.*, 1979). The states of interest are the types of employment (academic and non-academic). The exponential form prevents obtaining rates that are negative, which would be meaningless since the rate is the limit of a positive quantity. It also corresponds to a Poisson distribution of the expected number of moves, which is a classic way of describing the distribution of relatively rare events (Tuma *et al.*, 1979).

To estimate such models, we reorganized the data into pairs of jobs. One problem is that we do not know how certain jobs end: the last job each person holds is right censored. Not taking this into account could bias our results (Tuma and Hannan, 1978). The RATE program we used to estimate our models (Tuma, 1980) uses information on censored cases. Another problem is that the values of some variables change within a type of employer, a variation which might modify chances of moving. In particular, people could change rank, type of position, or employer within academia (or non-academia). We dealt with this problem by including *every* pair of jobs, including those within an employer type, but treating intra-sector moves as censored (see Petersen, 1986, for a justification of this procedure). Thus, someone who held two positions at one university and then moved to a non-academic employer would have three records: one for the pair of jobs in the first institutions, where the observation for time in this state would be censored; one for the pair of jobs covering the change of employer; and a final, censored observation for the last job. Someone who held only one job during the period of our observation would have one record, a censored one.

Still a third problem is that some people contribute more than one move to the data set, introducing heterogeneity that might not be controlled for by our independent variables. As Allison (1984) points out, while some researchers (e.g., Flinn and Heckman, 1982) have experimented with corrections for this problem, there are no generally recommended solutions yet. In lieu of a solution, the most one can do is try to specify the model well. Measures of previous mobility and type of career are included in our analysis in part as controls for otherwise unobserved heterogeneity.[9]

Results

Movement Out of Academia by the Sixth Year

All of our sample members began their post-Ph.D. careers within academia. Six years later, most were still there. At that career stage, 84 per cent held jobs in academic institutions (Table 1).[10] Individuals with clinical and counseling training and experience, however, were less likely than non-clinical psychologists to be in academia − 77 per cent compared with 92 per cent. Even this proportion is high, suggesting that the sample is indeed of academic psychologists.

Psychologists holding jobs outside academia tended to have private practice or other clinical positions or to be involved with administration. Individuals classified as non-clinical as compared with clinical differ in their distribution over types of non-academic jobs, with those labeled non-clinical being more likely to hold research or consulting positions and less likely to have jobs involving clinical work.

Logistic regressions predicting whether a person had a non-academic as compared with academic position six years after earning a Ph.D. provides some support for the idea that it is those who are less well situated and interested in academia who leave.[11] (See table 2.)

Table 1 Job Six Years After Earning Ph.D. in Percentages: APA Sample

Type of Position	Total	Clinical	Non-clinical
No position listed	1.7	1.6	1.7
Academic	84.3	76.9	92.0
Non-academic	14.0	21.5	6.2
Total	100.0	100.0	99.9
(N)	(592)	(303)	(289)
Type of Non-academic Position			
Consultant	3.6	1.5	11.1
Research	9.6	1.5	38.9
Clinical counseling	27.7	33.8	5.6
Administration	27.7	24.6	38.9
Other	2.4	3.1	0
Private practice	28.9	35.4	5.6
Total	99.9	99.9	100.1

NOTE: Totals for percentages differ from 100 due to rounding.

Those with non-clinical versus clinical backgrounds were more likely to hold academic jobs, as were those with more publications. Those who held first jobs at schools other than the top research universities were more likely to hold non-academic jobs, although most of these contrasts are not statistically significant. There is a period effect, as well. When the job held six years after finishing graduate school began after 1971, it was more likely to be non-academic, consistent with the idea that the academic market for psychologists was tighter after that date.

We had expected these effects to be stronger for individuals without the alternative opportunities open to psychologists with clinical and counseling experience and training. Here, however, the effects are stronger for clinical as compared with non-clinical psychologists. For clinical psychologists publications, type of first employer, and period have significant effects in predicting type of sixth-year location. The model as a whole is not even significant for the non-clinical sample members. This finding could mean either that the selection process operates more strongly among those with options outside of academia or that the small number of non-clinical psychologists who were outside of academia makes the results inconclusive.

Moving between Academia and Non-academia

Comparing the first position with that held six years later misses many moves made during the six years and afterwards and does not

Table 2 Logistic Regression for Whether Job Six Years After Earning Ph.D. is Non-academic: APA Sample

Independent Variables	Total	Clinical	Non-clinical
Field (1 = clinical, 2 = non-clinical)	−1.75**	—	—
Sex (0 = M, 1 = F)	−.09	−.03	−.62
Age when Ph.D. received	.007	.03	−.15#
R.A. ranking of Ph.D. department	−.005	−.008	.002
(1 = highest ranked, 90 = unranked)			
Year job began (0 = 72, 1 = 72)	1.32**	1.66**	.50
Origin position =			
tenure track	−.05	.03	−.39
no position listed	.03	.23	−.43
'other' university[a]	.78	1.02#	.06
4-yr college	1.02#	1.38#	.18
junior college[b]	.36	.80	—
unrated university[b]	.83	1.52#	—
Articles published by beginning of job	−.20*	−.20#	−.23
Intercept	−.80	−3.85**	1.97
Observed probability	.145	.235	.055
N 516			
	260	256	
Model X^2	63.0**	31.7**	6.7
R	.30	.19	0.0

#.05 p .10
*.01 p .05
**p .01

[a] Rating by Carnegie Commission (1971).
[b] For non-clinical, because of small number of cases in these cells, 'unrated' was classified with 'other' universities and 'junior' with '4-yr' colleges.

allow us to look at moves back into academia. In Table 3, we use complete career histories to describe movement out of and into academia. Job shifts in this table are any change of either title or employer.[12] Most completed job shifts for this sample are between academic jobs. Overall, however, almost 30 per cent are out of academic positions. It is possible, but relatively rare, to move from a non-academic back to an academic job, with only 7 per cent of the job shifts being this type.[13] Once again, there are differences in the mobility patterns of those classified as clinical compared with those classified as non-clinical. Those in the clinical category are more likely to move to and within the non-academic market. Overall movement back to academia, however, occurs with the same relative frequency for the jobs shifts of both groups, although as a proportion of moves other than within academia, moves back to academia are relatively more frequent for the non-clinical group.

What predicts the rate at which psychologists move out of academia? Table 4 provides answers to this question.[14] Productivity

Table 3 Description of Job Shifts in Percentages: APA Sample

(N) Shift type	Total (1527)[a]	Clinical (758)	Non-clinical (769)
Academic–non-academic	9.2	14.2	4.2
Non-academic–academic	2.4	2.9	2.0
Academic–academic	19.5	15.8	23.1
Non-academic–non-academic	2.9	4.6	1.2
Censored[b]	66.0	62.4	69.6
Total	100.0	99.9	100.1
Excluding censored shifts	(519)	(285)	(234)
Academic–non-academic	27.0	37.9	13.7
Non-academic–academic	7.1	7.7	6.4
Academic–academic	57.4	42.1	76.1
Non-academic–non-academic	8.5	12.2	3.8
Total	100.0	99.9	100.0

[a] Totals differ from 100 because of rounding.
[b] Job shifts within the same institution to 'no position listed' and from the last job of the history are right censored.

and interests are part of the story: those who publish at a higher rate and those with non-clinical versus clinical careers move out of academia more slowly. Position within academia shows some effect, with full and associate professors slower to move out of academic settings than assistant professors. The type of school has no effect, with type of position and publications controlled. Thus, the prediction of no net institution effect is supported here. When type of position and publications are not included, however, there is still no significant contrast among types of schools in their effects on mobility out of academia. Age at earning the Ph.D. probably represents an 'inertia' effect, with the older recipients slower to change positions overall. The hint of a negative effect in the previous analysis, however, might be in part a prestige effect.

One difference between these results and those obtained by treating the data as a panel is the effect of sex: women moved more quickly out of academia. This phenomenon could represent forces making academia less attractive for women or generally greater career discontinuity for them. Rank of graduate department, a resource especially early in an academic career, also has significant effects here but not in the panel analysis. Those with Ph.D.s from better departments (especially if they have clinical careers) leave academia more slowly. Period, on the other hand, which did have an effect when we looked at one particular career stage, has no significant effect here.

Table 4   Predicting Rates of Moving Out of Academia: APA Sample

Independent Variables	Total	Clinical	Non-clinical
Field (1 = clinical, 2 = non-clinical)	−1.35**	—	—
Sex (0 = M, 1 = F)	.58**	.50**	.72#
Age when Ph.D. received	−.03*	−.02	−.15*
R.A. ranking of Ph.D. department	−.006#	−.008*	.003
Year job began (0 = 72, 1 = 72)	−.04	−.06	.22
Origin position =			
associate professor	−.53#	−.39	−1.04
professor	−.19*	−.87	−10.76
non-tenure track	.25	.31	.21
Origin institution =			
'other' university	.05	−.08	.76
4-year college	.41	.46	.48
junior college	−.43	−.28	−9.92
unrated	.19	.26	−.32
No. articles published by beginning of origin job	.06	.05	.008
Articles/year in origin job	−.56*	−.48#	−.95#
No. institutional changes	−.11	−.11	−.02
Constant	−.61	−2.34**	−.50
Model X^2	100.77**	32.35**	34.96**
No. jobs	1174	525	649
No. transitions	123	96	27

.05   p   .10
* .01   p   .05
**p   .01

Disaggregating the sample by type of career interest does not give any additional insights. Unlike results from the panel data, the predictive power of the model is not necessarily stronger for the clinical group. For clinical and non-clinical psychologists, having more publications has a modest negative effect on movement out of academia, while other measures of career success have none.

Looking at prediction of rates of moving back to academia (in Table 5), we see some confirmation of our interpretation of the effects of some of the control variables. Being female accelerates the rate of returning to academia, suggesting that the effect of sex in predicting rates of leaving academia is one of career discontinuity.[15] Age when finishing graduate school again has a negative effect, consistent with its interpretation as a measure of increasing immobility.

Publishing is important for returning to academia: those who publish at a higher rate move more quickly back to academia (Table 5). Whether rate of publication is controlled or not, the type of position held outside academia has no effect. When number of tenure track positions replaces number of institutional changes, however, it

Table 5 Predicting Rates of Moving Into Academia: APA Sample

Independent Variables	Total	Clinical
Field (1 = clinical, 2 = non-clinical)	.30	—
Sex (0 = M, 1 = F)	1.25**	1.78**
Age when Ph.D. received	−.07#	−.08*
R.A. ranking of Ph.D. department	.008	.005
Year job began (0 = 72, 1 = 72)	−.63	−1.17*
Origin position[a]		
research	—	—
clinical (employee)	.05	.23
administration	−.80	—
private practice	−.25	.12
No. articles published by beginning of origin job	−.31#	−.36
Articles/year in origin job	.96**	1.48*
No. institutional changes	−.41	−.40
Constant	−.72	−.52
Model X^2	41.24**	26.02**
No. jobs	189	148
No. transitions	31	19

[a] Due to small numbers of cases, consulting is put in the 'other' contrast category for the combined group, and research, consulting, and administration are in the 'other' category for analysis of clinical psychologists.

\#.05 p .10
*.01 p .05
**p .01

has an effect opposite the one we had expected: having more jobs, which probably involved teaching, decreased the rate of moving back to academia. This could be because this variable measures career length and thus career age as well as teaching experience, with those farther along in their careers less likely to make any type of move.

For at least the clinical subsample, there is again a period effect: when a job began after 1971, the rate of return to academia was slower. This effect combined with the preceeding results suggests that the effect of a tight market is not so much to squeeze people out of academia as to make it more difficult for them to return. (Of course, those just beginning their careers might find it more difficult to find first jobs in academia, something we cannot test with our data).

Summary and Discussion

In this chapter, we followed the 1970s (and in some cases, late 1960s) careers of a sample of psychologists who began their careers in academic insitutions. Most of them were still in academia six years after finishing their Ph.D.s. Looking at all their jobs shifts, we found that while a sizeable proportion were out of academia, return to academia was relatively rare. In predicting non-academic versus academic location and mobility between academic and non-academic employment, we found evidence that both interests and success had effects. Those with clinical training and interests were more likely to be out of academia six years after finishing their doctoral training and quicker to leave academia (although not slower to return to academia). Those who published more and at a faster rate were more likely to remain within higher education. To some extent, those at the top research universities were less likely to be found outside academia after six years, and those with higher academic rank were slower to leave college and university employers. Type of institution, however, did not affect rate of exit from academia, nor did type of non-academic position affect rate of returning. Psychologists receiving their degrees from top-ranked departments, who could be seen as having more prestige within academia at the beginning of their careers, were also slower to leave academia. Those starting a particular job during the tight academic market of the 1970s were less likely to be in academic settings within six years of receiving their Ph.D.s and were slower to return to them, given that they had left. There was, however, no evidence that the tighter market squeezed people out of the academy once they had begun careers there. Women were faster to leave colleges and universities, but they were also faster to return, which is perhaps why there were no gender effects on sixth-year location. Individuals who were older when they received their Ph.D.s were slower to make any career shift, although they were also (among the non-clinical psychologists) less likely to be within academia six years after getting their degrees, suggesting both inertia and prestige effects.

In general, then, our results suggest that psychologists less successful within academia and with options outside it are those most likely to leave. These are the people who may well do better in terms of work satisfaction in non-academic positions. As Palmer and Patton (1981) point out, when these people leave academia they may free jobs for new Ph.D.s who are interested in academic careers. They suggest that more information on non-academic careers be made available (through universities and professional associations, perhaps) to those considering such a career change. As those of us helping to place new Ph.D.s know, lack of knowledge about non-academic employment is widespread and a problem in giving individuals enough information

to make decisions about the types of jobs they would like. Most of
graduate education is aimed at preparing and socializing students for
being professors. In thinking about graduate programs, we should
consider including not only knowledge about non-academic
employment, but also training that would prepare students for non-
academic jobs, something that clinical psychology programs seem to
do. Not only would students unsuited for or uninterested in academic
jobs have a better chance of getting established in non-academic
careers, but also those who do go into academia would have more
options in changing careers if they subsequently decided to do so.
Further, we might also help create jobs outside academia by showing
employers how they could use Ph.D.s in our disciplines.

As we have shown, people do leave academia, and when they do
so they rarely return. In other research (Rosenfeld and Jones, 1986),
we looked more generally at mobility and did not find being out of
academia a general barrier to re-entering. To the extent that those in
non-academic settings publish less than those in academia, as other
research suggests, leaving academia does make it harder to return.
Most of those who decide to change to a non-academic career spend a
considerable amount of time and energy making this decision (e.g.,
Palmer and Patton, 1981: 394), realizing that it can be an irreversible
move, especially in a tight market. Those who want to return to
academia, or at least have this as an option, need to keep in mind the
need to publish, even if this is not the activity rewarded in their new
career location.

In general, our models were not very powerful, in part because of
our relatively small sample size and few transitions of various kinds.
But lack of power could also be caused by the difficulty of predicting
career moves. In each case, individuals weigh career benefits and
losses from such a move. Even within academia, people trade prestige
for salary, rank, and other resources when moving among insiti-
tuions. Such trade-offs would be even more complicated when
moving out of academia. Individuals often are not just following their
own careers but are taking into consideration a spouse's career,
children's stage in school, and other personal factors. A non-academic
job, for example, might be seen as an option when a spouse has an
academic job in a particular location where there are no other
academic jobs open. Securing a job is not based simply on action and
decisions by the potential employees, but also requires a position to be
open and the potential employer to be making a hiring decision.
Changes in academia's reward structure relative to non-academe (e.g.,
the worsening relative salary position of academics), in academics'

families (with more dual-career families), and in the academic labor market (with an improvement of the market predicted in the next decade) may all affect what we see with respect to non-academic versus academic employment in the future. Those of us in academia should be more aware of the non-academic side of our disciplines, while those outside of academe should share information about their settings if we are to have a better sense of how careers can develop across types of employers.

Notes

1. Heinsler and Rosenfeld (1987) checked the reliability and validity of these data gathered from published sources with those from curriculum vitae provided by a sub-sample of the APA members included here. After two mail follow-ups, 52 per cent of those asked responded with a c.v. Those who did send us a c.v. seemed to be those involved and successful in academia. We are, therefore, more likely to include individuals who leave academia by relying on the APA data than by relying on our having tried to survey Ph.D.s directly. In general, the data from the sources we use here correlate highly with those on the c.v.s, and analyses using the c.v. data led to the same conclusions as those using the published data, such that there is no reason to believe the quality of the published information is lower than what we gathered directly.

    One could argue that by using a membership directory, however, we lose those who have left academia or the field entirely. To check whether using the 1981 Directory as a basis for our sample led us to overlook those who had left the APA or psychology earlier in their careers, we took a sample of ten men and ten women meeting out sample criteria from the 1968 Directory and followed them forward through the following membership lists and directories. Doing this, we lost three women before 1980 – one to what was obviously retirement, one immediately after her first appearance in the directory (perhaps because of a name change), and one for reasons that were not obvious from the listings. We also 'lost' one man because of what seemed to be a change in the spelling of his name. At the same time, using a more recent directory means we were less likely to lose women with name changes and temporary drop outs. Out of a random sub-sample of ten men and ten women in our APA sample, two men and two women were *not* in an earlier directory where they might be expected to be first listed after receiving their Ph.D.s..

2. Persons with ambiguous given names (e.g., Pat or Jan) were excluded from the sample.

3. We also collected information on books published by members of our sample. Very few people had published books. In other analyses, book publication had no significant effect on mobility outcomes (see Rosenfeld and Jones, 1987), so we do not include it in our analyses.

4. For an earlier cohort of academic psychologists, it was possible to find date of marriage and number of children in *American Men* (and later Women) of *Science* (AMWS) (see Rosenfeld, 1981). Almost no members of the cohorts included here were listed in AMWS. People at the AMWS office could give no real reason for this, other than that graduate departments and employers were not responding to their inquiries.

5. Since we are using cases from only one discipline, one might argue that we should use departmental rankings. The Quality I Carnegie category, however, overlaps heavily with the top psychology departments as ranked by Roose and Andersen (1970). All of the top ten departments are in the Quality I category, as were twenty-two of the top thirty departments. Conversely, only two of twenty-nine universities in the first category had psychology departments only rated 'good'; two had departments rated 'adequate'; and three had unrated departments. Further, one could argue that both quality of the department and of the university are important for a scholar. A top department in a top university is more likely to have good facilities, good colleagues from other departments, and good networks. For someone not in a psychology department (as was true for some of our sample members in some of their jobs), the university's prestige would be more important than the department's. One could also argue for the use of updated ratings or rankings which are available for both departments and universities. These later ratings, however, correlate very highly with the ones we use (e.g., Jones *et al.*, 1982). Further, the earlier ratings reflect the conditions under which our sample spent at least the early parts of their careers.

6. Long and McGinnis (1981) and Reskin (1977) define universities as schools that grant advanced degrees in the fields they study. There were a few instances in our data of people receiving their doctorates from what were classified as colleges. We recoded these schools into the appropriate university categories.

7. One might argue that this is too crude a measure of period, especially given that many of the sample members did not begin their careers until after 1971. We reanalysed all the analyses of this chapter using the actual year when a job began, rather than the dichotomous measure of period. This gave the same substantive results as using the dichotomous variable. When starting a job after 1971 had a negative effect, so did the year a job began, reflecting the worsening situation across the time we observed this sample.

8. This sort of argument suggests that the return to, say, publications will differ by sex. Other work, however, does not show that effects of geographic or institutional mobility differ by sex (Rosenfeld and Jones, 1986, 1987). Therefore, we do not generally look for interactions with sex here.

9. One phenomenon commonly observed in job and other sorts of mobility is that the longer someone has been in a given job or place, the slower his/her rate of mobility. It is difficult to test whether this is the result of unobserved heterogeneity or time dependency (and some argue that it is even difficult to distinguish these influences substantively; see Sørensen, 1983). One can, however, model the time dependence in various ways.

In an earlier article (Rosenfeld and Jones, 1987) on geographic mobility (very often associated with institutional mobility), we estimated Gompertz and Makeham's Law models of time dependency. We did not find them any improvement over the simpler model without explicit time dependency. We therefore use the simpler model here as well.

10. The N in Table 1 is less than 622 because not all sample members had six years of history. Someone who received a Ph.D. in 1974 but had last informed the APA of employment status in 1978 (as indicated by the recency date for that person's entry in the directory) would be an example of someone excluded here. Such short histories are not a problem for the event history analysis, because that analysis uses all pieces of the career history, rather than the pieces of career histories from certain stages.

11. Age had a cosiderable amount of data missing. Excluding age at receipt of Ph.D., however, did not greatly change the results. One might ask whether 'first job on tenure track' and type of school in which first job was held were somewhat redundant, given the greater number of non-tenure track positions available in the larger universities. The models in Table 2 were estimated including only one or the other set of variables without any substantive change in the results.

12. The 1,527 job pairs exclude those begun from a period for which we could not reconstruct the job history (thirty-six for men and seventy-seven for women), since for these periods we could not really specify the nature of mobility, but include censored jobs, i.e., the last in a history. The 1,527 job pairs contained 519 employer changes, less than one per person. This finding is inconsistent with the image of the 'mobile professor' (e.g., Brown, 1967), but is consistent with what others have observed recently (e.g., Long and McGinnis, 1981; Youn and Zelterman, 1985).

13. A possible explanation for the small number of transitions observed from non-academic to academic positions would be the comparatively short time sample members have spent outside academia: because of the selection criteria which required an academic first position, the sample members have had more time to leave academia than to re-enter it. To investigate this explanation, we took all those who listed their last jobs as non-academic in our sample and found their subsequent career history in the 1985 APA Directory (which was not available when we began our research), adding up to four years to their histories. The results of following the careers of these 120 people are as follows:

	Women %	Men %
to academic job	8.8	0
same position	60.3	61.5
to other non-academic position	16.2	30.7
retired	1.5	0
not found	13.2	7.7
Total	100.0	99.9
(N)	(68)	(52)

Of the six women who returned to academia, all accepted marginal jobs, e.g., adjunct faculty or contract lecturer. There thus seems to be a real lack of mobility back to academia.

14. One consequence of having multiple records from the same individuals is that the standard errors may be underestimated. We therefore are cautious about interpreting results significant only at the .10 level, despite our relatively small sample sizes.

15. To test further the extent to which moves into and out of academia indicate disruptions in a career rather than career building, especially for women, we estimated the models in Tables 4 and 5 including whether the job ended in a geographic move and an interaction of a geographic move with sex. There is a problem with considering geographic mobility a predictor of job changes, in that the decision to change jobs and locations is often made simultaneously. However, one could still reason that to the extent women's moves into and out of academia represent career disruption more than for men, geographic mobility would be more likely to involve a change in type of employer for women than for men. We found that jobs ending in geographic moves significantly increased the rate at which psychologists shifted between academia and non-academia, but that there was not an interaction with sex.

References

Allison, P. (1984) *Event History Analysis*, Beverley Hills, CA: Sage.

Boneau, A. (1972) 'On growing wiser: Learning from the employment problems of other disciplines', *American Psychologist* 27: 367–70.

Bowen, W. (1981) 'Market prospects for Ph.D.s in the United States', *Population and Development Review* 7: 475–88.

Brown, D. (1967) *The Mobile Professors*, Washington, DC: American Council on Education.

Caplow, T. and McGee, R. (1958) *The Academic Marketplace*, New York: Basic Books.

Carnegie Commission on Higher Education (1971) *A Classification of Institutions of Higher Education* (Technical Report), New York: McGraw-Hill.

Carroll, G. (1983) 'Dynamic analysis of discrete dependent variables: A didactic essay', *Quality and Quantity* 17: 425–60.

Chubin, D., Porter, A. and Boeckmann, M. (1981) 'Career patterns of scientists: A case for complementary data', *American Sociological Review* 46: 488–96.

Cole, J.P. (1979) *Fair Science: Women in the Scientific Community*, New York: The Free Press.

Cox, W. and Catt, V. (1977) 'Productivity ratings of graduate programs in psychology based on publications in the journals of the American Psychological Association', *American Psychologist* 32: 793–813.

Crowley, C. and Chubin, D. (1976) 'The occupational structure of science: A log-linear analysis of the intersectoral mobility of American sociologists', *Sociological Quarterly* 17: 197–217.

Flinn, C. and Heckman, J. (1982) 'New methods for analyzing individual event histories', in Leinhardt, S. (Ed.), *Sociological Methodology, 1982*, San Francisco: Jossey-Bass, pp. 99–140.

Hagstrom, W. (1965) *The Scientific Community*, New York: Basic Books.

Harmon, L. (1968) *Careers of Ph.D.s: Academic vs. Non-academic. Career Pattern Report 2*, Washington, DC: National Academy of Sciences.

Harrell, F. (1980) 'The LOGIST procedure', in *SAS Supplemental Library User's Guide: 1980 Ed.*, Cary, NC: SAS Institute, pp. 83–102.

Heinsler, J. and Rosenfeld, R. (1985) 'Type of data and academics' careers', paper presented at the annual meeting of the Southern Sociological Society, Charlotte, NC, April 1985.

Howard, S. (1978) *But We Will Persist: A Comparative Research Report on the Status of Women in Academe*, Washington, DC : American Association of University Women.

Jones, L., Gardner, L. and Coggeshall, P. (Eds) (1982) *An Assessment of Research-Doctorate Programs in the US: Social and Behavioral Sciences*, Washington, DC: National Academy Press.

Kapsis, R. and Murtha, J. (1985) 'Victims of a faculty layoff', *Sociology and Social Research* 70: 20–32.

Long, J.S., Allison, P.D. and McGinnis, R. (1979) 'Entrance into the academic career', *American Sociological Review* 44: 816–30.

Long, J.S. and McGinnis, R. (1981) 'Organizational context and scientific productivity', *American Sociological Review* 46: 422–42.

Long, J.S., McGinnis, R. and Allison, P. (1981) 'Reply to Chubin, Porter, and Boeckman', *American Sociological Review* 46: 496–98.

Marsh, J. and Stafford, F. (1967) 'The effects of values on pecuniary behavior: The case of academics', *American Sociological Review* 32: 740–54.

National Academy of Sciences (1979) *Climbing the Academic Ladder: Doctoral Women Scientists in Academe*, Washington, D.C.: Report of the Committee on the Education and Employment of Women in Science and Engineering, Commission on Human Resources.

Palmer, D. and Patton, C. (1981) 'Mid-career change options in academe: Experience and possibilities', *Journal of Higher Education* 52: 378–98.

Perloff, R. (1972) 'Enhancing psychology by assessing its manpower', *American Psychologist* 27: 355–61.

Perrucci, R., O'Flaherty, K. and Marshall, H. (1983) 'Market conditions, productivity, and promotion among university faculty', *Research in Higher Education* 19: 431–49.

Petersen, T. (1984) 'A method for incorporating time-dependent covariates in models for analysis of duration data', paper presented at the annual meeting of the American Sociological Association, San Antonio, TX, August 30.

Reskin, B. (1977) 'Scientific productivity and the reward structure of science', *American Sociological Review* 42: 491–504.

Roemer, R. and Schnitz, J. (1982) 'Academic employment as day labor', *Journal of Higher Education* 53: 514–31.

Roose, K.D. and Andersen, C.J. (1970) *A Rating of Graduate Programs*, Washington, DC: American Council on Education.

Rosenfeld, R. (1981) 'Academic men's and women's career mobility', *Social Science Research* 10: 337–63.
Rosenfeld, R. (1984) 'Academic career mobility for women and men psychologists', in Hass, V. and Perrucci, C. (Eds), *Women in Scientific and Engineering Professions*, Ann Arbor: University of Michigan Press, pp. 89–127.
Rosenfeld, R.A. and Jones, J.A. (1986) 'Institutional mobility among academics: The case of psychologists', *Sociology of Education* 59: 212–26.
Rosenfeld, R.A. and Jones, J.A. (1987) 'Patterns and effects of geographic mobility for academic women and men', *Journal of Higher Education* 58: 493–515.
Russo, N., Olmedo, E., Strapp, J. and Fulcher, R. (1981) 'Women and minorities in psychology', *American Psychologist* 36: 1315–63.
Sandefur, G. and Scott, W. (1981) 'A dynamic analysis of migration: An assessment of the effects of age, family and career variables', *Demography* 18: 355–68.
Smith, D.R. (1983) 'Mobility in professional occupational-internal labor markets', *American Sociological Review* 48 (June): 289–305.
Sorensen, A. (1983) 'Interpreting time dependency in career processes', discussion paper No. 733–83, University of Wisconsin-Madison, Institute for Research on Poverty.
Tuma, N. (1980) *Invoking RATE*, Stanford, CA: Stanford University.
Tuma, N. and Hannan, M. (1978) 'Approaches to the censoring problem in analysis of event histories', in Karl Schuessler (Ed.), *Sociological Methodology, 1979*, San Francisco: Jossey-Bass, pp. 209–40.
Tuma, N., Hannan, M. and Groneveld, L. (1979) 'Dynamic analysis of event histories', *American Journal of Sociology* 84: 820–54.
Youn, T.I.K. and Zelterman, D. (1986) 'Academic career mobility in multiple labor markets', a paper presented at the annual meeting of the American Sociological Association, Washington, D.C.
Zuckerman, H. (1970) 'Stratification in American science', pp. 235–57 in Edward Laumann (Ed.), *Social Stratification*, Indianapolis: Bobbs-Merrill.

5   Part-time Faculty and Part-time Academic Careers

Howard P. Tuckman and Karen L. Pickerill

Introduction

By the end of 1985 over a quarter of a million part-time positions
existed in academe. The number of these positions had continued to
grow throughout the 1970s and, as a consequence, an increasing
number of new faculty found part-time employment, the only entry
portal available to academe. Yet, despite the absolute and relative
growth in positions, the part-time population remained in the
shadows. Largely cut off from their full-time counterparts by the
hours at which they taught, lack of office space, and an inability to
attend faculty meetings, these part-timers were also hidden from the
larger society by lack of adequate data on their numbers and the short
duration of their employment. The 'typical' part-timer went largely
unnoticed on the campus green, except perhaps in those schools
where he (or more likely she) was in the majority.

   Surprisingly, little has been written about this group. Given the
above constraints, as well as their short-term employment contracts,
few part-timers have had the time to study and report on their
environment and the few written works that emerged tend to reflect
anger and frustration (Abel, 1984). These works convey only part of
the picture since many part-timers appear to be satisfied with their
work (Tuckman, 1978: Table 3). To date, relatively few full-timers
have shown an interest in studying issues related to part-timers, in
part because of the absence of adequate data. (For a discussion of the
issues, and for several sample solutions, see Biles and Tuckman,
1986). Thus, it is difficult for someone interested in part-time

employment as a career to obtain adequate information. The problem is further compounded by the fact that people have different motivations for becoming part-timers. Hence, the studies that are available must be viewed in terms of individual needs.

This chapter is designed to provide an insight into the nature of the part-time labor market for persons interested in considering part-time employment as a career option. It begins by drawing a distinction between voluntary and involuntary part-time employment and with an exploration of several definitions of 'part-time'. Data on the growth in the number of part-time persons in the US economy as a whole are analyzed and these are followed by an enumeration of the number of part-time positions in academe. In the process, several male–female differences are highlighted. The motives for seeking part-time employment are discussed and the issue of whether part-time employment leads to an academic career is considered. The chapter ends with an analysis of the social implications of the growing number of part-timers.

Voluntary versus Involuntary Part-time Employment

Less than full-time employment is desirable to persons with demands on their time, and/or interests, that would otherwise not allow them to enter the labor force. For those with responsibilities in the home, with poor health, with few remaining work years left, with conflicting educational or other demands on their time, with a high preference for leisure, or with a low tolerance for work, a part-time position provides a desirable form of labor force attachment. The person in this type of position can pursue other activities while, at the same time, maintaining an attachment to the labor force. Hence, the availability of this type of employment expands the panoply of career choices.

Part-time employment is not as desirable to people who are working part-time because they cannot find a better career option. Employed part-time because of a downturn in economy, decline in the demand for the product they produce, and/or a surplus in the number of job seekers within their field because of a wage level too high to accommodate the number of applicants, these persons bide their time, hoping that their part-time employment will simply be temporary. The data on part-time positions aggregated both groups until recent years when some of the data-gathering agencies began to differentiate between the two. As our results indicate, this difference is important in understanding the extent to which part-time employment is perceived as desirable.

Different Definitions of Part-time Employment

By its nature part-time employment involves less than a full-time commitment to the labor force but how this commitment is measured remains open to discussion. Several estimates of the number of part-time positions can be derived, depending on how part-time employment is defined. The potential measures delimit part-time employment in terms of: (1) whether a position carries less than full-time workload (usually as defined by the person answering a survey); (2) whether it involves less than thirty-five hours per week (an arbitrary cut-off point used by the Bureau of Labor Statistics (BLS) and subject to criticism in the last few years); (3) whether it involves a full-time workload borne for only part of a full year (also a criterion of the BLS).[1] A further question has been raised as to whether the position pool should be defined in terms of the jobs that part-timers actually hold or those they typically hold (Nardone, 1986: pp. 13–19). Because researchers define part-time in different ways, no single, universally accepted estimate of the part-time labor force is available. The lack of a consistent definition of part-time employment makes it difficult to compare the results of different research studies.

Part-time Employment in the US

The literature contains several different estimates of the number of part-time workers in the US.[2] These estimates differ from one another, primarily in terms of whom they include as part-timers. For the purposes of this section, we use Nardone's definition: 'part-timers' are all persons who primarily work part-time. This includes: (1) employed persons voluntarily working part-time, (2) employed persons not at work who usually work part-time, and (3) unemployed persons seeking part-time work (Nardone, 1986: 14). According to these criteria by the end of 1985 there were 18.6 million part-time workers employed in the US. This compared to 16.7 million in 1980, 14.3 million in 1975, and 11.9 million in 1970. For men 20 years of age and older the respective figures are 4.1 million, 3.4 million, 3.0 million, and 2.4 million. For women 20 years of age and over the figures are 10.6 million, 9.1 million, 7.5 million, and 6.3 million.

Figure 1 presents these data graphically. Note in the lower chart that the number of women in part time jobs exceeds that of men considerably, but the rate of growth in part-time employment is roughly the same for both sexes during the 1968–1985 period.

The top chart in Figure 1 traces the ratio of part-time to full-time workers in the US from 1968 to 1985. In this period the proportion of all employed persons working part-time increased from 14 per cent to 17 per cent, peaking at slightly over 18 per cent in 1983 before declining to just above 17 per cent thereafter. Approximately 24 per cent of all female workers and 7 per cent of all males over age 20 are part-timers: 72 per cent of the part-timers over age 20 are women. Nardone's data show that in 1985 15 per cent of all employed full-timers and 37 per cent of employed part-timers are in the age range 16–24. He explains this by school attendance:

> In October 1985, 6.3 million people between the ages of 16 and 24 were in school and employed. About four-fifths of these worked part-time. By comparison, of the 13.8 million in that age group who worked but were not in school, fewer than 15 per cent were part-timers.

Two other insights warrant comment. First, persons over age 65 are more likely to be employed part-time than full-time. This group represents 7.8 per cent of all part-timers but only 1.5 per cent of full-timers. Second, part-timers are more frequently employed in the retail trades and service industries than in manufacturing or related industries. The industrial shift within the US economy toward non-manufacturing enterprises has apparently helped to increase part-time employment.

Part-timers in Academe

Three major differences distinguish part-time employment in academe from part-time employment in other sectors of the economy. First, the academic part-timer is usually better educated and more likely to be from a middle-income family (Tuckman, 1978: Table 2). In contrast, the non-academic part-timer is more likely to be a high school dropout or a person with fewer years of schooling than an academic. He or she is also likely to come from a lower income family. Second, academic part-timers experience job instability due to changing conditions in academic labor markets rather than the larger economy. These include shifting student enrollments, fluctuating

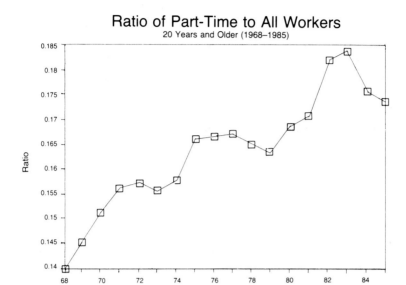

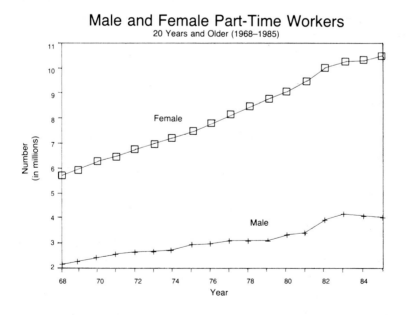

Figure 1

federal funds, and/or tightening budgets. In contrast, part-time employment outside academia is relatively more sensitive to fluctuations in the economy (Tuckman, 1986). Third, while the academic part-timer may have only attained 'marginal' status among his/her colleagues he/she usually commands full status from students. In academe, this type of position carries a measure of prestige and recognition whereas in most other industries, the part-timer is a truly 'marginal' worker (Doeringer and Piore, 1971).

The problems inherent in measuring part-time academic employment are also somewhat different from those described in the last section on national part-time employment. Because most of the available national time series data are obtained from surveys of institutions, at least three problems are raised. First, the surveys identify number of positions, not number of persons. Positions are reported rather than persons because institutions do not know how many positions their part-timers hold. Second, because most data-gathering agencies rely on the academic institutions to identify and report the number of part-timers they hire, differences arise in the institutional definitions, the ability to identify the number of part-timers on the payroll, and the willingness to release this information to outsiders. Third, in some years the sample size changes because of changes in the number of reporting institutions. This makes inter-year comparisons unreliable so that no single published source of data on part-timers is entirely acceptable.

The data reported in this section are compiled from institutional EEO-6 reports to the Equal Employment Opportunity Commission (EEOC). We believe that these represent the best available time series data to identify changes in the part-time position pool. The data are not as refined as the estimates presented in the last section but they are better than the available alternatives. Because these data are not generally available in published sources, we have tabulated the figures for four select years: 1975, 1979, 1981, and 1983. Unfortunately, 1983 is the last year for which the EEOC could provide data.

Between 1975 and 1983 the number of part-time positions at all institutions of higher education increased; from 212,000 to 261,000 (23 per cent). During the same period, the number of full-time positions increased from 446,000 to 471,000 (5.5 per cent). For every new full-time position nearly two new part-time positions were created. As a consequence, the 'market share' of part-timers grew from 32 per cent to 36 per cent of the total positions in academe. If we assume that the persons in these positions taught only one-quarter of a full-time load (a very conservative assumption) then the positions they occupied represent the equivalent of over 12,200 new full-time positions.[3] Clearly, part-time employment provided an important source of employment for those interested in a position in academe.

Unfortunately, the EEOC was unable to provide data to enable us to differentiate between employment at two-year colleges and at other types of institutions. There is, however, reason to believe that a large growth has been at the former. First, our 1976 study found that a majority of part-timers (53 per cent) are employed at two-year institutions and a majority of new positions are created at these institutions.[4] Second, more recent studies indicate that the expansion in part-time employment is heavily concentrated at two-year schools.[5]

Based on the trends evident in the national economy, one might expect to find that a majority of part-timers in academe are women. Examination of the data suggests that this is not true in academe. According to the EEOC data, 33 per cent of the part-timers in 1975 were female. Their numbers grew to 37 per cent in 1979 and 39 per cent in 1981. By 1983 40 per cent of part-time academics were women.[6] The bottom half of Figure 2 shows the number of academic part-timers by sex for the four years studied. Note that the number of males exceeds the number of females, that an increase occurs in the number of part-timers in both groups, and that the growth rate of female part-timers is exceeding the growth rate of male part-timers. The conclusion implied from this analysis is that while women are not a majority of the part-timers, their relative numbers are increasing.

The top half of Figure 2 shows the ratio of part-timers to all faculty. The first bar shows the ratio of all part-timers to all faculty, the second bar represents the ratio of male part-timers to male faculty, and the third bar indicates the ratio of female part-timers to female faculty. The diagram makes several points: (1) the ratio of part-timers to all faculty is increasing, albeit gradually (from 32 per cent in 1975 to 36 per cent in 1983), (2) the rate of increase is greater for females than for males, and (3) part-timers represent a larger proportion of female faculty than of male faculty (45 per cent vs 31 per cent in 1983). Although these data are basd on academic positions while those in the last section are for actual part-timers, they both indicate a similar finding with respect to sex. A larger proportion of women than of men are engaged in part-time as opposed to full-time employment. One reason for this find may be that women prefer part-time work as an employment option or because more females are involuntarily part-timers. The EEOC data do not enable us to differentiate between the two.

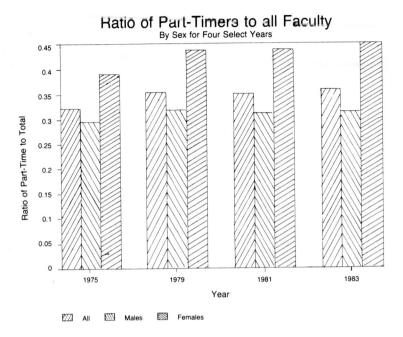

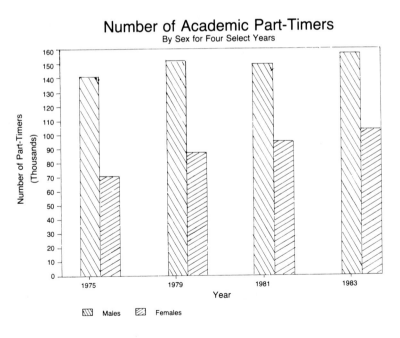

Figure 2

Possible Rationales for Choosing a Part-time Position

We have previously distinguished between voluntary and involuntary employment. This section considers these categories in greater detail. In an earlier paper, Tuckman proposed a taxonomy that can be used to classify people based on their reasons for becoming part-timers (Tuckman, 1978: pp. 307–8). Seven mutually exclusive categories are proposed: the semi-retired, students, those wishing to work full-time, full-mooners, those with home responsibilities, those with another part-time job, and all others. The semi-retired are the most distinct and easily identified. These part-timers are usually full-time persons in the process of phasing down their work commitment. Students represent the second category of part-timers. This category includes persons teaching in institutions other than the one at which they hope to receive a degree. Graduate students, teaching in their own departments, are excluded from the study. The Hopeful Full-timer category consists of the following: 1) those with no prior experience in academe gathering experience to become full-time, 2) those with prior experience working part-time because they could not find a full-time position. Full-Mooners are part-timers who hold a second job of 35 hours a week or more. Homeworkers are persons who work part-time primarily to care for children and other relatives. Part-Mooners are persons part-time in one academic institution with a second job elsewhere of at least one hour a week. Finally, Part-Unknowners are persons whose reasons for becoming part-time are unknown.

Table 1   *Protected Distribution of Part-timers in 1983*

Part-time Category	Percentage in 1976	Number Forecast in 1983
Semi-Retired	2.8	7,298
Student	21.2	55,257
Hopeful Full-time	16.6	43,267
Full-Mooner	27.6	71,939
Homeworker	6.4	16,681
Part-Mooner	13.6	35,448
Part-Unknowner	11.8	30,756
Total	100.0	260,646

See text for assumptions on which this table is based.

To classify persons into these categories it is necessary to have individual survey data that enable the data gatherer to determine the classification in which they belong. Unfortunately, in the last decade no national survey of part-timers has been conducted which can be used for this purpose. Hence, we employ the second best solution of utilizing the 1983 EEOC total number of part-timers and the 1976 survey percentages to provide a rough estimate of number of faculty falling into each category. To do this we implicitly assume that the survey percentages can be applied to the EEOC data and that the distribution of faculty across the seven categories has not changed. A test of the reliability of these estimates will have to await a new survey. Column 2 of Table 1 shows the percentages of faculty falling into each category in 1976 and column 3 shows the number of faculty who would be in this category in 1983.

Locational vs Gypsy Hopefuls

Several of the Tuckman *et al.* earlier papers argued the importance of the hopeful full-time group.[7] Subsequent discussions with part-timers and others suggest that within this group a voluntary segment exists that can be divided into two subgroups. The first, Locational Hopefuls, has three types of part-timers: the Captives – those who due to personal reasons (e.g., a working spouse) choose not to move, the Homing Pigeons – those who receive their degree from an institution and choose to return there even if no full-time position is available, and the Aesthetics – those who like a particular location and are willing to take part-time employment to remain in a geographic area. Locational Hopefuls, by choice, have limited their potential employment to a specific area, and as such can largely hope for full-time employment only as attrition or changes in the level of demand for faculty allow local institutions to hire more faculty. Their inability to find full-time employment is largely self-imposed.

Gypsy Hopefuls choose the part-time route because they enjoy the excitement of new people and places. Purists cannot find a place where they want to settle. These are people who move from one location to another in search of non-academic goals. In contrast, Hedonists accept temporary offers from institutions because they think they may enjoy working at them or living in a particular location. While they do not have the same need to constantly travel, as do the Gypsy Hopefuls, they do move on once their reason for settling is removed. A third group, the Losers, are those who, because of poor credentials or poor performance, must continually seek new employment as their short-term contracts expire. Many of these persons may also have voluntarily chosen part-time employment, despite their desire to be full-time. Unfortunately, no survey data are available to estimate the number of Locational and Gypsy Hopefuls in academe.

Economic Part-timers

The BLS uses a category entitled part-time for 'economic reasons'. Included here are persons with: slack work, material shortages or repair to their plant or equipment, a new job that started during the week, a job that terminated during the week, or those who could only find part-time work. Nardone argues that a person's placement in this category should depend not on these reasons, but rather on the type of work they usually perform (Nardone, 1986: p. 14). Persons who are usually full-time more closely resemble full-timers than part-timers, even if they report part-time work at the time a survey is conducted.

A similar argument can be made for persons reported as part-time in academe. Most aggregate counts are based on institutional data, hence, the 'usual' work patterns of positions are not known. This problem is particularly acute since many part-timers have been in their positions only a short period of time. Even those institutions utilizing individual survey data to report data on 'seeking full-time employment', such as the National Science Foundation and National Academy of Sciences, do not obtain sufficient information to determine if part-time employment is 'usual' or 'unusual'. Thus, the 'seeking full-time' category which corresponds most closely with the Hopeful Full-Time category contains both Locational and Geographic Hopefuls. The discrepancy between definitions of 'part-timers' may tend to overstate the true number of involuntarily Hopeful Full-Timers.

Despite this potential bias, our studies indicate that the percentage of Hopeful Full-Timers is field sensitive and that fields with an excess supply of faculty also tend to have the largest percentage of Hopeful Full-Timers (Tuckman and Tuckman, 1981). Our research also shows that this group is the one most dissatisfied with a part-time position (Tuckman, 1978: Table 3). Finally, existing evidence reveals that these persons do not subsequently find a full-time position (Abel, 1984: chs 2–3). On this basis, it seems reasonable to conclude that an economically unemployed market segment does exist among part-timers in academe and that its chances for advancement to a full-time position are not good.

Does Part-time Employment Give Rise to an Academic Career?

Part-time academic employment rarely gives rise to an academic career for at least five reasons. First, rarely does a career ladder exist for part-timers. Data from the 1976 study indicate that over 90 per cent of all the part-time positions in academe were unranked (Tuckman and Pickerill, 1986). Moreover, no evidence exists that part-time experience is weighed as heavily as full-time experience. Likewise, a person employed in a department as a part-timer has little or no advantage over an outsider seeking a full-time position; in fact, the reverse may be true because of the marginal status of the part-timers in the eyes of his full-time colleagues. Second, over 85 per cent of the part-time positions reported to the EEOC in 1983 did not carry tenure (Tuckman and Pickerill, 1986). Moreover, our earlier data indicated that a majority of part-timers are hired on one-semester contracts so that even long-term part-timers can be fired on short notice. The short contract period also indicates part-timers are potentially faced with layoffs before other academic faculty. Surprisingly, little research has been conducted to determine whether part-timers are, in fact, laid off more frequently than full-timers during downturns in academic markets.

Third, a study by one of the authors found that part-timers do not have normal salary progression over the course of their career.[8] Indeed, many institutions hold part-time remuneration constant over time while allowing full-time salaries to grow. Consequently, the salary differential between the two groups grows and this creates an incentive for increasing the use of part-timers within institutions.

Fourth, opportunities for promotion are limited or non-existent for most part-timers. Tuckman's 1976 study found that less than 3 per cent of all part-timers hold the rank of associate and less than 2 per cent hold the rank of full professor. The EEOC data cofirm this finding since only a small fraction of part-timers are in classified positions. The same data also indicate that the proportion of ranked positions is not changing over time. Thus, a person who accepts part-time employment with the hope that he will advance to a higher position is likely to be disappointed.

Finally, the 1976 study suggests that part-timers are not full fledged members of their employing departments. For example, less than 28 per cent felt that they were paid proportionately to their full-time counterparts (Tuckman, 1978: Table 3). Other studies have reported a lack of adequate office space and other facilities, and of opportunities to participate in governance activities.[9] Given these restraints, part-timers are unable to achieve the same career objectives and to engage in the same activities as their full-time counterparts. On the basis of these findings, we feel compelled to conclude that while part-time employment may provide a portal to academe, the person entering by this route is likely to be at a continuing disadvantage to an individual beginning his academic career in a full-time position. Moreover, there is little evidence that part-time employment opens up career ladder opportunities.

Social Implications of the Growing Ranks of Part-timers

The previous discussion raises several important issues. Perhaps the most important of these is whether the way academe treats part-timers is in agreement with the way they should be treated. Our current institutions are creating employment effects that have several social implications. In this final section we explore several of these and their potential meaning for the future.

The first implication is that faculty who take part-time positions without other employment will probably lack adequate fringe benefit coverage. An earlier article reported that only 47 per cent of all part-timers in the 1976 study had Social Security coverage, 19 per cent were covered by retirement plans, 11 per cent had workman's compensation, 8 per cent had medical insurance and 6 per cent had life insurance coverage (Tuckman and Vogler, 1978: p. 47). Little has changed since that article was written. Many insurance companies refuse to write coverage for part-time employees and, in the absence of national legislation, this is unlikely to change. A consequence is that those who choose a part-time career will find themselves ill-equipped either for retirement or to financially handle serious bouts of illness. In the absence of adequate salaries, they may be forced to rely on the goodness of the state.

A second implication involves the fact that part-time positions offer no time for paid research. In the absence of public programs which offer part-timers the opportunity to engage in research, a shift to part-time positions will mean a reduction in academic research. Moreover, persons who enter academe through part-time rather than full-time employment are likely to be lost to the formal research community. While some persons interested in doing research may deliberately accept part-time employment in order to engage in research, the number of such persons is likely to be limited.

Implication three is that the part-time labor pool represents a growing potential source of new faculty supply should the shortages predicted by some researchers develop in the full-time market. Research has shown that limited price-induced substitution of part-time faculty for full-timers does occur (Katz and Tuckman, 1984: pp. 85–90). For the part-time pool to be a meaningful source of new full-time faculty, better selection and hiring procedures need to be implemented. We have considered elsewhere how this might be done (Biles and Tuckman, 1986). Many academic labor markets models fail to explicitly incorporate the part-time pool as a source of supply and this deficiency is likely to affect their predictions.[10]

The data presented above show that academic part-time employment is often chosen by persons who cannot find a full-time job. This is true irrespective of the degree level of the part-timer. For example, a recent study found that among new doctorates employed in 1983, about 48 per cent of the women and 52 per cent of the males were seeking full-time employment (Tuckman and Belisle, 1987). Comparable data for new doctorates employed in 1979 were 51 per cent and 80 per cent. This group, previously referred to as 'Hopeful Full-Time', is part-time because it encountered barriers to full-time employment. There is a need to advise these people at the outset of the difficulties they are likely to encounter converting a part-time position to a full-time one. A need also exists to encourage academic institutions to integrate part-time faculty and offer them more equal standing with their full-time peers.

The growth of the part-time professoriate could have a very positive impact on the quality of instruction in the US. For many years the medical schools have hired outstanding specialists to lecture part-time. These persons bring to the classroom a unique blend of familiarity with the current academic journals and practical experience. Policies are needed which encourage the broader academic community to hire persons of this caliber. Progress or policies of this type might include temporary 'sabbatics' for outstanding practioners, particularly in disciplines where shortages exist or where large numbers of foreign instructors dominate the classrooms.

A danger exists that some institutions will hire such a high percentage of part-timers that they are unable to provide basic services. Public policy should discourage the staffing of institutions with a majority of part-timers. The absence of a cadre of research scholars, of faculty with the time to engage in governance and public service activities, and of normal advising and committee functions, can have a harmful effect on the quality of learning. To some extent accreditation rules may preclude this from happening but the pressures to relax these rules will increase if faculty shortages or budgetary problems develop.

Finally, a need exists to provide better time series data on part-timers. The federal data gathering agencies must be encouraged to collect better data on the number of part- and full-time positions in the US and an effort must be made to collect data on persons as well as positions. It is particularly important to provide more accurate data on those who are part-timers for economic reasons by field and to make these data available to persons making career choices. The research shows that students make good judgments when they are confronted with information on the labor market in the fields. As better data become available on the nature of this employment, potential participants in academe will be better able to judge what such employment means to them. Researchers will be better able to judge how many persons fall into each category and what determines the nature of satisfaction with a part-time career. At the same time, academic institutions will be in a better position to judge how the policies they adopt to part-timers affect attitudes of part-time workers. Given the large increase in the number of academic part-timers, the need for more studies is long overdue. The time is ripe for additional research on what promises to be a major labor market.

Notes

1. These criteria are discussed in National Commission on Employment and Unemployment Statistics, *Counting the Labor Force* (Washington: Government Printing Office, 1979). Data of this type are derived from the Current Population Survey and are reported in the Monthly Labor Review.
2. These are discussed in op. cit., National Commission.
3. The actual data on courses taught by part-timers indicate they teach more than 25 per cent. See 'Who is part-time in academe', *AAUP Bulletin*, Winter 1978, Table 3.
4. Ibid.
5. These are listed in the Appendix, Biles and Tuckman, op. cit.
6. Note that the 1976 study found that 39 per cent of the part-timers were women.

7. See, for example, H. Tuckman and W. Vogler, 'The "Part" in Part-time Wages', *AAUP Bulletin*, Summer 1978, pp. 46–48. See also Appendix, Biles and Tuckman op. cit. for a list of these papers.
8. H. Tuckman and J. Caldwell, 'The Reward Structure For Part-Timers in Academe', *Journal of Higher Education*, November/December 1979, pp. 745–61. For a discussion of how to provide such a structure see op. cit., Biles and Tuckman.
9. For a listing of these see Appendix, Biles and Tuckman, op. cit.
10. For a discussion of these see US Congress, Office of Technology Assessment, Demographic Trends and the Scientific and Engineering Work Force *A Technical Memorandum* (Washington: US Government Printing Office, OTA-TM-SET-35). December 1985.

References

Abel, E. (1984) *Terminal Degree*, New York: Praeger Publishers.

Biles, G. and Tuckman, H. (1986) *Part-time Faculty: Personnel Management*, New York: Macmillan.

Doeringer, P. and Piore, M. (1971) *Internal Labor Markets and Manpower Analysis*, Lexington: Lexington Press.

Katz, D. and Tuckman, H. (1984) 'Displacement of full-timers by part-timers – a model for projection', *Economics of Education Review*, Summer, pp. 85–90.

Nardone, T. (1986) 'Part-time workers: Who are they?', *Monthly Labor Review*, February, pp. 13–19.

Tuckman, H. (1978) 'Who is part-time in academe', *AAUP Bulletin*, December, Table 3.

Tuckman, H. (1986) *Testimony Before The House Committee on Science and Technology*, February 20th 1986, Washington D.C..

Tuckman, H. and Belisle, M. (1987) 'The career status of new doctorates one or two years later', *Educational Record*, Vol. 68, No. 1, 32–35.

Tuckman, H. and Pickerill, K. (1986) *Non-tenure Track Positions in Academe*, (unpublished paper).

Tuckman, H. and Tuckman B. (1981) 'Who are the part-timers and what are their colleges doing for them', *Current Issues in Higher Education*, 1981.

Tuckman, H. and Vogler, W. (1978) 'The "part" in part-time wages', *AAUP Bulletin*, Summer, pp.46–48.

6   Merit Pay in Higher Education

W. Lee Hansen

Introduction

The recent push by the President, various governors, and key educators for merit pay to elementary and secondary school teachers has launched a search for successful merit pay systems and their implementation. One place to turn for help is higher education where individual faculty members are regularly evaluated to determine their annual salary increases. Salary increases vary considerably, reflecting differences in the performance of individual faculty members. This contrasts sharply with the situation for public school teachers whose formal salary schedules provide uniform annual increases for everyone regardless of individual performance.

Research on merit pay in higher education is sparse and quite limited in scope.[1] Nonetheless, several distinct streams of literature exist. One is the literature from psychology that explores the relationship between pay and performance (McKeachie, 1979; Klass, 1986). Another is the economics literature that provides empirical estimates of the impact on earnings of productivity measures such as publications, teaching, and service activities (Tuckman, 1979). Still another is the literature from collective bargaining that touches on the uneasy trade-off between recognizing merit and giving essentially uniform increases to everyone irrespective of merit (Begin, 1977). Finally, a small body of literature touched on later focuses on administering merit-based systems in higher education (Brown, 1982, 1983, 1984). The abundant literature on merit-based pay in the private sector is not drawn on in this paper.

The uneven state of the literature can be attributed to several factors. The concept of merit pay is not well defined, and hence its

114

measurement poses conceptual issues. In addition, the task of assembling information on the characteristics of merit and non-merit pay systems is formidable, because salary systems differ so substantially among the nation's more than 3,400 colleges and universities. They each have somewhat different missions and varying strategies for accomplishing them. Moreover, this diversity extends to individual departments which often have extensive power in determining the distribution of annual salary increases. These characteristics make it difficult to ascertain how merit pay systems work. Thus, it is not surprising that so little research exists on merit pay in higher education.

This paper attempts to fill this void. Its purpose is to piece together a description of merit pay systems in post-secondary education, giving particular attention to how and to what extent salary systems recognize merit and how this in turn affects the distribution of faculty salary increases. We use scattered published references and also draw upon several sources of unpublished data. The result represents the best that can be done at this time.

The focus is on four questions. First, what are the principal types of salary systems in higher education and how does merit fit into these systems? Second, how do perceptions of merit differ? Third, how can we define merit pay? Fourth, how does the allocation of merit pay vary among different types of colleges and universities? The paper closes with a discussion of the gaps in our knowledge and the need for a research program to fill these gaps.

Pay Systems in Higher Education

Pay systems in higher education provide an odd mix of annual merit- and non-merit-based salary increases, reflecting adjustments for promotions, longevity, market conditions, price level changes, and pure merit.[2] These additional components complicate recognition of merit and yet are often directly related to it. At some institutions each component of annual salary increases is fully specified. At other institutions complete discretion is allowed in deciding how to allocate salary increase funds among the various components. In some cases all salary increase funds can go for merit, whereas in other cases nothing is allotted for merit increases. We turn now to consider these several types of adjustments.

Promotional salary increases are awarded each year to a relatively small fraction of all faculty members and represent a reward for merit in the career development of the individual recipient. Most institutions of higher education use the traditional hierarchial academic ranks – assistant professor, associate professor, (full) professor, and 'distinguished' professor – as a means of differentiating faculty members. Promotion from one rank to another is not automatic. Decision-makers typically employ some concept of 'merit' in recommending promotions, often relying on external assessments of a person's accomplishments. A promotion almost without exception brings with it an above-average salary increase.[3]

Several other factors, such as longevity, cost-of-living increases, and market factors, also affect salary increases but are not directly linked to merit. Longevity increases, when used, are awarded to everyone, perhaps every other year, in an effort to recognize the progressive growth of experience; frequently, longevity increases cease after, say, 20 years of experience (Kasper, 1986). As a result longevity increases cannot be viewed as a component of merit pay unless some discretion is exercised in deciding which individual faculty members receive these increases. A more selective approach used with salary schedules involves the creation of 'salary steps' through each rank; individuals move from step to step but only on the basis of some kind of evaluation that reflects merit. Cost-of-living adjustments as well as those for economic growth obviously have no relation to individual merit; these increases affect everyone equally.

Salary adjustment for market factors do reflect merit in part, although the connection is not a direct one. Market adjustments recognize differential changes in the supply-demand condition by discipline, and even subdiscipline, in the average levels of salaries required for institutions to remain competitive, and in what it takes to retain existing faculty members and to recruit new faculty members, both within the academic and the larger non-academic labor market. Frequently these adjustments come about because of widening disparities between 'inside' and 'outside' perceptions of merit. As this gap grows and ever-larger proportions of people in a field receive and accept outside offers, it becomes easier to justify increasing the salaries of all people in a field. In a sense, these increases reflect some combination of individual and group merit. For institutions these market adjustments provide a relatively simple but blunt instrument for responding to a long series of outside offers concentrated in particular fields. Recent salary adjustments for market forces have been most prevalent in the areas of business, engineering, and computer science.[4]

Annual salary increases can be distributed in a variety of ways. There are two principal approaches, one calling for the award of dollar increments, the other awarding percentage increments. Awarding dollar increments usually reflects a desire to change the relative distribution of salary increases and hence alter (typically to narrow) overall salary differences among academic ranks and between lower and higher paid faculty members. Awarding percentage increments preserves the relative salary structure, which is viewed as essential in maintaining competitive salaries and attracting new entrants to academe.

Because percentage increases are more typical and easier to analyze, we focus on them. We outline four different systems used by institutions to distribute merit salary increases:

1. Equal percentage increase for everyone

At one extreme are institutions that allocate equal annual percentage increases to all faculty members and give no recognition to merit. A variant on this system awards equal percentage increases to everyone but also automatically awards additional salary increases to reflect legislated scales that take into account longevity or length of service.

2. Equal percentage increases for everyone, plus a small allocation of total salary funds to reward merit

This approach, with or without longevity increases, diverts some portion of the total funds available for salary increases to recognize individual merit. In most cases these merit increases become a permanent part of the salary base; in some cases they are single-year increases equivalent to bonuses or prizes, and do not add to the recipient's salary base in calculating future salary increases.

3. Equal but small percentage increases for everyone, plus a large allocation of total salary funds to reward merit

This approach, with or without longevity increases, provides some minimum percentage increase for all faculty members but distributes most of the available funds so as to reward individual merit.

4. Unequal percentage increases for everyone, with all salary funds allocated to reward merit

This approach puts exclusive weight on merit and permits salary increases for individuals to range from zero to well above the average rate of increase.

Differing Perceptions of Merit Pay

What is merit pay and why is it important? Merit pay refers to the practice of granting annual salary increases that are intended to reflect the quality of the performances of individual faculty members during the prior year. In principle, it encourages faculty members to devote their efforts to teaching, research, and public service, thereby strengthening the institution and enhancing the benefits gained by students and society.

Most academic professors and administrators agree that teaching, research, and public service reflect the outputs that merit pay systems try to reward (Kirshling, 1978). However, they might well disagree about the weights assigned to each of these components, including the possibility that weights for one or more of these elements could be zero or even negative. Such disagreement would not necessarily divide faculty members from administrators; some would line up on each side of the issue.[5] Nor would disagreement signify institutional confusion about its mission. Instead, it would reflect the obvious fact that the missions of post-secondary educational institutions differ enormously. For example, research universities give heavy weight to research productivity, whereas liberal arts colleges emphasize teaching, with perhaps some limited attention to research among the more selective institutions. Public four-year institutions give primary attention to teaching and public service, whereas community colleges give considerable if not exclusive weight to teaching. Regardless of the dominant pattern of weights that might apply to different types of institutions, significant variation in these weights is likely to exist within these various groups of institutions, and to some degree among departments within each type of institution. These weights reflect the strength, focus, and values of institutions and their departments as they operate within the context of their missions.[6]

Efforts to reward merit are further complicated by its multi-dimensional nature and the difficulties of measuring the various elements of merit (Kirschling, 1978). Perhaps the easiest element to evaluate uniformly is research. The peer review provides an effective mechanism for assessing the quality of research and is applicable to publications, grants, honors, and the like. Another mechanism is the informal network of contacts that yield important helpful inter-pretative information on the quality of people's current research in a field.

Teaching, by contrast, is more difficult to assess, not necessarily in principle but in practice. Generally, relatively little emphasis is given to quality teaching. Even where it is given strong emphasis, formal mechanisms for evaluating teaching are rarely found. For example, few faculty members ever observe their colleagues teaching. Yet useful information on teaching performance can be obtained from student evaluations of teaching which are now common at most universities and colleges. Though little importance can be attached to small differences in the evaluation scores, the results are helpful in identifying the least and the most outstanding teachers. At the same time faculty members have numerous opportunities to observe their colleagues in teaching or near-teaching situations. Paradoxically, it is possible that these opportunities are more abundant at research universities where faculty members are more likely to present research papers at departmental seminars and colloquia, participate in jointly-taught courses, and make presentations at professional meetings.

Institutional and public service activities are susceptible to at least rough measurement by the volume and quality of activity. Public service typically receives greater emphasis at public institutions. Whatever the case, these activities are usually taken into account, even though subtle differences in the quality of these activities are difficult to assess.

Barring exceptional performance (or lack of it) on one or more of these dimensions, merit decisions are usually most heavily influenced by research and scholarship, followed by teaching performance, and then by institutional and public service. Only in rare instances do we know the precise details of how such a system works.[7]

Defining Merit Pay

The task of arriving at merit evaluations and translating them into salary increases is not easy. Perceptions of merit for individual faculty members will almost certainly differ among those who do the evaluating. Perhaps even more important, merit may mean one thing within an institution and something quite different within the context of the academic labor market. And as already suggested, merit is not necessarily the dominant consideration in developing recommendations for salary increases.

The narrow view of merit is that it recognizes differences in the performance of individuals within an institution. How well it recognizes these differences is a matter for argument. One approach is to try to develop agreement on the weights attached to different types of outputs and consistency in establishing true merit. A collegial approach that might at one extreme involve everyone in a department evaluating everyone else is likely to bring more and better information to the process and at the same time average the possibly divergent evaluations of different individuals.[8] Whatever the case, the resulting measure of merit and the salary increments attached to merit can probably best be viewed as rough approximations of overall performance.

The broader view is that merit serves as a critically important component of an institution's larger salary compensation scheme whose purpose is to improve the quality of the institution's outputs. Expressed another way, the goal of such a system is to offer economic rewards that are sufficiently high to attract, develop, and retain college faculty members who effectively perform their various duties. This must be done in light of the institution's mission, its fiscal capacity, and the constraints it faces as a result of tenure, academic governance, and collective bargaining agreements or legislated pay scales. Attainment of this goal requires offering a career pattern of salary increases that in the first instance must be capable of attracting promising young entrants into academic training and subsequently into academic careers. Once people have entered academic life the system must do two things. One is to recognize and reward quality performance of individual faculty members to prevent any significant number of defections to other institutions, and the other to enhance the likelihood of attracting talented people from competing institutions.

The presence of a merit system by itself may well affect both the initial and subsequent job choices of academics. For example, in making choices about what kinds of positions to apply for, individuals will usually seek to match their talents with the expectations of potential employing institutions. If faculty members subsequently find a mismatch between what they can do and what is expected of them or between their views and those of their institutions about the weights asssigned to different types of outputs, they will be dissatisfied. This leaves them several options: in the words of Hirschman (1970) they may want to move (exit) to the more congenial atmosphere at another institution, to try changing (voice) the system of weights at their institution, or to alter their own behavior to conform (loyalty) more closely to the institution's expectations.

Just as new faculty members will try to select institutions whose emphasis, and thus reward system, accord most closely with their own, institutions will seek to do the same. Institutions will search out new Ph.D.s entering the labor market and also faculty members currently at other institutions whose interests conform most closely to the institution's expectations. The same applies to experienced faculty members as institutions attempt to strengthen their capacity to produce their distinctive mix of outputs and to improve the quality of the outputs produced. This means that institutions will compete actively with each other and with employers outside the academic sector for both new and experienced personnel. It also means that they will have to work actively to prevent the most meritorious faculty members at their own institutions from being attracted by generous offers from other institutions.

For these reasons merit cannot be viewed on any universal absolute scale. Even if a merit system is designed to reflect differences in individual performance within particular institutions, it cannot help but be coloured by external assessments of merit. Such assessments may or may not be reflected through job offers from other institutions. Hence, the purpose and practice of merit pay produces or can produce conflict. The practice is not simply a matter of deciding what weights to use and what increments to award in recognition of meritorious performance. Practice must be tempered by the institution's goals of retaining and attracting experienced faculty members and of recruiting newly trained faculty members. Thus, merit salary increases must try simultaneously to elicit the kind of performance effort desired by the institution and at the same time be responsive to labor market activity that reflects meritorious performance.

What happens when this is not the case? Consider the situation in which perceptions of an individual's merit differ between the employing institution and other institutions. The salary paid by the employing institution may reflect quite accurately its perceptions of the individual's merit. But another institution's perception of that individual's merit may differ considerably, because it evaluates the various outputs differently (perhaps more accurately). It may place different weights on these outputs, or it may view an individual as playing a somewhat different role at its institution. As a result, the other institution assigns a higher merit rank than does the employing institution. This will likely lead the other institution to make a salary offer that exceeds the person's current salary and could cause the person to move. Of course, some seemingly equally meritorious colleagues might be viewed less favorably, with the result that salary offers, if made to them, would not be sufficiently large to induce a move.[9] Colleagues viewed by other institutions as being of less merit do not receive offers.

These differences between 'inside' and 'outside' perceptions of merit encourage ambiguity in the meaning of the term merit. Merit can be viewed narrowly as a device for rewarding outstanding performance within an institution, or merit can be viewed broadly as a device for rewarding outstanding performance viewed within the labor market as a whole. To the extent that inside merit equals outside merit, there will be little or no economic incentive for a person to move. But if perceived outside merit exceeds perceived inside merit, and the resulting salary offer is substantial enough to offset the 'costs' of moving to another institution, then we would expect to see the faculty member move.[10] The only way to prevent such movement is for institutions to ensure that the values of inside and outside merit-based salaries are approximately the same.

Ensuring that salary levels are kept in line with these differing perceptions of merit is difficult. For institutions it is costly to monitor outside perceptions of merit. For faculty members there are high costs of entering the market to obtain information on how other institutions regard their merit. Institutions that want to recruit meritorious faculty will willingly incur the costs of keeping informed. Hence, institutions must be alert to job offers received by their faculty members and be ready to respond. To the extent that an institution can assess an individual's outside merit and then pay a commensurate salary, it reduces the chance that outside offers will succeed in luring people away.

The moral of this analysis is that merit must always be viewed within the context of the labor market. Salary levels must be attuned to both outside and inside merit. The extent to which outside and inside merit differ depends on the attributes of individual faculty members. Scholarly and research–oriented faculty members are far more likely to be known beyond their own institutions, simply because more information is available to outsiders about them. For example, it is relatively easy to gain access to and evaluate published research. By contrast, academics whose primary activity is teaching are much less likely to be known elsewhere, even though they might be truly outstanding by any measure of inside merit and so rewarded. Hence, faculty members whose principal task is teaching will exhibit less mobility than the researcher-teachers. If, however, a market for outstanding teachers exists, it probably operates sluggishly because of the greater costs of acquiring information to evaluate merit as defined above. Thus, the potential increases for differences between inside and outside perceptions of merit as we move from teaching- to research-centered institutions.

Implications of Merit Pay

The implications of different methods of defining and measuring merit for the four quite different pay systems should be readily apparent, at least in terms of direct effects. System 1 completely excludes any consideration of meritorious performance by awarding equal increases to everyone, it yields highly predictable patterns of annual salary increases, and it produces an unchanged distribution of relative salaries both for individual faculty members and for their institutions. System 2 gives limited consideration to merit, but the overall salary distribution changes only if merit increases are sizable and permanent in their impact on the salary base of recipients. System 3 gives major consideration to merit but assures some minimum relative increase to everyone, irrespective of merit, with the result that the salary distribution widens over time. System 4 recognizes only merit and produces the widest spread of salary increases.[11]

The implications of these systems for the academic labor market are equally obvious. By awarding identical percentage increases to all faculty members regardless of field, institutions adhering to System 1 are likely to experience greater difficulty in recruiting potentially outstanding new faculty members, in attracting outstanding faculty members from other institutions, and in retaining outstanding faculty members. This occurs because outside evaluations of merit will generate salary offers exceeding the average (non-merit-based) salaries which are paid. The exact opposite situation will prevail for institutions with System 4 and to a somewhat lesser degree for those with System 3. Paradoxically, institutions with System 1 will be attractive only to less meritorious faculty from Systems 3 and 4 who, if given offers, might expect their salaries to increase! In addition, Systems 1 and 2 institutions will experience difficulty in matching salary offers received by faculty members in high-demand fields. In all of these examples, we see once again the results of different practices in how merit is assessed and rewarded. The disparities between inside and outside evaluations of merit will, by inducing job changes, alter somewhat the expected salary distributions.[12] Institutions with

System 4 will lose some of their less well-paid faculty members to lesser ranked institutions, thereby narrowing the distribution. If these same institutions attract people from System 1 institutions there will be an offsetting widening of the salary distribution in System 4, with little or no change in the distribution for System 1.

Despite these differences, it is quite conceivable that these salary systems could produce similar patterns of salaries over the professional lifetime and approximately similar increases across the age spectrum from year to year. Because all four systems coexist and institutions compete with each other, these systems do not operate independently of each other. Indeed, they are necessarily interdependent, affecting one another. In support of this proposition relative salary differences by academic rank have been found to be virtually constant over time and across institutions (Hansen, 1986).

Hidden behind these averages will be sharp differences in the career variance of earnings. This can be illustrated by assuming that newly hired assistant professors all receive similar starting salaries and that subsequent average salaries increase at some fixed percentage rate. Under System 1 everyone's salary will rise in lock step and the variance will not change. This will also be true for System 2 except that the one-time merit awards will widen the spread a little; but if these awards are distributed broadly, then eventually everyone will be back in their same relative position. The spread will be widest under System 4 because all salary increases are based on merit and hence the greatest differentiations occur. System 3 will produce a slightly narrower spread, depending on recent and past allocations between merit and across-the-board increases. Again, however, mobility will modify these results.

One way to recognize differences in performance while holding to a fixed salary schedule is to create a several-track salary schedule, with overlapping steps. As individuals diverge from the average in their performance, they can be moved ahead more rapidly or slowly along the different steps of the schedule. The resulting salary profiles can be thought of as reflecting some kind of multiple-track system. This variant of a salary schedule does not fully resolve the problem of recognizing merit, but it does allow considerable potential flexibility in recognizing merit in a salary schedule.

Evidence on Merit Pay

How merit systems actually function requires turning to the data. Several types of information are available for this exploratory effort.

One is collective bargaining contracts which contain provisions for merit pay increases. From them the distribution of annual salary increases can be estimated. Another is information on the distribution of salary increases across a variety of different institutions, all of which are part of major public systems of higher education.

What Do We Know?

The literature on merit pay in higher education, as noted earlier, is amazingly limited. Neither the AAUP's Committee Z on the Economic Status of the Profession nor the National Center of Educational Statistics' periodic surveys, which traditionally collect faculty salary data, has ever attempted to collect information on merit pay. The task of gathering regular salary data each year has been taxing enough.[13] While some thought has been given to the possibility of collecting such data, significant difficulties prevent going ahead with the project. A major obstacle has been formulating appropriate questions. Another is getting institutions to respond fully and carefully. A third problem, particularly among research universities, is trying to characterize in some simple way the great diversity of practices in different departments.

Individual researchers have also avoided the subject for many of the same reasons. There are no readily accessible data, and the task of trying to amass one's own data is formidable. Conceivably, faculty surveys such as those carried out periodically by the Carnegie Foundation Council could yield evidence on the distribution of salary increases, but these surveys have not been designed with that purpose in mind. Institutional researchers and university budget analysts apparently have given no more than cursory attention to the distribution of salary increases. On occasion they track the salaries of individual faculty members over particular time periods, but typically such information has been for internal use only.

Merit Pay in the Collective Bargaining Sector

Several recent studies examine the treatment of merit within collective bargaining contracts as part of the large effort to measure the impact of bargaining on faculty salary increases for colleges and universities. Mortimer (1982), summarizing a variety of studies, reports that in comparing unionized and non-unionized institutions, less than half of the former and more than three-quarters of the latter use merit as a criterion in awarding annual salary increases.[14] He reported that by 1978, as compared to 1968, fewer unionized institutions used merit in awarding salary increases, whereas no change occurred among non-union institutions. However, according to Guthrie-Morse (1979) the details of merit plans in collective bargaining agreements are rarely spelled out in any great detail. Douglas and Goldsmith (1981), based on an analysis of approximately 200 collective bargaining agreements, found merit pay funding plans included in only thirty-four collective bargaining agreements or 17 per cent of the total.

Merit pay has also been investigated at particular institutions, both those with and without bargaining authorization. In the bargaining sector Hollander and Turnbell (1984) discussed how merit is handled in the New Jersey public four-year colleges; typically, only a small fraction of total salary increase funds is allotted for merit increases, some of which takes the form of one-time bonuses or prizes. Musto (1984) outlines efforts to introduce the concept of merit into the University of Hawaii system, which operates under a collective bargaining agreement; that system also appears to give relatively small weight to merit in the award of salary increases.

To ascertain more precisely the place of merit pay in the collective bargaining sector, all AAUP-affiliated contracts that could be obtained through the AAUP's national office were examined for their provisions on merit pay. These agreements were grouped for analysis using the AAUP categories for classifying institutions.

The results of this analysis for 1985–86 are summarized in Table 1 for the fifty institutions with AAUP contracts. Twenty-four make some mention of merit pay, with fifteen offering merit rewards for merit as one-time bonuses, the equivalent of teaching awards; only four incorporate merit increases into the salary base (columns 1–4). No information is available for the other six institutions. In addition, a number of institutions impose rather restrictive maximums on the size of the merit awards, with the highest set at $1,500; for the three agreements with percentage maximums, the range of overall increases is from 4.9 to 8.0 per cent (column 5).

More important is information on the amount of the overall salary increase funds available for merit increases (columns 6–8). The weighted average of the merit increases for the fourteen institutions for which data were available is 1.1 per cent. If we assume that similar increases were available for the other 10 agreements that mention merit, the average percentage increase for merit, over all fifty institutions, comes to 0.5 per cent. In contrast, the increase in average salary at these same fifty institutions is 6.0 per cent. Thus, it appears

Table 1   Merit Pay Provisions in AAUP Collective Bargaining Agreements in Force in 1985–86

AAUP Classi-fication	No. of AAUP Agree-ments	No. wo. some info on merit	No. w. one-time bonus	No. w. base salary increase	Max. of listed increases*	Av. per cent of base for merit*	Av. per cent of salary increase	Prop. of inc. for merit (6)/(7)*
	(1)	(2)	(3)	(4)	(5)	(6)	(7)	(8)
I	14	9	6	1	$1,500(4)	1.4	6.3(5)	0.22
IIA	17	8	5	2	none listed 4.9–7.0% (2)	1.0(5)	8.4(5)	0.12
IIB	12	4	2	0	$500 8.0%(1)	0.5(2)	6.5(2)	0.08
IIC	2	1	0	1	$1,000(1)	1.5(1)	6.0(1)	0.25
III	4	2	2	0	$850	2.0(1)	3.8(1)	0.53
IV	1	0	0	0	none listed	—	—	—
Total	50	24	15	4				
Averages for those with merit provisions						1.1(14)	6.3(14)	0.17
Averages for all institutions with contracts						0.5(50)	6.0(50)	0.08

Notes: *Columns 5,6, and 7: the numbers of institutions are shown in parentheses.
Source: Columns 1-6 derived by author from AAUP collective bargaining agreements. Column 7 based on the reported average salary increase from 1984–85 to 1985–86.

that approximately 8 per cent of the total funds for salary increases are available to departments to reward merit.

What we would find from a similar examination of other collective bargaining agreements is not clear. It seems likely that the percentage allocated to merit would be even lower, inasmuch as non-AAUP contracts are less likely to emphasize quality performance by individuals. Unfortunately, other higher education contracts are not readily available to test this view.

It should be apparent that the range of relative salary increases, for the agreements examined here and very probably for all agreements, is sharply limited because so few incorporate merit into the salary base. In those that do, most treat it as equivalent to teaching prizes which have only a one-time effect and are likely to be 'passed around' over the years. Unfortunately, we have no way of measuring the overall distribution of salary increases without institutional data on the salary increases of individual faculty members.

Merit Pay in Public Higher Education

We know little more about merit pay increases in the non-bargaining sector. Explicit and publicly available descriptions of merit systems are absent. Consequently, we draw on the fragmentary literature and then employ a rather restricted set of data to identify what occurs.

Two pertinent studies have come to attention. Kasten (1982), through an evaluation of hypothetical faculty profiles by a panel of faculty members, documents the importance of research in determining merit pay increases among social sciences faculty members at the University of Wisconsin–Madison. McIntosh and Van Koevering (1986), in a careful and systematic study of peer review, merit ratings, and pay increases for a department at the University of Wisconsin–Green Bay, found that, of the various outputs of faculty members, the volume of their scholarly activity is directly associated with merit ratings. In turn, these ratings are closely related to salary increases which ranged from 17 to 76 per cent for the same individuals studied over a six-year period. This is an impressively wide spread. The authors concluded that merit increases account for 31 to 53 per cent of the observed percentage increase in average salaries.[15] Another view of the process of allocating merit salary increases emerges from unpublished data for the University of Wisconsin System. This System enrolls over 160,000 students and embraces a wide variety of institutions, including the University of Wisconsin–Madison, University of Wisconsin–Milwaukee, eleven 'cluster' universities (which include such institutions as University of Wisconsin–Oshkosh, and University of Wisconsin–Parkside), eleven two-year centers, and the University of Wisconsin System–Extension.

Because the missions of these institutions differ, it is reasonable to expect different allocations of salary increases. For example, UW–Madison has many and distinctive doctoral programs, ranks among the top ten research universities, and not surprisingly gives heavy emphasis to research productivity. The UW–Milwaukee, though less well-known, operates in much the same way, given its similar but somewhat less-intensive emphasis on research. The cluster universities are heavily oriented toward undergraduate education and place greater emphasis on teaching. The centers are even more heavily oriented to teaching because they offer only freshmen and sophomore coursework. The Extension Center's role is quite different in its mission, thereby creating difficulty in knowing what dominates.

We expect, as noted earlier in the paper, that the more heavily an institution is oriented toward graduate education and research the more likely it is to emphasize merit pay increases. Conversely, the more heavily an institution is oriented toward instruction the more difficult it is to assess merit, and the less important merit will be in determining annual salary increases.[16]

We examine the UW's merit pay system by comparing the percentage distributions of salary increases over the past several years, including academic years 1981–82, 1984–85 and 1986–87. These three periods are chosen because they are recent, the average percentage increases varied, and the allocations of these increases between merit and across the board increases differed.

The salary increase system prevailing within the University of Wisconsin System is not a pure merit system (System 4). Instead, some small portion of the merit increase funds is typically allocated across the board and is usually accomplished by specifying a minimum percentage increase in salary, thus making it an example of System 3. This minimum increase typically has two components. One is a state legislative mandate that requires a minimum increase of x per cent, with the remaining funds to be allocated for merit. (On occasion no such minimum has been specified, as in 1984–85, but that is the exception). The other component is the discretion granted to different parts of the System to allocate some portion of their remaining salary increase funds for across-the-board distribution; this means that in some parts of the System no one receives less than an x plus y per cent increase.

The variety of legislative and institutional allocations made in recent years is shown in Table 2. In 1981–82 when the overall increase was 8 per cent, a mandatory 2 per cent distribution was specified for everyone. The remaining funds were available for merit allocation at the doctoral institutions. The other elements opted for across-the-board allocations of from 1–2 per cent. The situation differed considerably in 1984–85 when the overall pay plan increase was 3.84 per cent. Because of the small amount, no mandatory distribution was specified. Individual elements of the UW System made different decisions, with two of them specifying no across-the-board distribution and the other two allocating roughly half their increases for across-the-board distribution.

The 1986–87 allocation proved to be quite special. The annual pay plan increase called for an average rise of 6 per cent, with 2 percentage points to be distributed across the board. Institutions then had the option of setting aside additional amounts. Only two elements specified additional across-the-board allocations, but the amounts proved to be relatively small, 0.5 per cent and 1.0 per cent. On top of the 6 per cent increase came the so-called 'catch-up' salary increase which allocated different amounts to the various institutions, in an effort to bring salary levels up to those of their peer institutions. At each campus unit catch-up funds were reallocated by the chancellors

Table 2 Percentage Increases in Pay Plan Levels, Allocations to Across-the-Board Increases, and Catch-up Increases, University of Wisconsin System

Year and Type of Increase	Doctoral Insts.		Cluster Univs.	Centers	Extension
		Element			
1980–81 to 1981–82					
Pay Plan Increase	8		8	8	8
Mandated Across-the-Board Increase	2		2	2	2
Campus Determined Across-the-Board Increase	0		2	1	2
Residual Merit Component	6		4	5	4
1983–84 to 1984–85					
Pay Plan Increase	3.84		3.84	3.84	3.84
Mandated Across-the-Board Increase	0		0	0	0
Campus Determined Across-the-Board Increase	0		2	2	0
Residual Merit Component	3.84		1.84	1.84	3.84
1985–86 to 1986–87	UW-Mad.	UW-Milw.			
Total Increase	15	13.2	12	15	14.4
Pay Plan Increase	6	6	6	6	6
Mandated Across-the-Board Increase	2	2	2	2	2
Campus Determined Across-the-Board Increase	0	0	0.5	1	0
Residual Merit Component	4	4	3.5	3	4
Catch-up Component*	9	7.2	6	9	8.4

Source: Annual University of Wisconsin System reports on salary increases for unclassified staff (faculty).

* These figures reflect the amounts provided to bring average salaries by rank up to the averages for peer institutions. This component was primarily distributed to individuals based on merit, with some differential allocations among colleges and universities.

to various colleges, in accordance with deviations in average salary levels from those of peer institutions.[17]

Two components of merit, representing substantial amounts of funds, were available for distribution by departments in 1986–87. One was the residual merit component of the pay plan which was handled in traditional fashion. The other was the amount of the catch-up available to different units for allocation to faculty members. Catch-up increases were allocated using merit, thereby introducing a greater emphasis on merit than would have occurred had there been larger average salary increases in prior years.

The resulting distributions of salary increases are presented in Tables 3 and 4; in Table 3 the distributions are plus or minus one percentage point around the average while in Table 4 the distributions are of plus or minus two percentage points around the average. (Because of the way the data are tabulated, the percentage ranges for 1984–85 are 0.7 and 1.7 per cent respectively in Tables 3 and 4).

Table 3   Distribution of Total Faculty Salary Increases, University of Wisconsin System Selected Years (in per cent)

	Element			
	Doctoral Insts.	Cluster Univs.	Centers	Extension
1981–82 – Overall Increase of 8%				
Per cent Below Average	29	13	21	27
Per cent Around Average (+/− 1.0%)	45	73	60	47
Per cent Above Average	26	14	19	26
1984–85 – Overall Increase of 3.84%				
Per cent Below Average	22	18	8	24
Per cent Around Average (+/− 0.7%)	55	66	78	50
Per cent Above Average	23	16	14	26
1986–87 – Differentiated Increases of 12–15% Pay System Elements	UW-Mad.	UW-Milw.		
Per cent Below Average	46	48	44	44	46
Per cent Around Average (+/− 1.0%)	17	25	31	32	17
Per cent Above Average	37	27	25	24	37

Source: Annual University of Wisconsin System reports on salary increases for unclassified staff (faculty).

Three conclusions emerge from these tabulations. First, the percentage increases vary widely around the average increase, indicating that merit plays a considerably greater role in these institutions than it could in the collective bargaining sector. Second, as we move from the research-doctoral institutions to the teaching oriented cluster universities in Tables 3 and 4, the distribution of relative salary increases narrows as might be expected. The Center System looks much like the cluster universities whereas Extension more closely resembles the doctoral institutions. Third, the relative spread in the distribution of salary increases is greater in 1986–87 than in 1981–82; the most appropriate comparison is with Table 3 data for 1981–82 and Table 4 data for 1986–87 which 'standardized' the comparisons,

Table 4   Distribution of Total Faculty Salary Increases, University of Wisconsin System Selected Years (in per cent)

	Element			
	Doctoral Insts.	Cluster Univs.	Centers	Extension
1981–82 – Overall Increase of 8%				
Per cent Below Average	16	5	7	0
Per cent Around Average (+/− 2.0%)	68	89	84	87
Per cent Above Average	16	6	9	4
1984–85 – Overall Increase of 3.84%				
Per cent Below Average	17	6	4	19
Per cent Around Average (+/− 1.7%)	67	85	87	63
Per cent Above Average	16	9	9	18
1986–87 – Differentiated Increases of 12–15% Pay System Elements	UW-Mad.	UW-Milw.		
Per cent Below Average	37	33	31	29	41
Per cent Around Average (+/− 2.0%)	34	49	53	57	30
Per cent Above Average	39	18	16	14	29

Source: Annual University of Wisconsin System reports on salary increases for unclassified staff (faculty).

showing a ± 1% range around the 8 per cent increase for 1981–82 and ± 2% range around the 12–15 per cent increase for 1986–87. The reasons for this pattern are not that surprising. And the results for 1984–85 are naturally more concentrated because the overall increase was so small; many departments found the increase to be too small to warrant fine differentiations. The wider spread for 1986–87 is striking but is explained by the need to be highly selective in allocating the substantially increased funds designed to eliminate the significant deterioration of salaries occurring in prior years.

Conclusion

The patterns of salary increases that emerge mesh closely with what most observers might have anticipated. Insitutions and faculty members operating under collective bargaining agreements allocate a relatively small proportion of their salary increase funds for merit. Outside the collective bargaining sector the weight given to merit is greatest in research institutions and smallest in institutions that emphasize teaching. Even among teaching institutions the emphasis on merit considerably exceeds that for the collective bargaining sector.

Were we to enlarge the time span of the analysis by following the distributions of salary increases for individual faculty members over a number of years, the differences would be even sharper. The fact is that faculty members who are regarded as most meritorious one year are likely to be similarly regarded the following year and perhaps in successive years as well. This will produce high correlations between year-to-year salary changes, thus increasing the variance of individual salaries for particular age cohorts. And because the most meritorious individuals in bargaining institutions will be rewarded less generously than their equally meritorious colleagues in the non-unionized sector, they will be on average more receptive to outside offers.

What insights does the experience of higher education have to offer the elementary-secondary sector as it considers adoption and implementation of merit pay? If K-12 teachers, who themselves are largely unionized, take as their model the unionized segment in higher education, then the prospects for introducing a merit system at the pre-college level are not good. The resistance to merit pay in K-12 has been and continues to be substantial, partly because the role of teachers in determining merit pay has been so limited. It is possible that case studies showing how merit pay 'works' in a variety of colleges and universities could point to ways of structuring merit pay proposals that would reduce teacher opposition by involving them in the process.

At the same time, we know far too little about merit pay in higher education. A comprehensive research program is needed to describe how merit pay systems operate, their effectiveness in rewarding meritorious faculty members, and the responses of faculty members to their merit increases. With such information we will be in a better position to predict the possible success of merit pay proposals for the nation's elementary and secondary schools.

Notes

The author acknowledges support from the Howard R. Bowen–Jack H. Schuster study of the American Professoriate that was sponsored by the American Association in Higher Education (AAHE) and the Teachers Insurance and Annuity Association and College Retirement Equities Fund (TIAA-CREF). Additional support was provided by the Wisconsin Center for Education Research with support from the National Institute of Education (NIE-G-84-0008) and also by the National Center for Postsecondary Governance and Finance with support from the US Department of Education's Office of Educational Research and Improvement (OERI-G-86-

0009). The opinions expressed in this paper do not necessarily reflect the position, policy, or endorsement of any of the above named organizations.

I also want to acknowledge the constructive comments of Howard R. Bowen, Maryse Eymonerie, Hirschel Kasper, Robert Lampman, Ulrich Lehmann, Donald Smith, Jacob Stampen, Martha Casey, and Bruce Beck. Helpful editorial comments were offered by Deborah M. Stewart and Marilyn H. Rhodes. Able research assistance was provided by Joanne Suffis.

1. The literature on merit pay is sparse, and that on faculty salary systems in general is not much more extensive. Perhaps the best introduction is by Brown (1982, 1983, 1984) who describes the concept of merit pay and how to evaluate performance for purposes of awarding merit pay. For additional references to recent faculty compensation studies see National Center (1986).

2. A good review of these elements is provided by Bowen and Schuster (1986). Several efforts have been made to place merit pay within the context of an overall salary compensation system. Steiner (1972) led the way, putting emphasis on 'maturation' as a neglected element that needed to be recognized along with merit. Eymonerie (1980) took up the issue again in the context of discussions about the advisability of establishing formal salary schedules in higher education. Simpson (1981) commented more generally on the problem of awarding merit salary increases when the rate of inflation outpaces the overall percentage increase in salaries; he suggested the need for a broader concept of faculty salary structure which encompasses general increases for cost of living, salary steps to reflect experience and provision for merit. Blitz and Tang (1981) also explored the difficulties of recognizing merit in periods of substantial inflation, as did Mortimer (1982), Hollander and Turnbell (1984), Musto (1984), and Spitzberg (1983).

3. For the small number of institutions that do not use ranks (i.e., everyone may have the title of instructor), promotion is not a part of the merit salary system.

4. This approach is best exemplified by the University of California which in 1983 established different salary schedules for faculty in several disciplines. Evidence on the patterns of disciplinary increases is from Hansen (1985, 1986).

5. A continuing concern is about who will make decisions on merit increases. To the extent that these decisions are made by administrators, faculty members will object because this violates the fundamental concept of peer review. Developing mechanisms for peer evaluations is not an easy task, however. Moreover, considerable trust is required to make such a system work. Where trust is lacking, among peers and between faculty and administrators, merit will be relegated to a minor role, as is typically the case in collective bargaining agreements.

6. Several readers of an earlier draft suggested that rewarding merit by granting well above or below average salary increases is probably easier in larger than in smaller departments. The impersonality of larger departments reduces the possibility of interpersonal frictions that might result from granting widely differing salary increases.

7. For one example, see McIntosh and Van Koevering (1986) whose paper is discussed below.
8. The chances for error are likely to be greater if all merit decisions are in the hands of a single individual.
9. As a practical matter if there is one open position elsewhere only one of two equally qualified people at an institution is likely to receive an offer. Subtle assessments of movability may dictate who gets the offer.
10. For individuals, the situation is obviously more complicated. Moving cost allowances which are quite common greatly reduce this barrier to job mobility. On the other hand the uncertainties involved are sufficient to prevent moving for small gains in salary.
11. This discussion ignores the effects of mobility which the presence of these from systems will induce.
12. This discussion ignores differences in average salary levels and institutional quality that shape the pattern of job shifts and hence affect the salary distributions.
13. These difficulties are described by the author in recent reports of the AAUP's Committee Z's Annual Report on the Economic Studies of the Profession which have appeared as special issues of *ACADEME: Bulletin of the AAUP* (see Hansen, 1986).
14. In 1985 411 colleges and universities were listed as having collective bargaining agreements (Douglas, 1986).
15. As is noted below, required across-the-board percentage increases limit the scope of increases that can be associated with merit.
16. The smaller the academic unit the more difficult it may be to reward merit because of the personal dynamics involved. To the extent that teaching institutions are smaller, their salary increases could be more compressed for this reason as well.
17. The details of allocating the catch-up pay increase are far too complex to be reported here.

References

Begin, J.P. (1979) 'Faculty bargaining and faculty reward systems,' in Lewis, D.R. and Becker, W.E., Jr. (Eds), *Academic Rewards in Higher Education*, Cambridge, MA: Ballinger.
Blitz, R.C. and Tang, A.M. (1981) 'Merit raises and academic tenure under inflation', *Economics of Education Review*, 1 (Spring), pp. 151–67.
Bowen, H.R. and Schuster, J.H. (1986) *American Professors: A National Resource Imperiled*. Oxford: Oxford University Press.
Brown, W.S. (1982) 'Merit pay in a university environment', *Journal of the College and University Personnel Association*, 33 (Spring), pp. 23–26.
Brown, W.S. (1983) 'Pay for performance: The merit pay concept in an academic environment', *Journal of the College and University Personnel Association*, 34 (Fall), pp. 23–26.
Brown, W.S. (1984) 'Performance review instruments and merit pay programs in an academic environment', *Journal of the College and University Personnel Association*, 35 (Spring), pp. 7–13.

Douglas, J.M. (1986) *Directory of Faculty Contracts and Bargaining Agents in Institutions of Higher Education*, National Center for the Study of Collective Bargaining in Higher Education and the Professions, Baruch College-CUNY.

Douglas, J.M. and Goldsmith, N.B. (1981) 'Analytical survey of contractual salary and compensation methodology in higher education collective bargaining', Excepted from Monograph No. 4, Summer 1981, National Center for the study of Collective Bargaining in Higher Education and the Professions, Baruch College-CUNY.

Eymonerie, M. (1980) 'Salary scales: Pros and cons', *Academe: Bulletin of the AAUP*, March, pp. 118–119.

Guthrie-Morse, B.J. (1979) *The Academic Incentive System: Some Effects of Collective Bargaining on Salary and Security in Four-Year Colleges and University*, unpublished Ph.D. Dissertation, University of Arizona.

Hansen, W.L. (1985) 'Salary differentials across disciplines', *Academe: Bulletin of the AAUP*, July-August, pp. 6–7.

Hansen, W.L. (1986) 'Changes in faculty salaries', in Bowen, H.R. and Schuster, J. *American Professors: A National Resource Imperiled*, Oxford: Oxford University Press.

Hansen, W.L. (1986) 'Continuing the upward climb', *Academe: Bulletin of the AAUP*, March–April, pp. 3–6.

Hirschman, A.O. (1970) *Exit, Voice, and Loyalty*, Cambridge, MA: Harvard University Press.

Hollander, T. and Turnbell, J. (1984) 'The merits of merit pay: Where's the merit in merit?' in Douglas, J.M. (Ed.), *Structural Reform in Higher Education Collective Bargaining*, Proceedings of Twelfth of Annual Conference, National Center for the Study of Collective Bargaining in Higher Education and the Professions, Baruch College-CUNY, April 1984, pp. 86–96.

Kasper, H. (1986) *Finding the Merit in Merit Pay for Faculty*, unpublished paper, Oberlin College.

Kasten, K.L. (1982) *Tenure and Merit Pay as Incentives for Research, Teaching, and Service at a Research University*, unpublished Ph.D. thesis, University of Wisconsin-Madison..

Kirschling, W.R. (Ed.) (1978) *Evaluating Faculty Performance and Vitality*, New Directions in Institutional Research, San Francisco, CA: Jossey-Bass.

Klass, B.S. (1986) *Merit Pay Allocations Decisions: A Review*, unpublished paper, Industrial Relations Research Institute, University of Wisconsin-Madison.

McIntosh, T.H. and Van Koevering, T.E. (1986) 'Six-year case study of faculty peer reviews, merit ratings, and pay awards in a multidisciplinary department', *Journal of the College and University Personnel Association*, 37 (Spring), pp. 5–14.

McKeachie, W.J. (1979) 'Perspectives from psychology: Financial incentives are ineffective for faculty', in Lewis, D.R. and Becker, W.E., Jr. (Eds), *Academic Rewards in Higher Education*, Cambridge, MA: Ballinger.

Mortimer, K.P. (1982) 'A decade of campus bargaining: An overview', in Douglas, J.M. (Ed.), *Campus Bargaining at the Crossroads*, Proceedings of the Tenth Annual Conference, National Center for the Study of Collective Bargaining in Higher Education and the Professions, Baruch College-CUNY, April 1982, pp. 97–105.

Musto, J.N. (1984) 'The merits of merit pay: Merit determination as a factor of faculty salary', in Douglas, J.M. (Ed.), *Structural Reform in Higher Education Collective Bargaining*, Proceedings of Twelfth Annual Conference, National Center for the Study of Collective Bargaining in Higher Education and the Professions, Baruch College-CUNY, April 1984. pp, 96–102.

Simpson, W.B. (1981) 'Faculty salary structure for a college or university', *Journal of Higher Education*, 52, pp. 219–36.

Spitzberg, I.J., Jr. (1983) 'Merit pay: Lessons learned', *Academe: Bulletin of the AAUP*, 68 (September/October), p. 48.

Steiner, P.O. (1972) 'Coping with Adversity: Report of the Economic Status of the Profession, 1971–72', *AAUP Bulletin*, 58 (June), pp. 187–94.

Tuckman, H.P. (1979) 'The academic reward structure in American higher education', in Lewis, D.R. and Becker, W.E., Jr. (Eds), *Academic Rewards in Higher Education*, Cambridge, MA: Ballinger.

7 Gender Differences in the Academic Reward System*

Debra Barbezat

Academics view the issue of discrimination differently compared with other types of workers. Many academics assume that similarly qualified individuals will be treated equally in a profession that they feel approaches a meritocracy. The possibility of salary discrimination may also be viewed somewhat differently by faculty members who, as Veblen noted, feel 'their salaries are not of the nature of wages and that there would be a species of moral obliquity in overtly so dealing with the matter' (Veblen, 1975: p. 118). But, how do the facts accord with the profession's contrary views?

In recent years, many researchers have turned their focus to this unusual labor market. Various types of data have been analyzed including longitudinal surveys and single cross-sectional data bases. We have debated the definition, measurement and sources of discrimination as well as possible remedies for unequal salary and employment opportunities. As yet, the verdict is split concerning the impact of affirmative action legislation designed to eliminate such disparities. This paper examines only one form of discrimination: salary discrimination by sex within academic institutions. Our goal is to present estimates of gender differences in the academic reward system as well as to examine alternative explanations of the source of such discrepancies.

Our study is consistent with the bulk of the discrimination literature in that it employs the residual approach for measuring salary

---

* A version of this manuscript appeared in *Population Research and Policy Review* (1987). Permission granted by Kluwer Academic Publisher.

discrimination. After estimating total male/female salary differentials, we decompose this total figure into a portion which is 'legitimate' in the sense that it reflects differences in qualifications between men and women, and an unexplained portion. The unexplained residual represents the salary difference remaining after we control for all available salary determinants and, therefore, constitutes our estimate of discrimination. A discussion of potential biases inherent in this approach accompanies the discussion of results.

The present investigation extends the literature on sex discrimination in academic labor markets in three important respects. First, considerable disagreement persists over which individual characteristics should be controlled in making comparisons between the earnings of faculty members. To the extent that currently observed differences between the sexes arose from previous discrimination, better measures of total discrimination may be had if these characteristics are not controlled. The data base[1] utilized for the present study contains detailed information on demographic characteristics, educational background, work experience, and employing institution; essentially all the predominant factors to which the salary differential is attributed. This permits us to derive several estimates of the salary differential while controlling for such explanatory variables as publication, field, type and quality of employing institution, and rank. Moreover, such detailed data are not obtained at the expense of limiting the investigation to a single institutional case study.[2]

This inquiry makes a second contribution in that we may compare estimates of the salary differential and discrimination between 1968 and 1977. During this nine-year period, both the turnaround in the academic labor market and the implementation of affirmative action legislation conceivably influenced the size of the earnings differential by sex. The bulk of the affirmative action legislation pertaining specifically to higher education, was implemented after 1968, when the first survey was conducted.[3] The time frame of the surveys, therefore, provides better indication of the long-run impact of antibias legislation compared with many existing studies.

Finally, the presence of specific data on work experience and marital and parental status allows us to test various hypotheses regarding the source of the male-female salary differential. Johnson and Stafford (1979) offer two explanations of disparities in the reward structure according to sex:

1. Women academics have an average lower productivity... and consequently, lower salaries. Because of the lifetime

pattern of their work attachment, the fall in the productivity of the average woman academic relative to men is especially acute during the first ten years of experience.

2. Women are, given equivalent training and experience, just as productive as men but receive lower salaries because of labor market discrimination against them – that is, they are paid lower salaries given their productivity than males are.

Johnson and Stafford have elaborated upon the first explanation, the life cycle theory, in several articles (Johnson and Stafford, 1974; 1977). While admitting that part of the salary differential is the result of discrimination, they argue that the proportionate salary differential accruing to male academics is generated primarily by the market's reaction to women's choices regarding training and labor force participation. We examine several implications of the Johnson/Stafford hypothesis with respect to the academic labor market.

The remainder of this paper is divided into five parts. The first section presents estimates of the total salary differential by sex for both 1968 and 1977. Several estimates are derived while alternately controlling for publication, academic discipline, and characteristics of the employing institution. The results of fitting separate equations for male and female academics are presented in the second section. In section three, we employ these separate regression models to perform an Oaxaca decomposition yielding a range of estimates of discrimination for the two periods. We use the survey results to investigate alternative explanations of the source of the male/female salary differential in section four. Conclusions and policy implications are presented in the final section.

Simple Measures of Discrimination

As a first step toward measuring the total salary differential by sex, we estimate a basic regression model using the logarithm of salary as the dependent variable. Only the top three academic ranks (assistant, associate and full professor) are analyzed. The independent variables included in the basic regression are: XPO (post-degree experience), calculated by taking the year of the survey minus the year in which the highest degree was received, XPO-squared, age, and dichotomous variables representing sex, region (northeast, midwest, west or south), race, type of contract (nine or eleven month), whether the respondent was primarily engaged in teaching or research, if the individual had earned an advanced degree[4] or had indicated spending a relatively large amount of time in administration.[5]

The coefficient on the sex dummy variable (which equals one for males) indicates that male faculty members received an annual salary that was approximately 21 per cent above that of their female colleagues in 1968. The comparable figures for 1975 and 1977 are 13 per cent and eight per cent (see Table 1).[6] Clearly, this coefficient may capture the effects of omitted variables. If, for example, male faculty members are generally more able than their female counterparts, the sex coefficient is biased upward. However, to the extent that all relevant criteria have been controlled, or, that omitted variables are distributed similarly for both sexes, this coefficient represents one estimate of salary discrimination. The findings suggest a marked decrease in discrimination over the period. The degree of salary discrimination also appears to be less than that discovered in other sectors of the economy.

Table 1 Coefficient of the Male Dummy Variable in Various Regressions for 1968, 1975, and 1977[a]

Number of Observations	1968 (N=13,613)	1975 (N=2,202)	1977 (N=3,021)
I Basic Regression	.2071 (.0147)	.1274 (.0136)	.0802 (.0102)
II Basic Regression with Rank Variables	.1508 (.0145)	.0989 (.0126)	.0489 (.0088)
III Regression I with Publication Variables (No Rank)	.1741 (.0145)	.1000 (.0130)	.0595 (.0094)
IV Regression III with Field Variables	.1651 (.0148)	.1044 (.0129)	.0463 (.0087)
V Regression IV with Institutional Type Variables	.1628 (.0148)	.0954 (.0126)	.0247 (.0066)

[a] Standard errors are shown in parenthesis.

The remainder of Table 1 documents the change in the sex coeficient as various additional explanatory factors are incorporated into the basic equation. Accounting for the fact that male academics tend to publish more than female academics reduces the differential, as measured by a lump sum advantage, from approximately 21 per cent to 17 per cent in 1968. The coefficient falls from 13 per cent to 6 per cent in 1975 and from 8 per cent to 6 per cent in 1977. Similarly, taking into consideration the possibility that men tend to be concentrated in fields that command relatively high pecuniary rewards also reduces the differential in both periods. Since the results are very sensitive to the specification of the productivity and discipline variables, we discuss their formation below.

The inclusion of field dummies is important due to the women's uneven distribution across disciplines, and also to adjust for varying demand conditions between fields. Originally, forty-two field dummy variables, representing the largest number of disciplines common to both surveys, were selected for inclusion. The number was eventually reduced to twenty-five[7] according to similarity of regression coefficients and discipline.

Productivity level was controlled by several methods. A number of publication measures were available in the survey, such as total number of published books, articles, and 'writings', as well as the same measures describing publication in the last two years only. After experimenting with all the variables, we constructed ten dummy variables representing six levels of article publication and four levels of book publication.[8]

The ability to control for publication represents an advancement over many previous discrimination studies. Nonetheless, the publication measures are inadequate in several respects. To begin with, it is important to recognize the differing publication rates between men and women may reflect discrimination on the part of journal editors, referees, and funding sources. Hence, the control variable is somewhat tainted.[9] This issue aside, more practical problems are associated with the productivity variables. While use of an interval variable enables the identification of nonlinearities in the data, the large differences in the interval size make it difficult to identify diminishing returns to increased publication. In addition, we cannot establish the quality of the published work. Data on citations or quality of the journal that accepted the articles would be useful, but one should recognize that these variables are also suspect. For example, a recent study by Ferber suggests that researchers tend to cite a larger proportion of authors of their own sex, thereby contaminating the citations variables.[10]

Finally, characteristics of the respondent's employing institution were controlled in order to analyze the impact of quality and type of institution on the salary differential. Women comprise a relatively large proportion of faculties at private colleges and other small institutions. However, controlling for this fact does not significantly alter the coefficient on the dichotomous sex variable in either period, as demonstrated in Table 1. The following discussion reviews the construction of the institutional type variables.

For the 1975 and 1977 data, the institutional type variables parallel the Carnegie classification system. The five dummy variables distinguish between Type I research universities; Type II research universities; Type I and II doctoral-granting universities; comprehensive colleges and universities; and liberal arts colleges (the standard in the regression equations). For example, in 1977 the regression results indicated a 13 per cent return to Type I academics, 7 per cent to Type II faculty members, 11 per cent to the employees of doctoral-granting universities, and the faculty of comprehensive colleges and universities enjoyed a 12 per cent proportionate salary advantage relative to their colleagues at liberal arts colleges.[11] Although the survey data confirm that women are more likely to be employed by a school with the lowest quality rating, and much less likely to be associated with a top ranked institution, controlling for quality,[12] in addition to type, did not reduce the male dummy coefficient any further than the estimates derived from controlling for type alone. This result is probably related to the fact that the Carnegie classifications also reflect institutional quality.

Since the schools were not classified along the Carnegie guidelines in 1968, we developed several alternative measures to test for the effect of institutional type on the male/female salary differential. We obtained the estimates in Table 1 by including a dichotomous variable representing universities and four-year colleges. The results indicate an 8 per cent return to university faculty above their college counterparts (significant at one per cent). Unfortunately, this broad classification of schools is less suited to capturing such differences as institutional quality or teaching load. The 1968 survey also separated institutions into the following mutually exclusive categories: Ivy League, (other) elite private university, elite private college, state university (Big Ten), state university (California system), state university (other), Black college/university, and 'other' (schools not already coded). Consequently, we incorporated dummy variables representing these general school characteristics into the salary equation. Relative to the omitted 'other' category, the results suggest a 5 per cent salary advantage accruing to academics at Ivy League universities, 14 per cent to those at elite private universities, 4 per cent to those employed by elite private colleges, 10 per cent to Big Ten faculty, and 13 per cent salary advantage to faculty members at both the California state university system and other state universities. The only negative coefficient was that of Black institutions, but it was not statistically different from zero.

Several authors have raised the question of whether it is appropriate to control for rank in the salary equations. Hoffman (1976) contends that sex discrimination may occur through slower promotion rates for females, in which case present rank reflects past discrimination. Consequently, estimates of sex discrimination that include rank variables are biased downward. The exclusion of rank from the equation is desirable on other grounds. Variables such as experience, highest degree, and number of publications are all closely related to rank. The multicollinearity that results from including rank makes it very difficult to explore the effects of other factors upon salary. Nevertheless, in order to evaluate the magnitude of the differance in estimates of the salary differential, Table 2 also presents the results of identical regressions, these with rank. Hoffman was correct in predicting more conservative estimates of measured discrimination. The inclusion of rank in the basic regression results in a decline in the male coefficient for all periods.

Finally, several other predictors of salary were tested for inclusion in the regression equation. A variable equal to the percentage of female academics in a given field was the most notable of these alternative explanatory variables. The rationale for including this factor derives from the comparable worth literature and the idea that the 'femaleness' of field depresses wages for men and/or women. The dearth of women in fields such as engineering, and their concentration in relatively low-paying disciplines, such as the humanities, supports this argument. In practice, the variable performed concentration in relatively low-paying disciplines, such as the humanities, supports this argument. In practice, the variable performed poorly in many different specifications of the salary model for 1968. The variable was negative and consistently significant at the 1 per cent level using 1977 data. However, the extremely small size of the regression coefficient does not support the view that a large proportion of women in a given field has any considerable influence on the average level of salaries. This finding is consistent with that of Fox (1981). Her case study of a major research university led to the conclusion that a high proportion of women has no significant adverse impact on the salaries of either men or women working in that department, school, or academic division.

Separate Regressions by Sex

It is dubious whether salary differences between the sexes can be adequately measured simply by inserting a dichotomous sex variable into the salary equations. To test the assertion that the underlying salary determination process is different for the two sexes, the basic regression was fitted for men and women separately, and then we compared the sum of squared deviations from these two equations to the sum of squared deviations in the basic equation in which both sexes were combined. The Chow tests indicated that the system of rewards was fundamentally different for male and female academics in both periods under investigation.

When we estimate separate equations for men and women, discrimination's effects may be evident in many ways. Table 2 summarizes the results obtained from a basic model with productivity and field variables. Upon comparing the men and women in 1968 it becomes clear that the male coefficients are higher than the corresponding female coefficients in several main areas including: all levels of article publication, all levels of book publication, the receipt of an advanced degree, and the return to an eleven-month contract. Some authors have noted that the impact of affirmative action may be to introduce discrimination against male faculty members (e.g., Koch and Chizmar, 1976). Although the men maintain their advantage in most categories in 1977, there are a few interesting reversals. The 21 per cent pecuniary return to women with an advanced degree, for instance, as opposed to 11 per cent for men, and the higher rates of return to book publication may signify changes in favor of the female professor. As a final note, Table 2 may also exhibit the impact on salaries of the turnaround in higher education. The conspicuous reduction in the article publication coefficients from 1968 to 1977, particularly for male academics, may be one consequence of financial constraints on institutions.

Previous studies, including Bayer and Astin (1975) lead one to expect that the fraction of explained variation would be greater in the men's equation than the women's equation. The reasoning is that discrimination may manifest itself in terms of an arbitrary or random reward structure for the minority faculty members. Surprisingly, the adjusted R-squared in 1968 is substantially lower for the male academics' salary regression. The reason for this result is not apparent. Perhaps if one imagines a broader definition of discrimination – one that considers discrimination in favor of particular men, as well as 'against' women – this result becomes more plausible. For example, a tendency to 'overcompensate' less-able men during a period of relatively abundant resources might decrease the extent to which men's observed characteristics are capable of explaining the determination of men's salaries. Clearly, as one draws closer to the mid-1970s, a number of forces encouraged departments to develop stricter salary schedules. Academic unionization, scarce funds, and affirmative action all increased the department's accountability regarding how salaries are determined.

Table 2 Regression Coefficients for Men and Women for 1968 and 1977 Including Productivity and Field[a]

	1968 Men	1968 Women	1977 Men	1977 Women
CONT 11	.178 (.011)	.09 (.011)	.173 (.008)	.174 (.020)
ARTICLE 1	.127 (.016)	.021 (.013)	.058 (.014)	.011 (.026)
ARTICLE 2	.141 (.018)	.059 (.017)	.088 (.015)	.019 (.030)
ARTICLE 3	.196 (.017)	.119 (.018)	.098 (.014)	.081 (.030)
ARTICLE 4	.254 (.019)	.142 (.023)	.145 (.015)	.148 (.035)
ARTICLE 5	.349 (.020)	.244 (.026)	.242 (.015)	.224 (.044)
BOOK 1	.046 (.011)	.037 (.012)	.021 (.008)	.026 (.019)
BOOK 2	.089 (.018)	.056 (.024)	.078 (.011)	.082 (.036)
BOOK 3	.116 (.021)	.046 (.032)	.104 (.012)	.125 (.037)
BLACK	−.049 (.050)	−.055 (.029)	.046 (.031)	.006 (.041)
NEAST	.068 (.013)	.044 (.013)	.051 (.009)	−.012 (.023)
MIDWEST	.078 (.013)	.013 (.014)	.026 (.009)	−.006 (.023)
WEST	.052 (.014)	.020 (.014)	.013 (.010)	.009 (.028)
TEACH	.015 (.014)	−.031 (.013)	−.024 (.012)	.012 (.026)
ADVDEG	.140	.184	.108	.213
CURADMIN	.149 (.019)	.161 (.020)	.118 (.010)	.094 (.024)
XPO	.013 (.002)	.009 (.002)	.026 (.001)	.018 (.003)
XPO-SQUARED	−.37E-03 (.4E-04)	−.20E-03 (.45E-04)	−.37E-03 (.32E-04)	−.33E-03 (.83E-04)
AGE	.0117 (.0009)	.0037 (.0007)	.0028 (.0006)	.0050 (.0012)
AGRICULTURE	.065 (.030)	.593 (.185)	.006 (.029)	−.189 (.122)
APPLIED PROF.	.188 (.034)	.119 (.027)	.124 (.028)	.079 (.058)
BIOSCIENCE	.108 (.021)	.003 (.023)	.017 (.022)	−.050 (.052)
BUSINESS	.249 (.026)	.061 (.040)	.207 (.021)	.036 (.056)
EDUCATION	.127 (.025)	.025 (.021)	.082 (.024)	−.029 (.049)
MECH. ENGINEER	.247 (.036)	.129 (.134)	.141 (.032)	N/A
ELEC. ENGINEER	.244 (.034)	.148 (.131)	.112 (.029)	−.244 (.169)
OTHER ENGINEER	.223 (.024)	.146 (.131)	.103 (.022)	−.110 (.071)
MEDICINE	.242 (.027)	.208 (.038)	.287 (.025)	.15 (.068)

Table 2 contd

	1968 Men	1968 Women	1977 Men	1977 Women
OTHER HEALTH	.170	.081	.130	.044
	(.037)	(.019)	(.030)	(.047)
ENGLISH	.074	−.039	−.009	−.134
	(.025)	(.023)	(.025)	(.053)
FOREIGN LANG.	.088	−.033	−.043	−.062
	(.027)	(.022)	(.027)	(.063)
HISTORY	.130	−.032	.036	.013
	(.028)	(.038)	(.026)	(.075)
PHILOSOPHY	.104	−.053	.009	−.222
	(.040)	(.048)	(.033)	(.102)
OTHER HUM.	.020	−.080	−.073	−.147
	(.040)	(.063)	(.039)	(.078)
LAW	.395	.155	.312	.361
	(.047)	(.076)	(.034)	(.120)
MATH/STAT	.228	.068	.071	−.055
	(.025)	(.032)	(.023)	(.063)
P.E./HEALTH	.076	.045	−.016	−.007
	(.042)	(.023)	(.035)	(.058)
CHEMISTRY	.113	−.055	−.017	−.055
	(.027)	(.039)	(.024)	(.079)
PHYSICS	.171	.053	.034	.003
	(.028)	(.063)	(.024)	(.084)
OTHER PHYS. SCI.	.139	−.129	.032	−.053
	(.032)	(.063)	(.029)	(.103)
ECONOMICS	.267	.083	.152	.138
	(.030)	(.057)	(.024)	(.064)
SOCIAL SCI.	.148	.022	.057	−.029
	(.020)	(.022)	(.020)	(.045)
ALL OTHER	.181	.115	.126	−.007
	(.043)	(.020)	(.029)	(.054)
CONSTANT	8.389	8.863	9.212	9.190
	(.035)	(.032)	(.029)	(.061)
$\bar{R}^2$	.226	.521	.722	.655
S.E.E.	.51	.18	.16	.16
N	12140	1473	2605	416

[a] Standard errors are shown in parentheses.

Differences between the sexes are also evident with respect to the field dummies.[13] The consistently positive field coefficients for males in 1968 are not so unusual when one recognizes that the omitted 'other' category is fine arts.[14] It is surprising, however, that women in areas such as physical science would earn less than those in fine arts. In general, the relatively high-paying fields were the same for men and women in 1968, although women received a lesser premium for membership in these fields than did male faculty members. The figures for women relative to men were roughly: 16 versus 40 per cent in law, 21 versus 24 per cent in medicine, 8 versus 27 per cent in economics, 13–15 versus 22–25 per cent in engineering, and 6 versus 25 per cent in business. In the 1977 regressions a relatively small sample size for women (N=416) hampered the regression's ability to sort out salary differentials by field. However, in certain fields women's position relative to men seems to have changed substantially over the period. By 1977, female law professors fared better than male law professors (36 versus 31 per cent for men). The proportional salary differential accruing to a female economist was almost equivalent to that of a male economist (which, by the way, had fallen since 1968). The salary premium for male medical professors had risen by 1977, while the return to female medical professors had fallen, thereby widening the salary gap between these academics. Finally, the financial penalty associated with teaching the humanities appears to have been much worse for women than for men.

Oaxaca Decompositions

In this section, we impose a formal structure upon the regressions for men and women in order to arrive at estimates of sex discrimination in salary. According to Oaxaca, discrimination is said to exist whenever the relative wage of males exceeds the relative wage that would have prevailed if males and females were paid according to the same criteria (Oaxaca, 1973). The 'discrimination coefficient', (D), is defined as follows:

$$(1) \qquad D = \frac{(W_m/W_f) - (W_m/W_f)^\circ}{(W_m/W_f)^\circ}$$

where (W_m/W_f) is the observed male/female earnings ratio and $(W_m/W_f)^\circ$ is the ratio that would exist if there were no discrimination. $(W_m/W_f)^\circ$, the ratio in the absence of discrimination, may be estimated in two ways: 1) the wage structure currently applicable to males would also apply to females, and 2) the wage structure currently applicable to females would apply to males. In practice, we estimate separate regressions for male and female academics. The estimated regression coefficients for one sex, male for example, are applied to the data for the other, female, and we can predict an average salary for females. This salary figure represents what the average female would be paid were she compensated according to the male pay structure. The residual between this figure and the average female salary derived from the women's equation is equal to (D), the measure of salary discrimination.

Table 3 provides an example of the Oaxaca decomposition procedure as applied to the basic regression for men and women in 1968. We estimate the total salary differential between the two groups by comparing the average (predicted) value of ln salary for the women's equation (9.344) to that of the men's equation (9.551). In order to compare the observed ratio of male/female earnings to the ratio that would prevail if discrimination did not exist, two estimates of $(W_m/W_f)^{\circ}$ are formed. First, assume that the males' wage structure also applies to females. The coefficients for the men's regression are applied to the average value of the women's characteristics, to obtain a predicted value of 9.498 for ln salary. Note that this value is higher than the average value of 9.344 derived from the women's equation. The result shows that even if women and men were equally compensated for their attributes, a 5 per cent salary differential would remain ($\exp^{9.551} - \exp^{9.498}$). This figure implies that approximately 17.6 percentage points of the total salary difference (23 per cent minus 5.4 per cent) are not based on unequal characteristics and may be viewed as an estimate of discrimination.

We may estimate the salary structure in the absence of discrimination, $(W_m/W_f)^{\circ}$, a second way. The coefficients for the female regression are applied to the average value of the men's characteristics to obtain a predicted value of 9.403. Note that this figure is less than the average value of 9.551 calculated for the men's equation. If men were rewarded as were their female colleagues, men's salaries would still exceed women's salaries by 6.1 per cent on average ($\exp^{9.403} - \exp^{9.344}$). Since the total per cent difference in salaries is 23 per cent, 16.9 percentage points of the salary differential may be attributed to discrimination.

Table 4 presents estimates of the total salary differential between male and female academics in 1968 and 1977. We fitted several specifications of the basic model for men and women separately, and formed corresponding estimates of discrimination using the Oaxaca procedure. In effect, a range of estimates results since $(W_m/W_f)^{\circ}$ was calculated using both methods described above. The table documents a general reduction in discrimination over the nine-year period. In 1968, approximately 12 to 18 percentage points of the 23 per cent total salary difference may be attributed to discrimination, depending upon

Table 3   Illustration of the Oaxaca Procedure for Basic Regression in 1968

Average Value of Ln Salary for Men	Average Value of Ln Salary for Women	Predicted Value of Ln Salary for Men in the Women's Equation	Predicted Value of Ln Salary for Women in the Men's Equation
9.551	9.344	9.403	9.498

I Total Percent Salary
  Difference
       $\exp(9.551) - \exp(9.344) = 14{,}058.746 - 11{,}430.037$
       Percent change is 22.998

II Two Estimates of the Percent Salary Difference in the Absence of
   Discrimination
   1) Compare the men's value with that of the women when women are
      compensated according to the men's salary structure
      $\exp(9.551) - \exp(9.498)$ implies a 5.443% salary difference
   2) Compare the women's value with that of the men when men are
      compensated according to the women's salary structure
      $\exp(9.403) - \exp(9.344)$ implies a 6.078% salary difference

III Two Estimates of Discrimination
    Discrimination is measured as a residual: the total salary difference minus the
    salary difference that exists due to differences in characteristics between the
    sexes.
    1) 22.998% − 5.443% = 17.555%
    2) 22.998% − 6.078% = 16.920%
    Estimate of Discrimination in 1968: 16.920−17.555%

Table 4   Estimates of the Total Salary Difference by Sex and Percentage Difference Due to Discrimination

Total Salary Difference Between Men and Women (From Basic Equation)	1968	1977
	22.998%	18.887%
	Estimates of Discrimination	Estimates of Discrimination
I Basic Regression	16.920–17.555%	9.470–11.529%
II Basic Regression with Rank Variables	11.764–12.433%	6.137–7.816%
III Add Publications to I (No Rank Vars.)	14.364–15.238%	6.484–6.551%
IV Add Fields to III	13.157–15.046%	6.019–7.453%
V Add Type of Institution to IV	11.562–13.626%	5.533–7.097%

Table 5   Mean Values of Explanatory Variables for Male and Female Academics in 1968 and 1977

	1968 Men	1968 Women	1977 Men	1977 Women
XPO	12.07	12.32	14.14	11.25
XPO-Sqrd	247.23	248.84	285.76	212.08
Age	43.03	46.04	44.12	44.04
Dummy Variables				
11 Month Contract	.37	.37	.27	.28
Article 1	.19	.25	.11	.24
Article 2	.13	.13	.12	.15
Article 3	.17	.12	.21	.20
Article 4	.13	.07	.19	.13
Article 5	.21	.06	.29	.10
Book 1	.28	.26	.31	.32
Book 2	.09	.05	.12	.06
Book 3	.07	.03	.11	.06
Black	.01	.03	.01	.04
Northeast	.26	.31	.31	.34
Midwest	.27	.23	.31	.31
West	.24	.22	.16	.14
Teaching	.61	.82	.49	.60
Advanced Degree	.81	.55	.90	.76
Current Administration	.07	.07	.14	.15
Full Professor	.36	.20	.46	.25
Associate Professor	.28	.28	.30	.27
Children	.76	.28	.82	.51
Ever Married	.94	.52	.94	.74
High Quality Institution	.35	.24	.32	.23
University	.81	.68		
Research University I			.44	.34
Research University II			.25	.21
Doctoral Grant University			.17	.27
Comprehensive College/University			.12	.14
Liberal Arts College			.03	.03

which factors are controlled. Estimates for 1977 are smaller, ranging from 6 to 12 percentage points of the 19 per cent observed salary difference. Regression II, which includes rank variables, reaffirms Hoffman's contention that measured discrimination is less when rank is included in the salary equations. In order to distinguish the predominant factors accounting for these results, Table 5 contains a comparison of credentials for male and female academics in the two periods.

The Source of Salary Differentials

Johnson and Stafford's (1974: p.890) explanation of the source of salary differentials by sex holds several implications regarding the relative earnings of men, single women and married women. First, this theory of voluntary choice stresses women's decision to reduce labor force participation during the childrearing years. The associated deterioration in skills, followed by renewed commitment to the workplace in later years, implies a prescribed path of relative earnings for men and women. The average salary of female academics relative to male academics should fall with years of potential experience, XPO, up to the end of the childrearing period, at which time women's relative earnings rise. A further implication of the life cycle explanation is that the salaries and career paths of single women should parallel men's more closely than those of married women. Also, regarding employment, Johnson and Stafford maintain that women's expectation of a shorter duration in the labor market leads them to prefer initial employment at particular types of academic institutions – those with relatively high starting salaries, but few training opportunities. Such choices lead to lower average salaries for women in the middle part of the life cycle.

In order to verify the pattern in relative earnings by sex, Johnson and Stafford examined cross-section data from the National Science Foundation for their 1974 study. In general, the authors have been faulted for not providing evidence that sufficiently supports their thesis. Strober and Quester (1977: p.20) offered the following critique:

> ... it is curious that the data with which J-S chose to work are absolutely unsuited to testing their life cycle human capital hypothesis, since the National Science Foundation Register provides no information at all on the registrant's work histories.

Again, if the life cycle explanation is correct, then the salaries and career paths of single women should parallel men's more closely than those of married women academics. One method of testing this hypothesis is to include dummies for marital and parental status in the earnings equation. A variable representing present marital status was evaluated as well as one denoting lifetime status; i.e., whether or not the respondent had ever been married. Because the life cycle explanation proposes that childrearing responsibilities impede productivity and lead to decreased participation, we included a variable representing the presence of children as well.

Table 6 presents the results of including variables for marital status (ever married) and parental status in separate equations for men and women. A faculty member's salary is not, apparently, affected by whether or not he/she has been married. Neither the male nor the

Table 6   *Regression Estimates of the Effect of Marriage and Children on Salary*[a]

	Men 1968 (N=12,140)	Women 1968 (N=1,473)	Men 1977 (N=2,605)	Women 1977 (N=416)
EVER WED	.0200 (.0217)	−.017 (.0121)	.0032 (.0155)	.0036 (.0223)
HAVE CHILD	.0739 (.0130)	−.0206 (.0137)	.0387 (.0100)	.0068 (.0199)

[a] Coefficients are derived from the basic regression controlling for publications and field. Standard errors are in parentheses.

female coefficients are significant at even the 10 per cent level in Table 6. As predicted by the life cycle hypothesis, the coefficient on Ever Wed is negative for women in 1968. But, again, the coefficient is not significant even with a relatively large sample size (N=1473). The presence of children is positively related to male academics' salary (7 per cent in 1968 and 4 per cent in 1977 – both significant at the 1 per cent level). The fact that the children variable is not significant at the 10 per cent level for women in either period weakens the theoretical link between children and productivity, as postulated by Johnson and Stafford. We might argue that the number of women is insufficient, leading to large standard errors, and thereby low t-statistics. Yet, even in the larger sample, (1968), the small size of the children coefficient (−.0206) makes it implausible that childbearing is primarily responsible for the large salary difference (12 percentage points of the 23 per cent total salary difference) that remains after controlling for the major salary determinants. The relatively small number of women who were ever married (52 per cent) or had children (28 per cent)[15] as of the 1968 survey also makes it less likely that the salary differential is related to family responsibilities, as does the positive coefficient on the children variable in 1977.

One criticism of the preceding analysis might be that the adverse effect of children on earnings occurs indirectly. For example, children may lead to decreased publication. By controlling for productivity, presence of children, as well as other factors affecting salary, the children coefficient may not exhibit a significant and independent effect on salary.

In deference to this objection, we examined the marital and parental status variables in a regression model in which publication was not controlled. If the presence of children (or marital status) is negatively related to the omitted productivity variables, then it is more likely that these variables will have negative (and significant) estimated coefficients. Under these conditions, the (negative) coefficient on children does become significant at the 10 per cent level for women in 1968 (coefficient equals $-.0242$). Again, despite this slight support for the life cycle hypothesis, the same inconsistencies remain using this amended equation: none of the other marital/parental coefficients for women are positive, and the estimated coefficient on the parental status variable for women in 1968 suggests a small effect relative to the total salary differential for that period.

The 1977 coefficient on children brings up the somewhat surprising possibility that children might be positively related to salary for female academics. Recent studies have dispelled much of the conventional wisdom in this area. Hamovitch and Morgenstern,[16] for example, found no evidence that child rearing affects either productivity or the probability that a woman will be judged 'outstanding' according to a ranking by her peers. Similarly, when Cole and Zuckerman (1987) investigated the persistent disparity in publication rates between men and women scientists, they also concluded that marriage and family obligations do not generally account for the gender differences. Single female scientists do not publish more than married women scientists with children.

In terms of the discrimination versus life cycle debate, one of the more important variables contained in the survey is the type of employing institution. According to Johnson and Stafford, women's expectations of a shorter duration in the labor market leads them to prefer initial employment at particular types of academic institutions – those with relatively high beginning salaries and fewer training opportunities. If one can assume that by the time they have obtained their degree most women academics are either already married or aware of their preferences in this area, one might expect differences between married and never-married women regarding initial job placement. The latter group is more likely to be located at top universities and research institutions. If the differences according to institutional type are not prevalent at the initial stage of job search, one might at least expect that they would surface later. At any point in time, the never-married women, who conceivably had fewer interferences or interruptions in their careers, should be found at the 'training institutions' in greater proportions.

As summarized in Table 7, figures for all individuals in the two surveys belie the possibility that never-married women are more prevalent at top research institutions. While married women are in some instances relatively numerous at two-year colleges, in percentage terms their representation surpasses that of single women at top research institutions in both 1968 and 1977.

Table 7   Representation of Men and Women by Institutional Type

Year: 1968 Institution Type:	University	Four-Year College	Foreign Institution	Two-Year College
First Job				
Men	72.2%	21.5%	2.7%	3.6%
All Women	60.60	30.80	2.00	6.60
Women: Never Married	57.00	35.60	2.00	5.40
Women: Ever Married	63.30	27.10	2.00	7.60
Present Job				
Men	76.7%	20.2%	N/A	3.1%
All Women	64.80	29.90	N/A	5.30
Women: Never Married	62.50	33.70	N/A	3.80
Women: Ever Married	66.60	26.90	N/A	6.50

Year: 1977 Institution Type[a]:	Research Univ. I & II Doc. Grant. Univ. I & II	Compre- hensive Univ. & Col.	Liberal Arts Colleges	Two-Year Colleges	Specialized Institutions
First Job					
Men	77.7%	12.6%	6.3%	2.4%	0.9%
All Women	68.20	14.70	10.60	5.10	1.40
Women: Never Married	63.90	12.00	16.50	6.00	1.50
Women: Ever Married	69.60	15.70	8.50	4.80	1.30

Institution Type[a]:	Research Univ. I & II	Doc. Grant. Univ. I & II	Compre- hensive Col. & Univ.	Liberal Arts Colleges	Two-Year Colleges
Present Job					
Men	66.0%	16.5%	11.8%	3.2%	2.3%
All Women	50.40	26.10	13.00	4.40	5.80
Women: Never Married	47.60	27.00	11.60	6.40	7.00
Women: Ever Married	51.20	26.00	13.70	3.70	5.40

[a] Institutional groupings correspond to the Carnegie classifications.

Finally, another implication of the Johnson/Stafford hypothesis is that the average salary of female relative to male academics will follow a prescribed course as years of post-degree experience, XPO, grow. According to their 1974 paper, the ratio of female to male earnings should be smallest at XPO = 0, where there has been no obsolescence of women's skills. The differential widens from five to fifteen years of XPO, 'the years when child care is most prevalent'. It narrows (or ceases to rise) during advanced years of post-degree experience when women renew their commitment to the labor market and consequently 'reacquire skills' (Johnson and Stafford, 1974: p. 895). To support this idea, the authors present evidence from six academic disciplines. They calculate the relative salary for comparable male and female academics at increasing levels of XPO. Pre-degree experience, highest degree, and quality of graduate school are controlled.

The following exercise, while not identical to Johnson and Stafford's, also estimates the relative salary of equivalent men and women faculty members at different levels of post-degree experience. However, we control for additional factors. Similar regressions were estimated for men and women controlling for: type of contract, publication, race, region, advanced degree, concentration in teaching versus research, current administrative activity, age, XPO and XPO-squared. In order to compare the salaries of similar men and women, the following characteristics were selected for the representative individuals: a white faculty member with a nine-month contract and an advanced degree who is employed in the midwest and primarily engaged in teaching.

Clearly, it is not realistic to assume that all characteristics remain constant over an academic's career. The extent of administrative work, publication, and age are three factors that tend to change with XPO. Therefore, cross tabulations were performed between XPO and several of the other independent variables. It was decided that the degree of current administration, which, for our sample, did not vary substantially with age, should be assumed to be permanently low (i.e., the dummy variable equals zero at all levels of XPO). The degree of publication, by contrast, varied significantly according to years of experience. Consequently, a publication cycle was generated for different levels of XPO. When salary comparisons are made, the appropriate average level of book and article publication for that level of XPO is used.[17] The age variable is handled in two ways. For the figures in Table 8 it is assumed that at zero years of postdegree experience the faculty member is 28 years old. Hereafter, age is incremented according to the change in XPO. Therefore, for the second salary comparison, when XPO = 3, age is set equal to 31. Another method was simply to use regressions that omitted the age variable. An ideal test of the variation in the male/female salary differential at various levels of experience clearly requires longitudinal data. Nevertheless, the methodology described above employs the cross-section data to sketch out a rough path of earnings for equivalent men and women over time, while keeping with the 'spirit' of the analogous Johnson/Stafford exercise.

The results, as summarized in Table 8, are generally not consistent with the predictions of Johnson and Stafford. In 1968, the female/male salary ratio declines continuously from XPO = 0 to XPO = 41. Although the difference is smallest at zero years of

Table 8   Estimated Female-Male Nine Month Salary Ratio by Experience for 1968 and 1977

Years of Post-degree Experience	Female-Male Salary Ratio 1968	Female-Male Salary Ratio 1977
0	.938	.948
3	.931	.938
8	.877	.986
13	.861	.978
18	.839	.955
23	.824	.931
28	.816	.906
33	.814	.858
38	.813	.856
41	.809	.816

experience, the revival in women's earnings does not occur. When age is omitted from the regression, a pattern more consistent with the life cycle explanation emerges. Starting from an approximate value of .92, the ratio falls continuously until XPO = 33, at which time an increase in relative earnings is apparent. A renewed work commitment might explain the trend in relative salaries. However, the improvement in earnings occurs rather late in life – especially for a group of women in which only 28 per cent have children. Moreover, the increase in relative salary could be caused by a number of other factors, including differential promotion rates.

In some ways the 1977 results run directly counter to the life cycle predictions. Table 8 documents a decrease in the salary ratio at XPO = 3 and then a rise at XPO = 8. After XPO = 8, women's relative salary declines without interruption. While the life cycle theory suggests that the ratio declines most dramatically from the first five to fifteen years of XPO, the ratio is actually highest for the periods XPO = 8 and XPO = 13. Women's relatively low slaries in the early years are in part caused by the productivity cycle and unequal rewards to publication. For example, at XPO = 3 the typical level of article publication becomes Article 2 (three to four articles).[18] For Article 2 the women's coefficient is .004 versus .078 for men. At XPO = 8 the typical level of productivity jumps to Article 3 (five to ten articles) and Book 1 (one to two published books). For this category of article publication the estimated male and female coefficients are much closer in size: .080 for women versus .096 for men. Also, the return to book publication is twice as great for women. Both of these circumstances add to women's improved earnings position as of XPO = 8. When the same exercise is conducted using the regressions without age, an identical pattern is uncovered. Women's relative salary is highest at XPO = 8 and XPO = 13. Again, the fact that the ratio declines continuously thereafter with increased levels of XPO, supports a cumulative discrimination hypothesis of the source of the salary differential by sex.

Conclusions

This paper has focused on salary differentials between male and female academics, in particular those that remain after controlling for various differences in productivity, experience, academic field and institution of employment. Whether one considers the return to an advanced degree, or the publication of articles and books, it has been shown that the system of pecuniary rewards is not identical for faculty members of both sexes. Moreover, the data indicate that a proportionate salary advantage accrues to men despite the inclusion of substantial control variables.

It has also been shown that the reward structure has changed over time. The most important finding, derived from the Oaxaca decompositions, is that the proportion of the observed salary differential attributable to discrimination has declined appreciably from 1968 to 1977. In 1968, the percentage salary difference due to discrimination ranged from 11.6 to 17.6 percentage points of the 23 per cent observed salary difference. In other words, anywhere from half (11.6/23) to two-thirds (17.6/23) of the observed salary difference might be attributed to discrimination. The corresponding figures for 1977, 5.5 to 11.5 percentage points of the 19 per cent total salary difference, reveal the decrease in the unexplained portion of the salary gap. A similar analysis of the 1975 data reveals a monotonic decline in measured discrimination. Interestingly, the total salary difference, 26 per cent, was larger than in either 1968 or 1977, but the Oaxaca decomposition produced discrimination estimates that fell between those for 1968 and 1977.

The present findings are interesting in light of recent pronouncements on the trend in the male/female salary differential in the overall economy. One commonly-held opinion is that the rise in women's relative earnings is primarily due to an improvement in women's characteristics relative to men, rather than any reduction in discrimination. The present findings do not support such a hypothesis. If 11.6 to 17.6 percentage points of the 23 per cent salary difference in 1968 is due to discrimination, then 5.4 to 11.4 points are attributable to unequal characteristics between the sexes. Using a similar procedure for 1977, the salary difference based on unequal characteristics is 7.5 to 13.5 percentage points. This increase occurs because while it is true that women's characteristics improved markedly over the nine-year period, the average level of attributes for the male academics improved by at least as much (see Table 5).[19] The improvement in the compensation of female academics relative to their male colleagues between 1968 and 1977 appears to be primarily the result of reduced discrimination rather than the enhanced characteristics of the average female faculty member.

In the final section, we also tested several implications of the life cycle theory of the source of male/female salary differentials using the survey data. The results do not, in general, support this explanation of the source of the male/female salary differential. Including marital and parental variables in the regression models did not have the predicted effect upon women's salaries. Neither were there significant differences in the institutional affiliation of single and married women as might be expected if married women invested less in the training options available at research institutions. Furthermore, the life cycle hypothesis suggests a specific pattern for the female/male salary ratio as years of experience increase. The pattern, as estimated here, did not follow the prescribed course. Rather, the growth in salary differentials as post-degree experience rose, was more compatible with a cumulative discrimination explanation.

In 1978, the terminal year for our surveys, Leob, Ferber and Lowry (1978) wrote that 'affirmative action programs have apparently somewhat eased women's access to academic employment, especially at universities. The rising proportion of women in higher education was undeniable as indicated by a Carnegie Council report noting that from 1971 to 1974–75, the proportion of women faculty in four-year colleges and universities had risen from 20.7 per cent of the total faculty to 26.3 per cent.[20] But entry into the profession was not the only goal. By the late seventies, there was a new concern over the possibility of a 'choke up' of women and minorities in the academic profession. In other words, recently hired academics, while admitted to the profession, would be unable to successfully pass through the system to the tenured ranks and the relatively highly paid positions. In fact, the proportion of women in the tenured ranks did not change substantially throughout the seventies and a number of empirical studies concluded that salary differentials among faculty members were as persistent as those found in other sectors of the economy.

Nevertheless, this study presents an optimistic view of federal legislation to provide equal employment opportunity. The large 'residual' salary differences that we calculate for 1968, equal to between one-half and two-thirds of the total salary gap, provide evidence of the need for antibias regulations. Moreover, affirmative action legislation appears to have been effective in reducing measured discrimination during the 1970s. In addition to the fall in the total male/female salary gap, the proportion of the salary gap that is not explained by unequal attributes declined substantially between 1968 and 1977.

Just as implementation of antibias legislation corresponded to a period of reduced salary discrimination during the 1970s, waning commitment to affirmative action during the 1980s may have reversed earlier gains. Data from a 1984 national faculty survey suggest that the total male/female salary differential rose to 21.5 per cent in 1984. Between 40 and 60 per cent of this differential could be attributed to discrimination, depending upon which factors are controlled.

While noting the marked reduction in discrimination estimates between 1968 and 1977, we must still exercise caution in interpreting these results. First we note that after controlling for all available faculty characteristics, roughly 30 per cent of the salary gap in 1977 could be attributed to discrimination. Moreover, according to our methodology, gender differences in professional qualifications such as publication rates and institutional affiliation do not constitute evidence of discrimination. Only differences in the rewards to characteristics are discriminatory. For whatever reason, the qualifications of the average female faculty member, while improving between 1968 and 1978, were not progressing at the same rate as those of the average male professor. If we extend our scope to consider other forms of discrimination, such as varying promotion rates, our estimates probably represent a lower bound on the extent of discrimination. Of course researchers and administrators might be less concerned about salary differences resulting from unequal characteristics if they were to subscribe to the theory that women, primarily due to family obligations, make different choices with respect to their careers and training opportunities. The final section of this paper found little evidence supporting the life cycle explanation of observed salary differentials. Consequently, we should not assume that unequal results are always the product of voluntary choices.

Notes

1. Three national faculty surveys comprise the data base for this study. The 1968–69 faculty study, which is part of *The Carnegie*

Commission National Surveys of Higher Education, was directed by Martin Trow. Everett Ladd and Seymour Lipset conducted the *Survey of the American Professoriate* for 1975 and 1977 in conjunction with the Roper Center of the University of Connecticut. The surveys are very similar in terms of design and sampling methodology. Neither the original collectors of data, nor the agencies mentioned, bear any responsibility for the analysis or interpretations presented here.

2. For this paper, community colleges were not included in the sample of institutions, although they were analyzed at an earlier stage of the study. Two-year college patterns of promotion and salary determination are decidedly different from those of four-year colleges and universities.

3. It was not until 1968 that Executive Order 11246, requiring written affirmative action programs, was extended to cover sex discrimination. In 1972, the Equal Employment Opportunity Act extended Title VII to educational institutions and the Equal Pay Act was broadened to cover faculty and administrative salaries.

4. Since many disciplines are represented in the survey, the advanced degree could be any of the following: Ph.D., Ed.D., other doctorate, medical, or law degree.

5. The omitted categories for the dummy variables represent: female, employment in the south, race other than Black, nine-month contract, no advanced degree, emphasis on research, and relatively less time spent in administration work. Men and women are equally represented in all of the omitted categories with the following exceptions: women are less likely to be primarily engaged in research (18 per cent versus 39 per cent in 1968 and 35 per cent versus 51 per cent in 1977), less likely to have an advanced degree (55 per cent versus 81 per cent in 1968 and 76 per cent versus 90 per cent in 1977), and less likely to be Black (3 per cent versus 1 per cent in 1968 and 4 per cent versus 1 per cent in 1977).

6. The regression coefficients offer approximate estimates of the proportionate salary advantage accruing to male faculty members. To obtain a precise estimate it is necessary to take the antilog of the regression coefficient. For example, a regression coefficient equal to .2071 suggests a 23 per cent salary difference in favor of male academics ($e^{.2071} - 1$). The antilog correction only results in substantially different estimates when the coefficients are relatively large.

7. The fields are agriculture, applied professional, bioscience, business, education, mechanical engineering, electrical engineering, other engineering, fine arts, medicine, other health fields (e.g., public health), English, foreign language, history, philosophy, other humanities, law, math and statistics, physical education and health, chemistry, physics, other physical science, economics, social science, and an 'other' category. Equality of field coefficients was treated using the following statistic:

$$\frac{\beta_j - \beta_k}{{}^s\beta_j - \beta_k} \approx t_{n-k}$$

See Jan Kmenta, *Elements of Econometrics* (New York: Macmillan Publishing Co., Inc., 1971), p. 372.

8. Specifically, the categories Article 1 – Article 5 denote 1–2 articles, 3–4, 5–10, 11–20, and more than 20 articles, respectively. For books, Book 1

- Book 3 represent 1–2 books, 3–4, 5 or more. The omitted dummies denote no published articles or books.

9. For evidence on disparities in the evaluation of articles by men and women, see Mary R. Lefkowitz, 'Education for women in a man's world', *Chronicle of Higher Education*, 6 Aug. 1979, p. 56.

10. Marianne A. Ferber, 'Citations: Are they an objective measure of merit?', *CSWEP Newsletter* (Fall 1984), p. 6. Another notable complication in controlling for publication concerns the fact that the frequency of publication varies tremendously across academic disciplines, reaching a peak with the physical sciences. Consequently, we made several attempts to standardize the publication variables across fields. Two variables, representing the number of standard deviations from the mean level of book publication in one's field, and the number of standard deviations from the mean level of article publication in the respondent's field, were constructed and tested in the salary equations. Two alternative publication measures represented normalized variables of publication points ranging from twenty to eight. Note, however, that even these corrected productivity measures entail some conceptual difficulties, such as the problem of evaluating and comparing the production levels of new scholars. Since the results using the standardized variables were qualitatively the same, and their construction involved a substantial loss of cases, the interval publication variables are used for the remainder of this paper.

11. All coefficients are significant at the 1 per cent level.

12. To illustrate how the quality ratings were formed, in 1968 this index combined three equally weighted items: SAT scores required for admission (Selectivity), research expenditures adjusted for number of students (Research), and total institutional expenditures, also adjusted to a per-student basis (Affluence).

13. F-tests comparing the sum of squared deviations of the regression equations with and without discipline variables verified that the fields are relevant in explaining the variation in ln salary in all cases except males in 1968.

14. The mean salary for fine arts faculty was the lowest of all academic fields for every year examined.

15. The comparable statistics for men in 1968 are 94 per cent and 76 per cent respectively.

16. William Hamovitch and Richard Morgenstern, 'Children and the productivity of academic women', *Journal of Higher Education*, 48 (Nov./ Dec. 1977). The authors reconcile their findings with earlier results that imply an inverse relationship between such factors as productivity and fertility as follows. Hamovitch and Morgenstern examined a sample of women currently in the labor force. Previous studies included women who were not at the time employed. Since one reason that women may not be in the labor force is because they have left to raise children, by including them in the sample there is a greater tendency to find a trade-off between fertility and productivity. Such trade-offs are not, however, apparent in a sample of fully-employed women.

17. The average levels of article and book publication were derived from examining the entire sample of respondents.

18. The typical level of book publication is Book 0, indicating no published books.
19. For example, from 1968 to 1977 women's average publication rates increased. By 1977, 10 per cent of the women were in the highest publication category, as opposed to 6 per cent in 1968. However, 21 per cent of the male faculty members were in the highest category in 1968 and this figure rose to 29 per cent by 1977. The average level of post-degree experience for men rose from twelve to fourteen years throughout the period, while the average level for women fell from twelve to eleven years. Five per cent more women were full professors in 1977, but 10 per cent more men had achieved this rank as well.
20. Figures are quoted from Reed, p. 338.

References

Barbezat, D.A. (1988) 'Affirmative action in higher education: Have two decades altered salary differentials by sex and race?', *Research in Labor Economics, 10,* Forthcoming.

Bayer, A.E. and Astin, H.S. (1975) 'Sex differentials in the academic reward system', *Science,* 188 (May), 796–802.

Cole, R. and Zuckerman, H. (1987) 'Marriage, motherhood and research performance in science', *Scientific American,* 256 (Feb.) 119–125.

Ferber, M.A. (1984) 'Citations: Are they an objective measure of merit?', *CSWEP Newsletter* (Fall) p. 6.

Fox, M.F. (1981) 'Sex segregation and salary structure in academia', *Sociology of Work and Occupations,* 8 (Feb.) 39–60.

Hamovitch, W. and Morgenstern, R. (1977) 'Children and the productivity of academic women', *Journal of Higher Education,* 48 (Nov./Dec.) 633–645.

Hoffman, E.P. (1976) 'Faculty salaries: Is there discrimination by sex, race, and discipline?', *American Economic Review,* 66 (March) 196–198.

Johnson, G.E. and Stafford, F.P. (1974) 'The earnings and promotion of women faculty', *American Economic Review,* 64 (Dec.) 888–903.

– (1977) 'The earnings and promotion of women faculty: Reply', *American Economic Review,* 67 (March), 214–217.

– (1979) 'Pecuniary rewards to men and women faculty', in *Academic Rewards in Higher Education,* Lewis, D.R. and Becker, W.E., (Eds) Cambridge, MA: Ballinger Publishing Company, pp. 231–243.

Kmenta, J. (1971) *Elements of Econometrics,* New York: Macmillan Publishing Co.

Koch, J.V. and Chizmar, J.F., Jr. (1976) 'Sex discrimination and affirmative action in faculty salaries', *Economic Inquiry,* 14 (March) 16–24.

Lefkovitz, M.R. (1979) 'Education for women in a man's world', *Chronicle of Higher Education,* (6 Aug). p. 56.

Leob, J., Ferber, M. and Lowry, H. (1978) 'The effectiveness of affirmative action for women', *Journal of Higher Education,* 49 (May/June) 218–230.

Oaxaca, R. (1973) 'Male-female wage differentials in urban labor markets', *International Economic Review,* 14 (Oct.) 693–709.

Read, R. (1983) 'Affirmative action in higher education: Is it necessary?', *Journal of Higher Education*, 52, 332–349.

Strober, M.H. and Quester, A.O. (1977) 'The earnings and promotion of women faculty: Comment', *American Economic Review*, 67 (March), 207–213.

Veblen, T. (1957) *The Higher Learning in America*, New York: Hill and Wang.

8 University Scientists as Entrepreneurs*

Maurice N. Richter, Jr.

Business corporations, in search of university-based knowledge and expertise, and universities, in search of financial support from business, have been developing a wide variety of relationships. In addition, a number of business corporations have created university-like research facilities of their own, while universities and their scientists have become increasingly involved in business activities.[1] This paper seeks to contribute to our understanding of one aspect of this latter development: the formation of business firms by academic scientists for the purpose of commercially exploiting their own discoveries and expertise. Such firms may provide products as diverse as industrial enzymes, integrated circuits, new methods for locating mineral deposits, and market surveys (Etzkowitz, 1983).

According to Frank A. Darknell (personal communication), there are grounds for believing that approximately 3.3 per cent of scientists and engineers who are employed full-time as professors in American four-year higher-educational institutions also work as consultants for commercial companies of which they are owners or part-owners. This is, of course, a small percentage. It is probably much smaller for scientists than for engineers, although we have no precise data on that point.

But the importance of the phenomenon is much greater than the facts about its low rate of occurrence might suggest, for two reasons: (1) even if there is only one faculty member at an entire university

* This is an expanded and modified version of a paper presented at the annual meeting of the American Sociological Association, August 1985, and published in *Society*, vol. 23 no. 5, July–August 1986, pp. 81–83. I thank *Society* for permission to include the paper in this volume.

who is engaged in entrepreneurship, this single venture may sometimes raise crucial issues, make important contributions, involve large sums of money, and/or attract considerable publicity; (2) faculty entrepreneurship appears to be growing.

The Significance of Academic Entrepreneurship

In several ways this phenomenon challenges established academic/scientific values and norms. One professor – one of twenty-eight university scientists, engineers and administrators in a major private university who were interviewed about this and related topics – noted that the time and energy needed to set up and run a business 'may be so great that even if you do all the things you have to do at the university, like meeting your classes, there are lots of intangibles that may slide'. He also pointed out that other kinds of conflict-of-interest may arise: 'a professor with his own firm may have to decide whether external funds he got should be used for research in his own firm or should be channeled through the university' (cited by Richter, 1985: 461). Further, a professor's relationships with other university personnel may be complicated by relationships with the same people in a business context: e.g., if a professor, as a business person, competes with, hires, or has business dealings with his/her university colleagues, students or administrative superiors. The interests of a professor's own firm may also affect his/her choice of research topics in a way which would be detrimental to academic-scientific values, and may create temptations for the use of university resources for private entrepreneurial purposes.

But that is only one side of the story. Conflicts of interest which *might* arise do not *necessarily* arise. One interviewed university scientist pointed out that a firm established by a professor, if fully separated from the university, may involve less potential conflict-of-interest in certain respects than is involved in ordinary consulting if the latter utilizes university laboratory facilities and graduate-student labor. Furthermore, entrepreneurship among professors may also confer certain benefits on the university: it may, for example, (1) enable the university to retain the services of valued professors who would find employment elsewhere if they could not combine their academic work with entrepreneurial activities, (2) help to finance the research of some professors, (3) give some professors experiences which enable them to prepare students more adequately for careers in the business world, (4) stimulate economic development in the community surrounding the university, and (5) provide university laboratories with equipment, supplies or services which would be unavailable, or available only at higher prices, from other sources (one of my interviewees, for example, has provided his own laboratory at the university with equipment at below-market prices from his own firm).

We have here, then, a phenomenon which may seriously challenge the integrity of academic life in certain respects, but which universities may nevertheless be unable to ban completely without thereby significantly harming some of their own legitimate interests.[2]

Routes to Academic Entrepreneurship

Etzkowitz (1983) has suggested that firm-formation among faculty members develops as an outgrowth of (1) the tendency for academic research to be conducted by research teams rather than by isolated individuals, and (2) the tendency for key research professors to behave increasingly like 'entrepreneurs' in their efforts to obtain funding for their research from outside sources. Etzkowitz describes academic research teams as 'quasi-firms' which differ from real firms only in that they do not involve financial investments made in anticipation of financial profits. According to Etzkowitz, the introduction of such investment is a small but decisive step which transforms, into a firm, a kind of structure that has already developed within the framework of the university in legitimate pursuit of academic-research objectives. This step, in turn, as he describes it, is facilitated by a tendency for university scientists to view their own entrepreneurial activities as only minimally inconsistent, or even fully consistent, with traditional academic/scientific norms: for example, Etzkowitz cites one such scientist who described his own entrepreneurship as merely 'intensive consulting' (1983: 228).

This latter interpretation suggests, and comments by my own interview respondents also suggest, a way in which faculty entrepreneurship may arise that is quite different from the way Etzkowitz emphasizes. University scientists who do considerable consulting often 'incorporate themselves' for tax purposes. Having thus established their own one-person consulting firms, these scientists can then relatively easily move beyond ordinary consulting into additional, entrepreneurial, activities, alone or with others. For those university scientists who enter entrepreneurship by this alternate route, the process begins with ordinary consulting together with incorporation

induced by tax considerations, rather than beginninng with collabora-
tive research among colleagues and with the seeking of external
research funding.

Just as there is more than one route from academic science to
faculty entrepreneurship, so likewise there is more than one way in
which faculty members may seek to relate their entrepreneurial
activities to academic/scientific norms. One way, which Etzkowitz
has noted, involves minimizing the contrast between these norms and
entrepreneurial requirements: e.g., insisting that the temporary
withholding of certain limited items of information to protect the
proprietary interests of a corporation does not really interfere
significantly with the university's commitment to open communication of research findings. Another way involves admitting that
entrepreneurial requirements *are* significantly incompatible with traditional academic/scientific norms, but insisting that these norms have
been largely undermined already by circumstances in which entrepreneurship has played no part: e.g., claiming that the norm of open
communication has been damaged so much by *governmental* secrecy
requirements that additional secrecy-requirements imposed by business corporations will hardly make much difference. Many statements
by my own interviewees reflect this latter point of view.

Academic Entrepreneurship and the Occupational System

To understand academic entrepreneurship we must view it within the
wider context of developments involving the entire academic occupational system and the larger occupational system of society as a whole.

The most recent (1977) edition of the *Dictionary of Occupational
Titles* published by the United States Department of Labor lists
approximately 20,000 distinguishable occupations in the United
States, including (to name only a very few assorted examples) goat-
truck driver, returned-telephone-equipment-appraiser, nursery-school
attendant, orthodontist, helicopter pilot, and fig sorter. This extreme
differentiation in occupations has been paralleled by a comparable
development of academic specialization, which has produced a
striking contrast between the universities of earlier times and those of
today: it is hard for us today to grasp the fact that 'Yale in 1802 had a
professor of mathematics and natural philosophy who also taught
whatever chemistry and natural history was offered' (Daniels, 1968:
35). Some university systems have accommodated themselves to

increased academic specialization more effectively than have others: the nineteenth century shift in the center of world science from France to Germany may be at least partly attributable to the greater acceptance of specialization in German universities (Ben-David, 1971).

Clark (1983) has presented one conception of academic specialization and its effects. He states that 'No one has yet found a way to slow the division of labor in society. No one is about to find a way to stop the division of knowledge in *academic* society' (p. 16). While recognizing that 'each field borders some others' (p. 14) and that a few disciplines such as mathematics have widespread application, Clark nevertheless describes 'a steady distancing of the specialities from one another' (p. 16): thus, 'law does not need archaeology, English literature does not need physics' (p. 41). The academic profession is 'heavily fragmented' (p. 36) and 'universities as organizations are relatively disintegrated' (p. 15).

Within the framework of this approach, an explanation of academic entrepreneurship suggests itself: under the impact of academic fragmentation and distintegration, the traditional norms of university life have been weakened, and some professors, no longer strongly constrained by these norms, have been lured into money-making activities. However, trends concerning academic and societal organization can also be reasonably interpreted in a very different way, which suggests, in turn, a very different perspective on academic entrepreneurship.

This alternative perspective involves the following points:

(1) Although modern social systems are characterized by much more occupational specialization than their pre-modern predecessors, they are also nevertheless *less* highly specialized than they *could* be. As I have noted elsewhere, in a typical American university;

> we will often find people who are teachers *and* researchers, teachers *and* administrators, teachers *and* (graduate) students, etc. If the division of labor were maximized, each of these roles would, by definition, be separated from the others. (Richter, 1984: 319)

(2) Academic specialization does not mean that specialties are becoming increasingly divergent. On the contrary, as Price (1965: 26) has noted, although 'science has indeed continued to specialize at an accelerating rate', it is also true that the sciences 'in their basic concepts or techniques...are growing more and more together': thus, 'it's not always easy to tell a biologist from a physicist...; either one is likely to turn out as a biophysicist before he is through'.

(3) The tendency for differentiated elements to achieve new modes of integration applies not only to academic specialties but also to major social institutions. In comparatively small and simple societies in the past, various institutions with which we are familiar had not yet become as clearly differentiated from one another as they were later to become: for example, in the Plymouth colony of the seventeenth century, the family was also a 'business', a 'school', a 'vocational institute', a 'church', a 'house of correction', and a 'welfare institution' (Demos, 1970: 183–184). As societies have become more complex, new institutional distinctions have emerged, but institutions have also become intertwined in ways which create the appearance that the boundaries separating them are 'breaking down'. Thus, Price (1965: 24) has described a tendency toward 'the breakdown of boundaries' among different spheres of American life: e.g., between agriculture and industry, between economic affairs and political affairs, between science and engineering, and between government and universities.

Within this frame of reference, academic entrepreneurship appears not as a manifestation of any deterioration of academic values, but rather as a manifestation of a broad social trend involving increasingly close integration among major social institutions: what is 'breaking down', according to this view, is not the academic system itself but rather a barrier which has previously separated academia from other institutions including business.

Academic Entrepreneurship and Unionization

In a movement which acquired strong momentum in the 1960s, academic personnel on many American university campuses have become unionized. There was considerable comment, in the sixties, about the fact that professors, in forming unions, were coming to behave like blue-collar workers. In 'moonlighting' – i.e., doing additional work for extra income on top of a full-time job – some professors are doing what is also done by blue-collar workers and by business managers as well. In engaging in the particular form of moonlighting which involves entrepreneurial firm-formation, some professors are coming to behave specifically like business people, in two respects: (1) they are engaging in business activity, and (2) they are moonlighting in a particular way which is more characteristic of business managers than of blue-collar workers. In fact, academic concerns about faculty entrepreneurship on a 'moonlighting' basis are paralleled by similar concerns within some business corporations about entrepreneurial moonlighting among their managerial personnel (Hymowitz, 1983), although the two situations involve slightly different problems. In the business world, managerial moonlighting may involve disloyalty if a manager earns extra money by competing with, or assisting others to compete with, his or her own primary employer. In the academic world, professorial moonlighting involves a somewhat different set of issues arising from the fact that the responsibilities of professors to their own regular university employers are characteristically defined only in extremely vague ways.

Although faculty unionization, and faculty entrepreneurial 'moonlighting', are obviously quite different phenomena, and although they have, in a sense, quite different origins (one involving faculty imitation of workers, the other involving faculty imitation of business people) there are nevertheless certain important features which these developments share:

First, they both involve the intrusion, into academic life, of organizational arrangements which have originated in other sectors of society. Academic life had previously been insulated to a large extent from these arrangements. Now its insulation from them has ceased to be effective.

Second, both faculty unionization and faculty firm-formation represent attempts by faculty not only to obtain more money, but also to protect their professional autonomy against certain challenges to it, unionization being an attempt to achieve these goals collectively, and firm-formation being an attempt to achieve them for the individual faculty involved. There is a paradoxical situation here: as previously noted, entrepreneurship may divert faculty attention away from academic matters, but it may also enhance the professional autonomy of faculty by giving them organizational and financial footings completely separate from the bureaucratic structures of their own universities and completely separate from the funding sources on which many of them have become dependent.

Conclusion

University-scientist entrepreneurship has emerged in a societal context in which entrepreneurship is highly valued and in which obstacles to the diffusion of ideas and practices from one sphere of activity to another have been significantly weakened. It has emerged in an institutional context characterized by ambivalence toward it, and hence some tolerance of it, among university administrations, and by vague definitions of professorial responsibilities. Within these contexts, university-scientist entrepreneurship has been facilitated by certain pre-existing structural patterns ('quasi-firms' as described by Etzkowitz, and faculty-consulting arrangements) which represent 'stepping stones' in this direction, and by motivational patterns involving faculty efforts not only to make money but also to use entrepreneurial ventures to compensate for limitations on professional autonomy in the university environment.

This interpretation, in turn, involves a conception of 'scientists in industry' which is fundamentally different from the conception presented long ago by Kornhauser (1963). According to Kornhauser, scientists who go into industrial work thereby give up more autonomy than do their counterparts who enter instead into academic life. Now, under conditions quite different from those which prevailed when Kornhauser wrote about this matter, a limited involvement of university scientists in the business world apears to have an autonomy-enhancing effect. The point is not that a business environment provides greater autonomy to scientists, or more favorable working conditions in other respects, than an academic environment, but rather that autonomy (with its associated benefits) is facilitated by multiple organizational ties rather than by ties to a single organization exclusively.[3]

Notes

1. For discussions of these trends from diverse points of view, see Langfitt *et al.* (1983), National Science Board (1982, 1983), Eveland *et al.* (1982), Tornatzky *et al.* (1982), Peters (1984), Bouton (1983), and Walsh (1985).
2. Ways in which universities have dealt with this situation, and recommendations concerning ways in which they might deal with it, are discussed by Giamatti (1982), Varrin *et al.* (1985), Etzkowitz (1984), Richter (1985), American Association of University Professors (1983), and the publications cited in footnote No. 1 above.
3. I have discussed the concept of autonomy with particular reference to science, in Richter (1981).

References

American Association of University Professors, Committee A (1983) 'Corporate funding of academic research', *Academe* Nov. – Dec.: 18a–23a.

Ben-David, J. (1971) *The Scientist's Role in Society*, Englewood Cliffs, New Jersey: Prentice-Hall.

Bouton, K. (1983) 'Academic research and big business: A delicate balance', *New York Times Magazine* Sept. 11.

Clark, B.R. (1983) *The Higher Education System: Academic Organization in Cross-National Perspective*, Berkeley: University of California Press.

Daniels, G.H. (1968) *American Science in the Age of Jackson*, New York: Columbia University Press.

Demos, J. (1970) *A Little Commonwealth: Family Life in Plymouth Colony*, Oxford: Oxford University Press.

Etzkowitz, H. (1983) 'Entrepreneurial scientists and entrepreneurial universities in American academic science', *Minerva* 21: 198–233.

Etzkowitz, H. (1984) 'A research university in flux: university-industry interactions in two departments', *Report to National Science Foundation*, 83-GB-0040.

Eveland, J.D. and Hetzner, W. (1982) *Development of University-Industry Cooperative Research Centers: Historical Profiles*, Washington: National Science Foundation, NSF/ISI-82003.

Giamatti, A.B. (1982) 'The university, industry and cooperative research', *Science* 218: 1278-1280, Dec. 24.

Hymowitz, C. (1983) 'More managers try moonlighting to boost income and fulfillment', *Wall Street Journal* 63 (210) Dec. 24, p. 1.

Kornhauser, W. (1963) *Scientists in Industry: Conflict and Accommodation*, Berkeley: University of California Press.

Langfitt, T.W., Hackney, S., Fishman, A.P. and Glowasky, A.V. (Eds) 1983 *Partners in the Research Enterprise: University-Corporate Relations in Science and Technology*, Philadelphia: University of Pennsylvania Press.

National Science Board (1982) *University-Industry Research Relationships: Myths, Realities and Potentials*, Washington: National Science Foundation, NSB 82-1.

National Science Board (1983) *University-Industry Research Relationships: Selected Studies*, Washington: National Science Foundation, NSB 82-2.

Peters, L.S. (1984) *A US Medical Center and Its Research Connections with Industry*, New York: Center for Science and Technology Policy, Graduate School of Business Administration, New York University.

Price, D.K. (1965) *The Scientific Estate*, Cambridge, MA: Belknap Press of Harvard University Press.

Richter, M.N., Jr. (1981) *The Autonomy of Science*, Cambridge, MA: Schenkman.

Richter, M.N., Jr. (1984) 'A comparative analysis of academic organization', *Review of Education* 10: 316-321.

Richter, M.N., Jr. (1985) 'Industrial funding of faculty research', *Humanity and Society* 9: 459-485.

Tornatzky, L.G., Hetzner, W.A., Eveland, J.D., Schwarzkopf, A. and Colton, R.M. (1982) *University-Industry Cooperative Research Centers: A Practice Manual*, Washington: National Science Foundation, NSF/ISI-82002.

Varrin, R.D. and Kukich, D.S. (1985) 'Guidelines for industry-sponsored research at universities', *Science* 227: 385-388, Jan. 25.

Walsh, J. (1985) 'New R & D centers will test university ties', *Science* 227: 150-152.

9 The Economics of Academic Tenure: A Relational Perspective

Michael S. McPherson and Gordon C. Winston*

Introduction

The main argument advanced in favor of the institution of tenure is the protection it provides for academic freedom.[1] Defenders of tenure seem ready to concede its economic inefficiency, but see it as a necessary price to pay to protect scholarly independence. Those who question the value of academic freedom, or see other ways to protect it, then see little to recommend the institution of tenure. Indeed, in one of the few economic articles on tenure, Armen Alchian (n.d.) explained its existence cynically as an expensive and wasteful luxury indulged in by a professoriate freed through the non-profit status of colleges and universities from the rigors of the competitive economy.

Such a negative view of the economic role and consequences of tenure seems to us one-sided and, importantly, misleading. The implicit assumption that the world outside the academy provides most workers with little effective job security is false, and the idea that colleges and universities could function efficiently by operating on the basis of personnel policies analogous to the longshoreman's shape-up is mistaken. Indeed, some of the most interesting empirical work in

* Reprinted from *Journal of Economic Behavior and Organization* by permission of Elsevier Science Publishers. We are grateful to the Faculty Development Program at Williams College for support of this research. The views presented in this paper are those of the authors. We have been helped by comments from Richard Chait, Lee Alston, Joseph Kershaw, and members of the Williams College Economics Department. Throughout the paper we follow the convention of using the masculine pronoun to refer to both men and women.

174

labor economics of late has emphasized what Robert Hall (1982) calls, in the title of one of his papers, 'The Importance of Lifetime Jobs in the U.S. Economy'. Much of the most exciting recent work in analytical labor economics, and in macroeconomics as well, has aimed at understanding the mutual interest workers and firms have in sustaining stable long-term employment relations, and in protecting each other from the vagaries of the market.[2]

Academic tenure, of course, differs importantly from the kind of job protection seniority affords to production workers or (more to the point for comparison with academics) the kind that corporate employment policies provide to middle-level managers. But, we suggest, the difference lies less in the degree of job security afforded[3] than in the nature of the job guarantee and, surprisingly, in the explicit and risky probation that precedes obtaining the guarantee. To put the latter point somewhat polemically: the striking thing about the university, compared to a typical corporation, is not the number of college graduates employed there with secure jobs, but the number of high-level employees who don't expect to be allowed to stay. This point is closely related to our first point, the nature of the job guarantee. For academic employees are assured not only continued employment with the 'firm', but continued employment in a highly specific and well-defined position: teaching, for instance, eighteen-century French literature. The system of rigorous probation followed by tenure is a reasonable way of solving the peculiar personnel problems that arise in employing expensively trained and narrowly specialized people to spend their lifetimes at well-defined and narrowly specialized tasks. The character of this problem, and of this solution, moreover, helps to explain a good deal about academic employment.

It is these themes that we shall develop. They will show that the tenure institution has some desirable efficiency properties that are often overlooked. This, of course, does not prove that tenure should not be reformed or abolished, especially in light of an emerging situation which may raise some of the costs of tenure. Neither does it suggest that we dismiss arguments for tenure based on academic freedom; we merely put them to one side. But we do suggest that any serious proposal for the reform of tenure has to show how alternative arrangements would solve the personnel problems tenure solves; both theory and experience suggest that the implicit alternative of providing faculty with no job guarantee does not solve these problems. Our major aim, in any event, is not to evaluate alternative policies, but to contribute to understanding how tenure actually works in the context of the university.

In developing this analysis, we draw heavily on the emerging literature in a field which we call – generalizing a term of Victor Goldberg's – 'relational economics'. The predominant theme of this literature is that the fact of uncertainty in economic life undermines the usual assumption of anonymity in economic transactions and instead makes it valuable for the parties to economic transactions to develop sustained relationships with one another. This perspective has been applied to good purpose in studying the economics of organizations (Arrow, 1974; Williamson, 1975, 1980), the economics of law and contract (Goldberg, 1980; MacNeil, 1974), labor economics (Leibenstein, 1976), macroeconomics (Okun, 1980) and elsewhere. The analysis of tenure is only one of its many potential applications to the operation of academic institutions.

Our analysis will proceed by contrasting 'stylized' or 'ideal-typical' pictures of the corporation and the academic institution. Corporate employees, we will assume, are hired with an effective lifetime job guarantee, perhaps following a brief and largely perfunctory probationary period and barring gross malfeasance or severe economic hardship for the corporation (these latter qualifications corresponding to comparable limitations on the academic tenure commitment). Corporate employees are not, however, guaranteed a particular assignment, with well defined tasks and perquisites, but rather face an array of possible career paths along which the corporation has discretion to move them at varying rates. University employees in contrast do not receive an immediate employment guarantee, but face instead an extended and serious probation. But when they *are* guaranteed employment, it is a guarantee of employment in a specific set of tasks with well defined perquisites.

These pictures are exaggerations, but, we think, recognizable ones. The notoriety of corporation jobs that lack an implicit employment guarantee – those of CEOs or advertising executives – only stress the contrast with the more usual case. And the narrowly defined and well ensured tasks of the academic fit the picture of the research universities and the more prestigious colleges better than they fit other places. But we think accounting for the differences in our extreme cases will shed light on the wider range of corporate and university personnel policies encountered in the real world.

Our analysis proceeds in several steps. First is a brief explanation for why employers and employees (outside and inside academics) value secure employment relationships and a brief statement of the difference it makes when the commitment is to a narrowly defined job. In section three is an analysis of the reasons why academic institutions commit themselves to providing faculty with security in a specific job. There follows an analysis in section four of the central implications of this specific job commitment for the character of the academic employment relationship and of academic life more generally. Section five discusses alternatives to tenure, and conclusions appear in section six.

Job Security, Job Specificity and Organizational Effectiveness

One of the central insights of analytical labor economics over the last decade has been the recognition that the productivity of an organization depends heavily on the character of the work environment it is able to provide. The classical picture is of the profit-maximizing firm, sensitively adjusting the wage rates of workers and hiring and firing ruthlessly to get the most out of its work force at minimum cost—such a firm turns out on a careful view of its internal requirements not to be maximizing profits at all. Most obviously, the implicit assumption of 'no transactions costs' embodied in this picture of the rapidly adjusting firm is wrong. Turnover is costly to firms because of training costs and the value of accumulated information about present employees, information that cannot be cheaply or reliably purchased in the market. At the same time, mobility is expensive to workers – they value job security – because of search and relocation costs, and because of information they accumulate about the firm they work for. So firms can hire a labor force of a given quality more cheaply by pursuing a policy that reduces involuntary turnover of employees.[4]

Within the firm, moreover, workers need to train other workers, which they will be reluctant to do if the trainee is a viable candidate for the trainer's job (Thurow, 1975; Solow, (1980). It is also often cheaper for employers to evaluate the performance of a team or group of workers than to judge the performance of individuals within the group, so that neither wage nor dismissal incentives may be easily targeted at individuals (Alchian and Demsetz, 1972; Williamson, 1975). More subtly, firms need to create an 'atmosphere' (to borrow Williamson's word) within the work group that conduces to a cooperative attitude; elements of wage and employment competition within the group may poison the atmosphere and discourage workers from revealing information to higher management that might be useful in reassigning tasks, making judgments about promotions, and the like.

Williamson, Wachter and Harris (1975) have analyzed the resulting structure of 'internal' labor markets at length. Firms will maintain an active position in the 'external' labor market only for a relatively few positions in the job structure: the bulk of positions in the job hierarchy will be filled by promotion from within. The wage attaching to a particular job in the hierarchy will be largely independent of who occupies it; differential success in performance will be rewarded by more rapid promotion through the hierarchy rather than by more pay for better workers within a rank. The perennial prospect of promotion provides workers with an individual incentive to stay with the firm and produce, without exacerbating the tendency toward destructive competition between workers at the same grade.

The wage and promotion structure also helps to cement the relation between the worker and the firm. The firm invests in the worker, both by training and – importantly – by accumulating information about his particular strengths and weaknesses. The worker signals his willingness to stay through and past the initial investment period by accepting a relatively low initial wage: a strategy which makes sense only if he plans to stay. He is willing to do so in part because he believes the firm will find a 'slot' for him that fits his capacities and interests. Within limits, the resulting wage/promotion arrangement will be self-enforcing: the worker and the firm will have a mutual interest in getting the worker into a job where his productivity is high and where his pay is high enough both to ensure continued employment with the firm and to make other workers in the firm aspire to such high productivity jobs. The need for the firm to present itself to employment candidates as a good place to work provides it with an additional incentive for 'honest' promotion and job assignment practices.

Esential to this picture, however, is the presumption that there exists in the firm a variety of jobs of varying wage and productivity which workers might be willing to accept. One might see the firm as having internalized some of the functions of a placement agency: because information about worker capabilities is a by-product of the production process, it makes sense for firms to offer to workers the service of finding the job that fits them best. Other things being equal, the firm will be more attractive to workers the wider the array of potential jobs it offers.[5]

In academic employment there is very little of this internal job mobility: it is a crucial fact that people who are hired to the faculty either stay on the faculty or are dismissed: they do not move to alternative employment within the institution, except for the relatively few who move into academic administration. And, of course, non-academic employees are hardly ever promoted to the faculty. Reasons for this crucial fact will be discussed shortly, but first it is important to note that it radically reshapes the structure of the employment problem that colleges and universities face, compared to that of large corporations.

To the degree that firms can freely assign workers to jobs and career paths with differing wages and productivities, they can avoid the risk of radical mismatches between wage and productivity for individual workers while still avoiding the costs of high turnover. Moreover, the return on investment in information about worker performance will be increased by its dual role in the organization: the same information which is useful in monitoring the worker's performance in his present job also has value in determining when and whether to reassign him.

The university, lacking this flexibility in assigning responsibilities to workers, is thus in a difficult spot. When a worker is inflexibly attached to a particular job, mismatches between wage and productivity can only be avoided by (a) adjusting wages to match individual productivities, (b) accepting the costs of higher turnover by dismissing low productivity employees, or (c) introducing more intensive and costly initial screening. Alternative (a) is of course used within limits, but unrestrained use of wage differentials is unattractive because it requires costly monitoring of the performance of every individual faculty member throughout his career and because of the disruptive and demoralizing effects of introducing large wage differentials for faculty with comparable rank and responsibilities. Freeman (1976) notes the constraints academic institutions feel in establishing wage differentials between and within academic departments. (Notice that, without extensive initial screening for faculty quality, wage differentials might need to be very large indeed to reflect productivity differences. With such screening in place, the expected productivity of the monitoring needed to sustain wage differentials is lower.) Alternative (b), if seriously pursued throughout every employee's career, also requires expensive monitoring throughout the career (which itself has negative 'atmospheric' effects) and introduces employment insecurity which is costly to both workers and the firm.

Academic employers have thus settled on a version of alternative (c) – more intensive initial screening – as a central element of their personnel policies. This takes the form both of more intensive pre-employment screening than corporations undertake for entry level positions and of intensive on-the-job screening concentrated in the first few years of employment. These considerations help account for several of the key features of academic employment policy.

First, and most centrally, we can understand why such a 'big deal' is made out of promotion and tenure decisions. The decision to employ a person permanently in a well-defined position is momentous both for the worker and the firm: the worker gets not merely employment security but something close to a guarantee of status and lifetime income prospects; the firm is locked into not only a stream of future wage payments, but a stream of future productivity from the worker over which it will have very little control. It follows therefore that firms will invest quite heavily in the scrutiny of their non-tenured employees, and that workers will attach great importance to perceived fairness of the institutions for making tenure and promotion decisions. The result is a concentration of everyone's energy and attention on that single point in the career, which is quite the opposite of the more diffuse but more sustained attention to worker performance in the corporation.

The obverse of close attention to the academic worker's performance prior to tenure is the marked inattention to performance after tenure. This too can be seen as a rational response to the academic employment situation. In the corporation, with its flexible job assignment policies, a principal role for the continual monitoring of employee performance is the making of continual marginal adjustments in workers' job assignments: increasing the productivity of the existing labor force by re-allocating tasks among workers. But in the university, where the tasks are final once the employment guarantee is made, monitoring performance has little value, for there is little to do with the information. To be sure, information about tenured faculty can influence the rate of wage advance to some degree and can serve as a basis for moral suasion, but the central use to which such information is put in the corporation, to shape the path of the worker's career advance, is markedly less available within an academic institution.

These considerations also help account for the existence in academia of a sharply defined 'nodal point' by which time a decision of 'up-or-out' on tenure must be made. Personnel decisions in the corporation are almost always taken at the margin: to hasten or delay promotions; to expand or contract the range of responsibility. In academics, the possible decisions at any time are two: the marginal one of continuing employment for another year or the dramatically non-marginal one of terminating employment. If the former decision is always available, there will be an almost inevitable tendency to evade the latter one, which is bound to be difficult and unpleasant. To force a decision by a fixed moment serves both to legitimize the harsh decision to let someone go – the option of another chance just isn't available – and provides an incentive to gather the large amounts of costly information needed to make such weighty decision responsibly (see Brewster, 1972).

These remarks show the fundamental differences between the personnel problems of the academic institution and the corporation that follow from the narrowness and specificity of the academic job commitment. Much more remains to be said in elaboration of the implications of these points for the operation of colleges and universities. But it is time now to examine with care the reasons for this crucial structural difference between the university and the corporation: why do universities not offer – and why do faculty not seek – the wide range of career paths offered within a typical corporation?

Sources of Job Specificity in the University

The fact that individuals are hired to do quite narrowly defined and rigidly specified jobs is central to the economics of tenure, and describes the major structural contrast between university and corporate employment. The sources of this difference lie on both the production and demand sides of the market. The 'organizational technology' of the university is such that it attaches relatively little value to preserving its freedom to change the job assignments of particular workers. At the same time, worker preferences are such that a faculty member would typically prefer to continue his occupation (say, teaching physics) at another institution than to stay with the 'firm' in a different job. Behind these differences in organizational technology and preferences lies an important difference between the corporation and the university in the kinds of 'knowledge capital' workers acquire to do their jobs. In the university, this knowledge is predominantly tied to the worker's academic subject: it is specific to the *occupation* and not to the firm. In the corporation, there is likely to be a greater premium on *firm-specific* human capital: knowledge of the particular codes, practices, and procedures of *that* corporation as opposed to others. (For the importance of firm-specific human capital in the corporation see Arrow, 1974; Becker, 1964). The distinction between occupation- and firm-specific human capital is drawn in Rosen, 1977.

This contrast is reflected in the differences in training patterns for corporate and university work. In academic employment, training is for a specific academic discipline and not for a specific employment or firm. Academic training is an extreme case of the classic 'non-appropriability' of worker training – the fact that firms are reluctant to invest their resources in the training of their employees and more so the less specific is that training to that firm – the more generally valuable it is in other firms. Training for university employment is so extreme a case of non-appropriability that the firm – the hiring university – refuses to provide any training and, instead, hires its employees with virtually their full complement of training (the Ph.D.) secured elsewhere and at someone else's expense. This is underscored by the curious, if familiar, fact that the new academic employee does the same thing – teaches the same sorts of classes in the same way and writes the same sorts of articles and books – as the thirty year veteran. Quality, it is hoped, improves with maturity, but the duties of faculty members remain remarkably the same.[6]

Again, the corporation presents the antithesis in its widespread employment of individuals trained as generalists who are subsequently put through a highly firm-specific training followed by a career of additional training in different, again firm-specific activities. The multiplicity of suitable corporate jobs with their often differentiated internal training requirements and the individual worker's multiple job assignments, *seriatim*, over his career are aspects of the high degree of substitutability among those jobs. An important reason for the substitutability appears to be the absence of high levels of requisite prior training; conversely, the absence of much prior training before workers enter the firm tends to make all jobs similar for the generally-talented but not specifically-trained individual.

This difference in training and human capital accumulation patterns naturally shapes worker interests in the character of the job guarantee they will seek. Individual academics will typically prefer to substitute one employer for another while retaining their occupations rather than to scrap their costly training in favor of taking a different job at the same institution. Moreover, it is reasonable to expect that only workers with a relatively strong prior commitment to the occupation will undertake training in the first place, so that the commitment to the profession is a result of preferences as well as the opportunity cost of the specialized investment in training. The academic worker will thus put little value on a guarantee of employment which is not specific about the kind of employment guaranteed.[7] The new corporate employee, on the other hand, with less investment in occupation-specific training, and less knowledge about where his skills and interests lie, will care more about job security as such, and may put positive value on the corporation's implicit offer to match his job assignment to his aptitudes, as information about those aptitudes emerges.

The tendency to job rigidity in the university is compounded by its objectives of doing its job of education and research (producing its product) at reasonable cost. An important aspect of the technology of university production, the result of the specialized human capital possessed by academics, is that it is rarely as easy to substitute employees among jobs as it is to hire new employees from outside for those particular jobs. If the university has an opening for a worker to teach and do research in particle physics, the productivity in that job of a professor of French literature currently employed by the university is unlikely to be nearly as high as that of a new employee trained specifically in particle physics – someone currently in graduate school or employed in the physics department of another university. The occasional Renaissance Man, of course, is the exception that proves the rule. It will similarly be unlikely that the best person for a non-academic job opening will be a faculty member – in many cases it seems true that intense academic training does as much to *dis*qualify as to prepare people for other kinds of work. So on pure productivity grounds, too, the university will accommodate these sharp technological differences in productivity among individuals and will hire French scholars to teach French and physicists to teach physics.

The corporation, of course, shows that this employment pattern is far from inevitable. It hires the liberal arts graduate – often a history or English major – for a broadly defined 'management' training program from which he or she may be assigned to a specific job in production management or financial management or sales or . . . and even a cursory examination of corporate management careers makes it clear that once assigned to sales or production or finance, the corporate employee will often be reassigned to quite different sorts of managerial employment throughout his career with the firm. Indeed, even employees (like engineers) who may be hired for their specific skills will often, if successful, 'graduate' into jobs that do not depend on those skills.

So both sides of the market lead to narrowness and rigidity of academic employment: the technology of production sharply reduces flexibility in inter-job substitution at the same time that the preferences of workers sharply reduce their willingness to change fields rather than changing firms. Neither appears dominant.[8]

It is understandable, then, in light of the important differences in the interests at work in the academic and corporate employment settings, that the form of the agreements ensuring job security will differ. As Simon (1957) has stressed, the contract governing any employment relation will be importantly 'incomplete', with the worker ceding an important amount of discretionary authority to the firm about exactly what activities he must undertake. In the corporate setting, the firm's authority generally extends to granting the firm considerable freedom to determine what position in the firm the worker will fill, not only to begin with but through the career. The *quid pro quo* is an implicit commitment by the firm to retain the employee in some capacity, barring markedly unusual circumstances. But in the university, the faculty member cedes much less authority to the 'firm' to determine the content of his job. Indeed, it can be argued that this is one of the most attractive features of academic employment – the fact the workers are, to a remarkable extent, asked to do very little they don't choose to do. They get paid for reading, thinking, talking and writing about those things that they find interesting and rewarding. The result, of course, is that the university has little authority to re-assign workers to different work; it may make offers and suggestions, but the presumption is that an academic worker always has the right to stick to his job. An offer of tenure ensures this security in a specific job permanently. The *quid pro quo* is, however, a little different than in the corporate world: job security comes only following a lengthy and rigorous period of probation.

Personnel Decisions in the University[9]

The university and the corporation, then, face sharply different sorts of personnel problems. The corporation can feel relatively relaxed about the 'quality' and characteristics of the person it hires into entry level positions, and can follow an implicit policy of 'instant (or almost instant) tenure' simply because it has available a wide range of job slots requiring differing capacities and offering different wages, and because it retains freedom to allocate employees among those jobs, and to re-allocate employees as time goes on. The essence of the corporate personnel management problem is to ensure a steady and reliable flow of information about employee performance and to maintain a responsive institutional structure to re-allocate employee responsibilities on the basis of that flow of information. Economists, notably Arrow (1974) and Williamson (1975), are beginning to appreciate what a subtle and important problem this is.

The university, however, essentially *knows* what its people are going to do and, if it is to attract good employees, it cannot allow itself very much discretion about how much it will pay people to do it.[10] Its problem then is to ensure that it gets good quality workers into the 'firm' and to ensure that they stay motivated in the absence of sensitive marginal incentives. The probation-tenure system is a reasonable response to this distinctive employment problem. We shall discuss in turn some aspects of the probation period, the tenure decision and the problem of motivating senior faculty.

The Probation Period

It is possible to identify four distinct ways in which a lengthy and explicit probationary period is valuable.

(1) *Performance monitoring*

In any economic transaction, people need to know what they are buying. The productive organization – including the university – must have ways of knowing about the performance of its employees in doing the things that produce the firm's output. But among workers and jobs, there is very great variety in the ease with which that performance can be measured by the firm: the ditch-digger quite unambiguously has or has not moved a specific amount of dirt by noon: the theoretical biologist may or may not have spent the morning in pursuit of his research objectives – he may have been day-dreaming about making a killing in the stock market. Differences in the inherent measurability of different occupations are essentially technological, attaching irreducibly to the specific activity (Leibenstein, 1976). Given these inherent technological measurement problems, incentives to misrepresent performance may compound the difficulties of measurements. Workers and firms may both try to give a misleading picture of what the worker is actually doing, but absent the underlying technological measurement problems in the first place, incentive distortions cannot persist: if performance can easily be monitored, there is no room for attempted misrepresentation.

The performance of the activities of academic workers – teaching and scholarship – is certainly hard to measure.[11] These activities do not produce concrete, measurable products of easily discernible quality; neither their output nor their input are easily observable or measurable.

It is not necessary to this analysis to assert that corporate productive activities are any easier to measure than those of academia. What counts for the present analysis in differentiating the two organizations and their labor markets is, simply, that the university combines measurement difficulties *and* job-specific employment while the corporation combines its measurement difficulties with job-flexible employment: the corporation can second-guess and the university cannot.

But 'hard to measure' is rather too imprecise for our purposes. What it means is that a worker's actual job performance can be known by the firm only with the expenditure of resources – on things like record keeping but most importantly in the form of attention, time and effort. Performance that is inherently harder to measure simply takes more of those resources. Of course, it may be both undesirable and exorbitantly expensive to try to know with certainty the quality of a performance. So what's relevant is often the achievement of a given level of confidence in that knowledge. Again, the 'harder to measure', the more resources are needed to get to that level of confidence.

This applies to measurement of the performance of an individual worker at a particular point in time. There are two important additional dimensions. Spence and Williamson note the frequently greater ease – the lower cost – of measuring the performance of a group of workers than that of an individual worker alone. Alchian and Demsetz (1972) relied on such 'non-separability' of performance measurement for their influential analysis of internal organizations – their illustration was the difficulty of the separate measurement of the work performance of two men lifting a box onto a truck. As a group, their performance is easily measured; individually it is not.

The even more relevant – and neglected – dimension of measurement is simply the duration of the period over which the performance is measured. A repetitive activity – like either teaching or scholarship – may be very costly to monitor quickly, but be quite easy to judge over a longer period. So in addition to the differences among jobs in their inherent static costs of performance measurement, there will also be differences in the way performance information accumulates with the duration of observation.

The relevance of this time dimension for academic employment is obvious. Academic job performance is unusually difficult to measure quickly. The ease with which accurate judgments can be made clearly increases with a longer period of observation. While it would be very difficult to judge scholarly potential, for instance, in a week of even very intensive observation, it is easy to achieve a reasonable judgment over a five-year period. In general, a longer period of observation of any repetitive activity yields a given degree of measurement accuracy at lower total resource cost. For these reasons, the lengthy probationary period for faculty can be a useful method of quality control.

(2) Self-selection[12]

One hazard facing the university is analogous to the problems of moral hazard and adverse selection in the insurance industry. Given the assured status and security of the tenured academic position, there is danger of persons misrepresenting themselves – their basic attitudes, work habit, goals, etc. – in order to obtain tenure and showing their 'true colors' afterwards. This problem, of course, exists for the corporation too, but is mitigated by the fact of job flexibility. The worker who has led his superiors to overestimate his potential can be either down-graded or 'kicked upstairs' in response.

The interposition of a probationary period, with relatively low pay and a relatively high dismissal probability, reduces the incentive for misrepresentation of this kind. The longer the period over which one has to 'fake' desirable attitudes, the greater the cost of doing so and since levels of performance after tenure are not so intensively monitored or enforced, there is a strong premium on granting tenure to those who genuinely enjoy their work. The longer the probationary period, the greater the tendency to screen out those who don't. (One might add to this a point originally due to Pascal, who noted that merely acting out religious ritual may eventually produce real belief. There may be a tendency for one who tries to act the part of a well-motivated academic to actually become such eventually. Those among us who feel surprised at how hard they continue to work after receiving tenure may be cases in point.)

(3) Time to tenure as an economic variable

With relatively rigid wages and job descriptions, the university faces a problem in adjusting the attractiveness of its employment offering to changes in market conditions. The corporation, of course, faces a comparable problem which it solves in part by varying promotion prospects and rates of promotion in response to market conditions. The university can, in a similar way, use variations in the likelihood of promotion and in the length of the probationary period to vary the value of its employmet offer as market conditions change. There is extensive empirical evidence that such variation is in fact an important feature of the academic labor market (Kuh, 1977 and Weiss, 1981).

(4) *The focusing of monitoring resources*

As noted earlier, fixing a terminal point to the probationary period enforces a concentration of attention and monitoring effort that encourages careful evaluation of candidates for promotion. In the absence of such a focal point, the tendency will be encouraged to postpone the difficult decision to fire anyone and to dissipate the energies needed to stage a serious evaluation.

The Tenure Decision

While it is useful in some contexts to speak of the 'university' as making decisions on tenure and job security, in fact specific individuals within the institution are charged with making them. The arrangements in the university are quite different from typical corporate arrangements, and these differences can be at least partly understood in terms of the analysis developed here.

In the corporation, decisions about promotions are typically made in a hierarchical manner, with those at higher levels in the hierarchy deciding on those lower down, and with a well articulated structure of levels shaping the whole. In the university, however, while Deans and Presidents may be involved in decisions, most of the weight of the tenure decision is typically borne by those members of the discipline who have already been given tenure: peer review is the order of the day.

Several aspects of these arrangements can be addressed in our framework. Why is it disciplinary peers, rather than 'higher ups' within the institution, who bear the weight of the decision? Why is it peers within the institution rather than peers outside the institution who are central? And why is it tenured faculty, rather than all those in the discipline at the institution, who decide?

The rationale for peer, rather than hierarchical, authority is clearly linked to the specialized nature of academic job assignments: judgment of an employee's performance during the probationary period must be made by those who are competent in his field since his main productive activities are specific to that field.[13] Just as the university cannot usually hire a French professor to teach particle physics, so it cannot rely on a French professor (or a dean or president trained for that role) to judge the performance of a particle physicist. Of course, formally the role of peers may only be advisory to those with hierarchical authority, but Higher-ups will rarely have ground to over-rule strong recommendations from departments and, if such recommendations are often over-ruled the Higher-ups will undermine the incentive for departments to put much effort into evaluations.

Peer judgments could, in principle, be made by committees of outsiders. Their advice is, of course, sometimes obtained, but rarely given weight comparable to that of the candidate's colleagues. This is so despite the fact that it is sometimes alleged that outsiders could be more fair and objective. One reason for the importance of 'locals' is that they can more cheaply be informed about aspects of a colleague's performance other than published work. Such information could only be made available to outsiders through extensive visits and observation. This fact is especially important since (as we discuss further below) an important part of the judgment is a forecast about the candidate's likely behavior *after* receiving tenure, and this requires a subtle view of the candidate's motivations, which is harder for outsiders to obtain.

Another, perhaps more important, reason for giving weight to local views concerns the motivation of the evaluators. The fact that local evaluators must live with the results of their decision and they presumably care about the reputation and quality of the department they are affiliated with, gives them a stronger reason to judge with care than outsiders would have. We should add, of course, that insider evaluation is subject to abuse, for which the obtaining of outside views may be a partial corrective. The attribution of motivation may become an intrusive and arbitrary exercise, and the concern with needing to 'live with' a colleague may lead to undue emphasis on traits of congeniality or even obsequiousness. But it is not clear that there is any feasible system for evaluating academic personnel which can avoid these hazards.

Last is the question why non-tenured people are typically excluded from the group of peers who decide on tenure. One obvious reason is the potential conflict of interest in evaluating a potential competitor – or conversely the potential conspiracy on the part of candidates to support one another's interests. Indeed, the need for objective evaluations has been cited by some observers (we think wrongly) as the key rationale for the institution of tenure itself:

without job security, faculty would be motivated to resist retaining workers superior to themselves (Freeman, 1980). A separate reason for excluding non-tenured personnel from tenure decisions is the relatively brief time over which they can expect to be associated with the institution, which may lead them to give undue weight to the short-term interests of the institution in making decisions.

Motivating Senior Faculty

Like universities, corporations generally avoid instituting wide merit based pay differentials for different workers doing similar jobs: wages within grade, in fact, are closely linked to seniority (Medoff and Abraham, 1981). But corporations can use promotion ladders and job reassignment as devices to continue to motivate effort among workers who are not threatened with dismissal. As we have argued, these options are much less available to universities. So the question arises: how *does* one motivate senior faculty? This is a large question, worthy of a paper (at least) in its own right, but a few observations related to the themes developed here are warranted.

First, a negative point: given the logic of the academic employment structure, it is far from obvious that intensive hierarchical effort to evaluate and motivate senior faculty in fact make much sense. Monitoring worker performance is an expensive activity, and it may in itself have a negative impact on morale. It may be perfectly sensible, if there is little to be done with the information that is gathered anyway, to limit monitoring to what is needed to detect gross malfeasance, to the spontaneous monitoring of each colleague by his peers, and to accept that a certain amount of 'deadwood' is an unavoidable by-product of the system.

An interesting extension of this point has been suggested by Oliver Williamson (1975, pp. 55–56). If in fact it is difficult to monitor or regulate the performance of faculty in their central activities of teaching and scholarship it may prove *counterproductive* to monitor those ancillary activities (like use of the telephone or of paperclips) where regulation is possible. If there is no alternative but to trust faculty on important matters, it may be prudent to trust them on small matters as well, in order to make that attitude of trust as visible and pervasive as possible. More broadly, the general attitude of autonomy and mutual respect which universities try to foster among faculty can be seen as a reasonable response to their inability to monitor and regulate their central activities.

The fact that marginal incentives are hard to supply for senior faculty affects importantly the character of the screening process for non-tenured faculty. It is necessary to determine not only what faculty are capable of doing, but also to form a judgment about what they will be *inclined* to do, in the absence of marginal incentives. It is crucial to select for promotion faculty who have a strong 'internal' motivation to perform, or, alternatively, faculty who are readily subject to 'moral suasion' or 'peer pressure' in regulating their performance levels. This is plainly a difficult judgment to reach, since it involves inferring by observing someone who is subject to sanctions how he will behave when he is not subject to those sanctions. The point made earlier about the self-selection function of the probationary period is relevant here, since the longer the probation, the higher the cost to the candidate of acting against his inclination. A further implication is that the need to form judgments about a candidate's inclinations and motivations argues against reducing the tenure decision to a set of purely 'objective' indicators, like number of publications. As noted, reaching judgments about motivation and about likely performance under changed conditions creates opportunities for abuse, but they seem to be unavoidable.

The discussion to this point has focused on incentives internal to the institution. It is necessary to note as well the incentive for tenured faculty to perform well in the hope of achieving a better position at another university – 'better' in terms of pay, prestige, or other factors that matter to the person in question. Active markets for senior faculty only exist, however, at a relatively small number of institutions. Predictably, they are the ones where research figures most prominently in the work of the faculty, since research performance is much easier for 'outsiders' to evaluate and so to provide a basis for competing offers. At this group of universities, the external market functions as a partial substitute for the other motivating factors discussed here.

Term Contracts as an Alternative to Tenure

The logic of the present analysis may be usefully underscored by a brief comparison of tenure arrangements to the most familiar kind of employment arrangement commonly thought of as an alternative to the tenure/probation system.[14] This is the alternative of term contracts: appointing faculty to renewable contracts of relatively short (three to five years) duration. Under a term-contract system, faculty are offered a series of fixed-period renewable contracts. The notion is that under such a system each faculty member's performance is constantly reviewed during his career, with each contract renewal contingent on performance in the preceding contract period. The 'naturalness' of this alternative no doubt stems from the rather odd idea – derived from taking textbook economic theory too literally – that this is how 'real world' employment markets work. Indeed, judged by textbook criteria of the working of timeless markets, term contracts have a strong appeal in economic efficiency terms: 'deadwood' workers are constantly being got rid of on the basis of their recent performance and everyone is continually spurred to strong efforts by the threat of dismissal.

Our theoretical perspective, however, makes us strongly doubtful that things will work out this way in practice. Moreover, a valuable recent book on tenure by Richard Chait and Andrew Ford (1982) provides strong case study evidence supporting our theoretical view. If the decision about contract renewal were more than nominal, it would prove very costly to universities committed to it. The resources required to evaluate everybody seriously every few years would be simply enormous. If such evaluations did not result in many dismissals, they would be largely wasted. If they did, the university would bear the costs of greater turnover. Moreover, the threat of job insecurity might make it more difficult to hire good faculty at wages comparable to those at places offering more security, and against the potential incentive advantages of more intense monitoring would have to be weighed the potential negative morale implications of that practice.

In fact the more likely outcome is that contract renewals will become routine, and the system will approximate instant tenure. Two strong incentives contribute to such a shift from nominal job insecurity to actual job security. First, in perpetual re-evaluation there is no moment of truth: no special time when the resources of the institution need be brought to bear on evaluating an employee's performance. Since that evaluation is both time and resource consuming, and it risks a quite unpleasant outcome – and since another opportunity for evaluation will come along soon – the incentives are there to prevent a real and meaningful evaluation with each (or any) termination of a fixed-period contract. In a tenure decision, where the issue is a lifetime commitment, it is much more difficult to be slack and to procrastinate.

The second incentive is the simple fact of mutuality – the judges are also judged. Since everyone on the faculty is in the same contract renewal boat, there is obvious pressure for the judges to be gentle and compassionate and not to evaluate their fellows too harshly – when one's own turn is on the horizon, only the slightest imagination is needed to see the value of such a precedent.

The schools employing term contracts that Chait and Ford examined (Hampshire College, Evergreen State College, and the University of Texas at Permian Basin) support this view of the consequences. Reappointments become routine and turnover is quite low. Chait and Ford (1982, p.12) quote a Task Force established at Hampshire to review the term contract policy as asserting that:

> The current system also has an adverse impact on the faculty's quality by diverting inordinate faculty time away from teaching (and other work). The involvement of so many faculty in the review of over twenty of their colleagues a year seriously drains important resources from the main educational functions of the college.

The authors (p.13) further note that the faculty, 'referees today and candidates for re-appointment tomorrow, fear retribution as well as strained relationships'. Hampshire has since moved to create a 'tenure-like' decision for a ten-year reappointment after the first two three-year appointments to create a 'crunch decision' that will focus attention and resources. Evergreen has not made such a shift, but the absence of pressure for making difficult decisions seems to have been felt there too. The authors report an interview with the President of Evergreen in which he said, 'Sometimes I say to myself, "My God, we have instant tenure!"'.

Instant tenure, of course, is precisely what, in our analysis, corporations have. But, to repeat our earlier point, they do not provide instant tenure to a specific job with specific responsibilities and perquisites. Universities with instant tenure are likely to be forced either toward extremely intensive pre-screening of candidates for appointment, which is intrinsically quite difficult, since close observation of the candidate, over a long period of time doing work like that he will be asked to, is required; or else to accept a decline in quality of personnel.

One perhaps surprising point here is the potential advantage of a probation/tenure system over term contracts from the standpoint of minority employment. To the degree that term contracts amount to instant tenure, the cost to the university of making 'mistakes' will rise, and there will be pressure in hiring to rely on established channels of historic reliability in locating candidates. (An illustration is the practice at Oxford, which has instant tenure through term contracts, to hire its own graduates.) To the degree that those historic channels embody past policies of discrimination, instant *de facto* tenure will militate against change and experiment. A similar problem arises to the degree that disadvantaged groups are victims of 'statistical discrimination', having their individual qualities discounted because of (correct or incorrect) beliefs about average characteristics of their group (characteristics which may themselves be the result of discrimination) (see Akerlof, 1970 and Thurow, 1975). The opportunity to observe an individual during probation will reduce the reluctance to judge the individual on his own merits rather than on group averages, and may also over time lead to the undermining of the beliefs that sustain the statistical discrimination. This line of reasoning may apply not just to racially and sexually disadvantaged groups, but to graduates of less prestigious universities as well.

Conclusion

The central message of this paper can be summed up as follows: the institution of tenure is not simply a constraint imposed on universities, whether to protect faculty jobs or to ensure academic freedom, but an integral part of the way universities function. The tenure/probation system is a reasonable response to the highly specialized nature of academic work and to the long training such work requires. An intelligent understanding of the operation of universities and a constructive approach to the reform of their personnel policies needs to take these realities into account.

This conclusion need not be so complacent as it may sound. One could, for example, question whether academic training needs necessarily to be so specialized as it has become. It is also true that our analysis presents a somewhat idealized picture of how tenure and promotion decisions are made, and there is room for argument about how close to these ideals various colleges and universities come in practice. Our point, however, is that criticism of the tenure system and proposals for reform must come to grips with the quite real and special academic personnel problems the tenure system responds to. Much existing criticism, by failing to understand the economic functions of tenure, fails to do that.

A further step away from complacency may be taken by recalling some of the special pressures that may arise for the tenure system in the near future. Our analysis incorporates two key assumptions about the workings of the academic labor market: one, that the typical individual will enter the academic career with a stronger commitment to the occupation than to a particular institution; the other, that the granting of tenure amounts to a lifetime employment guarantee in practice. Both these have for the most part been true over the fifty years or so that the institution of tenure has been in full force in America. But of course tenure is always granted subject to financial exigency for the institution, and people can only pursue a lifetime commitment to academic employment if jobs are available.

Many observers expect the impending decline in college-age population to produce substantial strains on the academic labor market (Carter, 1976; Dresch, 1975; Freeman, 1976; Bowen, 1981 and Oi, 1979).[15] As the likelihood of financial crises at academic institutions rises, the value of obtaining a tenured position falls. At the same time, the familiar academic career pattern of starting out at a prestigious institution and then moving on to tenure at a less prestigious institution if necessary has ceased to be viable in many fields. For the next fifteen years, fewer people will enter academe with the expectation that it will be a lifetime career. Thus, some of the basic assumptions of our analysis will be at least partly undermined in the future. The operation of the tenure system has in the past been closely tied to the background of an expanding university and college system. A period of contraction is likely to stimulate a search for alternatives on the part of both employers and workers. Whether the pressures will be sufficient to cause such an alternative to emerge is difficult to say. But constructive thought about the form such an alternative to tenure might take, and especially analysis of its likely consequences for the performance of universities and colleges, will need to draw on the kind of functional analysis of tenure we have begun to develop here.

We would like, finally, to point toward two kinds of further work that need to be done both to extend and to strengthen the foundations of this study. First, our analysis contains a number of implications about the behaviour of academic institutions which it would be desirable to test. We would expect, for example, that institutions where faculty play more specialized roles would be more likely to conform to the 'ideal typical' tenure model. We would also expect that academic hiring practices in fields where there is closer substitution between academic and non-academic employment of skills (business and medicine may be examples) will be less likely to adhere to the classic probation/tenure pattern. These and other implications should be developed and tested. Second, it is possible to think of some segments of industry with labor market institutions similar to tenure (e.g., the Army's up-or-out policy) and also to think of occupations with similar characteristics (rigid job description and high costs of measuring performance) to academics (accounting and medicine may be examples). It would be valuable to see if there is indeed a match, as our view would suggest, between tenure-like labor market institutions and academic-like occupation characteristics.

Notes

1. A representative sample of writings is Smith (1973). Valuable material on the legal and historical aspects of academic tenure is in Keast and Macy (1973).
2. Two recent papers concerned with the academic labor market that build on this literature are Freeman (1977) and James (1980). Neither is centrally concerned with the topics of interest in this paper.
3. Legally, of course, tenure is not a job guarantee. In institutions following AAUP guidelines, tenured faculty are (a) appointed 'without regard to term' – that is, without a specific end-date, and (b) are assured of a certain formal procedure prior to dismissal. Dismissal must be for cause, but the cause quite explicitly can be incompetence or economic exigency. That few people get fired is a practical more than legal consequence of the working of these rules in an academic setting.
4. This literature is usefully condensed and cited in Okun (1980, ch. 3).
5. It might seem that all that matters is the number of 'good' jobs available. But this is not so, since for workers who are uncertain about their productivity, the absence of low-productivity jobs means not assurance of a good job but a higher probability of dismissal.
6. This shifting of the training function entirely out of the employing institution is especially interesting in light of the fact that the same institutions are involved in both roles, even while keeping separate. Not only does the firm have the competence to train its own workers but it is often engaged in just that activity in its own graduate schools. So MIT hires a new Standard Ph.D. to train its Ph.D. candidates at the same time that Stanford hires a new MIT Ph.D. to train its Ph.D. candidates. Even when the formal identity of competence is not so glaring, much of the anomaly remains: when Kermit Gordon and Emile Despres were on the Williams faculty, Charles Kindelberger referred to Williams as 'the best graduate school in economics in the country, only you've got to be an Assistant Professor to get in'.
7. Presumably, he'd like to have his cake and eat it too. Both sorts of security – especially since they are rights and not obligations – are nice to have. The point here is simply that if one has to choose, the choice will typically be in favor of keeping the occupation and not the employer.
8. It is futile to ask whether it is workers' rigid preferences or universities' rigid productivity requirements that explains the job specificity and

rigidity of academic employment. The more flexible, adaptable job environment into which the corporate employee is hired, too, is the result both of greater flexibility in production and greater indifference on the part of the worker whether he is assigned to one job or another within the firm.

9. Many of the points in this section emerge, from a somewhat different perspective, in section IV of James and Neuberger (1979).

10. This latter point deserves elaboration. The corporation, we assume, will fix a wage for a given job. But people's expected incomes will vary with the jobs (and career paths) they are assigned to. Why could the university not achieve a similar result by varying pay according to teacher performance? Besides the general arguments about morale implications and difficulties of productivity measurement noted earlier, there is a further problem. With a flexible array of jobs, the corporation has an interest in putting high-productivity people in high-paying jobs. This tends to keep the corporation 'honest' since to put a potentially high-productivity person in a low-paying job costs the firm product, as well as costing the worker income. But with the job assigment fixed, the university could save itself money by asserting falsely that a particular professor had low productivity. So there would be more ground for suspicion that the university might use its power to set wages in 'unfair' ways that don't match productivity differences.

11. But not equally. There seems little doubt that teaching performance is even harder to measure than scholarship, if only because the inherent qualitative judgments made about both are made by more knowledge-able people and more publicly in the case of scholarship. Furthermore, those judgments are made by much the same people over time – there is continuity in the population of judges in the case of scholarship but a constantly changing group in the case of teaching. This difference between teaching and scholarship, while not directly relevant to the present analysis, would certainly be central in any analysis that differentiated between university and college faculties.

12. The phenomenon of self-selection in labor markets has received much attention recently. See Spence (1974), Salop and Salop (1976) and the articles referred to in Okun (1980, ch. 3).

13. This is more clearly the case in scholarship than in teaching. This would lead us to hypothesize that the role of disciplinary peers in tenure decisions is stronger at schools that put more emphasis on research.

14. A different and in some ways rather intriguing alternative to a tenure/probation system would be the adoption of an 'instant tenure' system, like that of the corporation. This could only work efficiently if universities retained more discretion over the job assignments of faculty than they now do, and if there were a wider range of jobs available in universities than now. This could conceivably come about if universities were branches of multi-product corporations. To pursue the 'thought-experiment' of organizing universities in that way would take us away from the main point of this paper, but it may be worth attempting on another occasion.

15. For a sceptical view of these projections, see Ahlburg *et al.* (1983).

References

Ahlburg, D., Crimmings, E.M. and Easterlin, R.A. (1981) 'The outlook for higher education: A cohort size model of enrollment of the college age population, 1948–2000', *Review of Public Data Use* 9, 211–227.

Akerlof, G. (1970) 'The market for "lemons": Quality uncertainty and the market mechanism', *Quarterly Journal of Economics* 84, Aug., 488–500.

Alchian, A. (n.d.) *Private property and the relative cost of tenure.*

Alchian, A. and Demsetz, H. (1972) 'Production, information cost, and economic organization', *The American Economic Review* 62, no. 5, Dec., 777–795.

Arrow, K.J. (1974) *The limits of organization* New York: W.W. Norton.

Becker, G.S. (1964) *Human capital: A theoretical and empirical analysis, with special reference to education*, New York: National Bureau of Economic Research.

Bowen, W. (1981) *Report of the President: Graduate education in the arts and sciences: Prospects for the future*, Princeton, NJ: Princeton University.

Brewster, K., Jr. (1972) 'On tenure', *AAUP Bulletin* 58, Dec., 381–383.

Cartter, A. (1976) *Ph.D.s and the academic labor market*, New York: McGraw Hill.

Chait, R. and Ford, A. (1982) *Beyond traditional tenure*, San Francisco, CA: Jossey-Bass.

Dresch, S. (1975) 'Demography, technology, and higher education: Toward a formal model of educational adaptation', *Journal of Political Economy* 83, June, 535–569.

Freeman, R.B. (1976) *The overeducated American*, New York: Academic Press.

Freeman, R.B. (1980) 'The job market for college faculty', in: McPherson, M. (Ed.) *The demand for new faculty in science and engineering*, Washington, DC: National Academy of Science.

Freeman, S. (1977) 'Wage trends as performance displays productive potential: A model and application to academic early retirement', *Bell Journal of Economics and Management Science* 8, 419–443.

Goldberg, V. (1980) 'Relational exchange: Economics and complex contracts', *American Behavioral Scientist* 23, Jan./Feb., 337–352.

Hall, R. (1982) 'The importance of lifetime jobs in the US economy', *American Economic Review* 72, March.

James, E. (1980) *Job-based lending and insurance: Wage structure in tenured labor markets, Working paper no. 228*, State University of New York at Stony Brook: Economic Research Bureau.

James, E. and Neuberger, E. (1979) *The university department as a non-profit labor cooperative*, revised version of paper presented at the US-UK Conference on Collective Choice in Education, Boston, MA, Dec, Mimeo.

Keat, W.R. and Macy, J.W., Jr. (Eds) (1973) *Faculty tenure*, San Francisco, CA: Jossey-Bass.

Kuh, C. (1977) *Market conditions and tenure for Ph.D.s in US higher education*, a report for the Carnegie Council on Policy Studies in Higher Education, Mimeo.

Leibenstein, H. (1976) *Beyond economic man: A new foundation for micro-economics*, Cambridge, MA: Harvard University Press.

MacNeil, I.R. (1974) 'The many futures of contract', *Southern California Law Review* 47, May, 691–816.

Medoff, J. and Abraham, K. (1981) *The role of seniority at US work places: A report on some new evidence, Working paper no. 618*, National Bureau of Economic Research.

Oi, W. (1979) 'Academic tenure and mandatory retirement under the new law', *Science* 206, Dec. 21, 1373–1378.

Okun, A. (1980) *Prices and quantities: A macroeconomic analysis*, Washington, DC: The Brookings Institution.

Rosen, S. (1977) 'Human capital: A survey of empirical research', in Ehrenberg, R. (Ed.), *Research in labor economics: An annual compilation of research*, Vol. 1 (JAI Press, Greenwich, CT) 3–40.

Salop, J. and Salop, S. (1976) 'Self-selection and turnover in the labor market', *Quarterly Journal of Economics* 90, No., 619–629.

Simon, H. (1957) 'A formal theory of the employment relationship', in: *Models of man* pp. 183–195, New York: John Wiley.

Smith, B. (Ed.) (1973) *The tenure debate*, San Francisco, CA: Jossey-Bass.

Solow, R. (1980 'On theories of unemployment', *American Economic Review* 70, March.

Spence, A.M. (1974) *Market signaling: Informational transfer in hiring and related screening processes*, Cambridge, MS: Harvard University Press.

Thurow, L.C. (1975) *Generating inequality: Mechanisms of distribution in the US economy*, New York: Basic Books.

Weiss, Y. (1981) *Output variability, academic labor contracts and waiting times for promotion, Working paper no. 26–81*, Foerder Institute for Economic Research, Faculty of Social Sciences, Tel Aviv University, Ramat Aviv.

Williamson, O.E. (1975) *Market and hierarchies: Analysis and anti-trust implications*, New York: Free Press.

Williamson, O.E. (1980) 'Transaction-cost economics: The governance of contractual relations', *Journal of Law and Economics.*

Williamson, O.E., Wachter, M.Z. and Harris, J.E. (1975) 'Understanding the employment relation: The analysis of idiosyncratic exchange', *The Bell Journal of Economics* 6, no. 1, Spring.

10 Research on Academic Labor Markets: Past and Future

David W. Breneman

When Ted Youn and I began talking about this volume two years ago, our principal purpose was to gather together the best recent writings of economists and sociologists on trends in academic labor markets, with an eye toward a more realistic and integrated analysis than either discipline alone has supplied in the past. We hoped that the economist's theory of human capital could be strengthened by addition of the sociologist's focus on institutional aspects of the market and by that discipline's emphasis on status attainment. We also hoped to increase our knowledge of how academic labor markets function, with particular reference to the nature of academic careers over time.

Our first objective has been achieved only to a limited degree, primarily because the chapters were not co-authored by economists and sociologists working together on a common problem. Instead, each chapter bears the marks of the research style or paradigm of the individual disciplines. The nature of the subject matter, however, often forces good social scientists to develop more eclectic approaches than a strict adherence to narrow methodological techniques would permit. Thus, we see economist Hansen grappling with the institutional and political features of merit pay systems, sociologists Rosenfeld and Jones concentrating on the market processes that influence exit and re-entry to the academy, and economists McPherson and Winston presenting a subtle institutional analysis to explain the logic behind academic tenure. In that sense, the nature of the questions that the authors pursued forced them to consider a wider range of explanatory variables than might have been normally expected.

Our second objective – increased knowledge of the functioning of academic labor markets – has clearly been achieved. The papers explore and flesh out our understanding of adjustments made within higher education in the past decade of slow growth. To provide a context for that statement, it will be helpful if we review briefly the state of labor market analysis for faculty inherited from the 1960s and early 1970s.

The seminal works in this field are those of economist Allan M. Cartter, published in a series of articles in the mid-1960s on supply and demand for college teachers (Cartter, 1965, 1966). Prior to his work, the prevailing view was that the country faced an unending and dangerous shortage of Ph.D.s, described by President John F. Kennedy as 'our greatest national problem'. Cartter had observed that, contrary to projections, the proportion of college faculty with Ph.D.s had not declined during the high-growth years of the late 1950s–early 1960s. This fact prompted him to review supply–demand projections that others had done, and led to his own forecasts that supply would sharply exceed demand in colleges and universities by the mid-1970s in most academic disciplines. The demographic techniques that he employed in his analyses are presented thoroughly in his final work, *Ph.D.s and the Academic Labor Market* (Cartter, 1976), published by the Carnegie Commission on Higher Education. Cartter's projections, as many young academics learned to their dismay, were remarkably accurate, as the labor market for new doctorates in most fields turned sour in the mid-1970s.

Cartter's methodology relied primarily on a series of fixed-coefficient models that link enrollments from one year to the next and tie faculty demand to those enrollments in fixed relationships. His approach was improved by the work of economist Richard B. Freeman, first presented in his doctoral dissertation, *The Market for College-Trained Manpower* (Freeman, 1971). Freeman introduced a relatively simple econometric model of the labor market for highly-educated people that treated supply as a dynamic response of students to the current state of the relevant markets. Because advanced degrees require several years to complete, however, supply is constantly out of phase with the market in a pattern known in economics as the 'cobweb model'. In simplest terms, a shortage of engineers causes entry wages to rise, which prompts large numbers of students to enroll in engineering programs, becoming part of the supply four years later. By that time, supply may exceed demand, causing wages to fall (or rise more slowly), which in turn leads to smaller entering classes in schools of engineering, giving rise to the cycle all over again. Freeman applied this model to numerous occupations that require advanced schooling, including college teaching, and argued that a period of excess supply will generate its own correction, albeit with a time-lag of several years. The implication for the labor market for Ph.D.s was that the enormous imbalance between supply and demand that Cartter projected would not, in fact, occur, for students would respond rationally by seeking other occupations not requiring the Ph.D. Freeman and I developed this analysis in some detail in *Forecasting the Ph.D. Labor Market: Pitfalls for Policy* (Freeman and Breneman, 1974), a report of the National Board on Graduate Education.

My own research at Berkeley on the Ph.D. production process also extended the analysis of supply and demand by considering the behavior of academic departments that award the doctorate. Cartter's and Freeman's work ignored the role that academic departments play in governing the supply of new doctorates. In a detailed investigation of the doctoral output of twenty-eight departments at Berkeley covering the 21-year period, 1947–1968, I demonstrated the dramatic differences in Ph.D. output among departments, differences far greater than departmental graduate enrollments would imply. My analysis led me to view academic departments as prestige-maximizing entities, with definite objectives regarding the number of graduate students to enroll and to receive the degree. This research, completed in 1970, was published by the National Bureau of Economic Research in an edited volume, *Education as an Industry* (Breneman, 1976). Use of a prestige model for understanding university behavior involves a construct often used by other social scientists, particularly sociologists.

A final work I will mention as part of the intellectual backdrop for this field through the mid-1970s is an essay prepared by economist Stephen P. Dresch for the National Board on Graduate Education, *An Economic Perspective on the Evolution of Graduate Education* (Dresch, 1974). In this provocative work, Dresch sought to relate the development of graduate education to demographic, technological, and economic trends in the broader society. He argued that the late-1950s and early-1960s represented a fleeting 'Golden Age' for graduate education, marked by rapidly expanding enrollments, sharp increases in federal support for research, increased social significance of the educated elite, and rapidly rising faculty salaries. Dresch went on to argue that this brief 'Golden Age' could not last, and that the task facing graduate education in the balance of this century was adjustment to a more normal time of slower growth and fewer resources.

It is apparent from this brief review that the dominant policy issue of the 1960s–early 1970s concerned the quantitative balance between supply of new doctorates and demand for their services. The period began with belief that we faced continuing, chronic shortages of highly educated people, and ended with concerns about the oversupply of such persons. Richard Freeman summed up the situation we had reached by the mid-1970s in a book aptly titled, *The Overeducated American* (Freeman, 1976). Two points emerge from this history that are relevant to the current volume.

First, with the emphasis on supply and demand that marked the earlier decades, one can understand why so little attention was paid to the career development of those already in the system. Attention was focused instead on the factors that influence the flow of new entrants to the various fields, not what happened to them once they were there. Second, it is also clear why research in the 1980s has shifted away from supply and demand and toward analysis of career development of current faculty. Most observers realized in the mid-1970s that the existing stock of faculty was going to be with us for two more decades, and attention understandably turned to the conditions facing those faculty. The pertinent questions now became those that focused on the adjustment of colleges and universities to an era of slow (or no) growth. The essays in this volume can be seen as a contribution to that analysis.

Apart from the specific findings of each chapter, what general conclusions emerge from the papers in this volume? First, it is apparent that colleges and universities have adapted personnel practices to fit the changed economic environment of the last ten years. Increased use of part-time faculty is one obvious example, and the paper by Tuckman and Pickerill documents both this trend and the policy and educational issues that it raises. Career mobility has also been reduced, and the papers by McGinnis and Long and by Youn and Zelterman trace those patterns and their implications for faculty and for institutions. The terms under which a faculty member can exit higher education as a place of employment and subsequently return are explored by Rosenfeld and Jones, while Hansen examines the role of merit pay in an increasingly unionized market. Barbezat's paper assesses the impact of affirmative action guidelines on wage discrimination between male and female faculty, while Richter explores the relatively new entrepreneurial role adopted by many science faculty.

Clearly, institutions of higher education and the men and women in them have changed behavior and expectations in ways that were not foreseen a decade ago.

One also sees in several of the papers, primarily by the sociologists, the enormous importance of institutional and personal prestige and the system of mentorship in shaping academic careers. The existence and functioning of this prestige system seems to be of such potentially great explanatory power that one can only hope that further work will be done to refine and more precisely identify and measure its influence on the topics examined in this volume.

The papers also demonstrate, albeit unsystematically, the importance of institutional decisions on academic careers. We would seem to have reached a point where such decisions, and an understanding of the underlying behavior of academic departments and institutions, could not be ignored by those conducting research in this area. Much more work of the type reported by David Garvin in his book, *The Economics of University Behavior* (Garvin, 1980) needs to be done if researchers are to have this necessary background knowledge.

Although few papers in this book deal in any depth with such policy tools as fellowships, postdoctoral grants, or early retirement policies, one does come away from these essays with a sense of how important an intelligent use of such tools might be in easing the adjustment of this complex system to changing economic circumstances. One of the clear lessons from the earlier work on supply and demand for Ph.D.s was the necessity of counter-cyclical policies because of the long time-lag in Ph.D. production. Unfortunately, few agencies absorbed that lesson and acted on it. One of the few examples of sensible policies is the pre-doctoral fellowship program in the humanities begun several years ago by the Andrew W. Mellon Foundation. By encouraging and supporting over 100 new doctoral students each year, this private fellowship program will ensure a continuing supply of bright young faculty for the 1990s, when large numbers of current faculty will retire.

A further conclusion that follows from these papers concerns both the value and the limitations of the study of individual disciplines found in most chapters. A closely related matter involves the data problems encountered by most of the authors in attempting to trace careers over time. One is frustrated by the lack of strong conclusions in several of the papers, and by the sense that the researchers were laboring under severe data limitations. One is also properly reluctant to generalize from the findings for specific fields such as biochemistry or clinical psychology, and yet most policy recommendations require the ability to generalize. I see no easy solution to this dilemma, for surely different factors are at work in the various disciplines, and should not be ignored. Nonetheless, as our knowledge base grows, interpreters will be needed who can absorb the findings from the several disciplines and translate them into meaningful and intelligent policies.

My suggestions for future research follow directly from the brief historical overview and from conclusions derived from the papers in this volume. First, the time is right for a return to the broad supply and demand studies that typified the 1960s and early 1970s. The coming decade will witness the retirement of many faculty who entered the system during the high-growth years, and we must avoid a return to the 'boom or bust' psychology that has characterized these markets for so long. A good start in this direction has been provided by Howard R. Bowen and Jack H. Schuster in their book, *American Professors: A National Resource Imperiled* (Bowen and Schuster, 1980). Their work, however, focuses almost entirely on aggregate figures for Ph.D. supply and demand, and a valuable complement would be field-by-field analysis. It is surely time now for faculty to begin encouraging bright undergraduates to consider careers in teaching, and yet my experience suggests that far too few faculty are doing that. Federal and state agencies, as well as private foundations, also need to be alerted to the prospective shortages of highly trained people so that fellowship programs and other forms of graduate student financial aid can be increased.

Second, as I suggested above, further work on both the analysis of college and university behavior and on the determinants of the prestige system in higher education is warranted. Sociologists should have a natural advantage in conducting such research, and if economists would incorporate such concepts in their work, they could provide richer analyses of academic labor markets.

From the standpoint of public policy, few areas are more important than further understanding of the factors that influence women and minorities to undertake doctoral education. Most people in higher education are aware that racial and ethnic minority groups constitute a rapidly growing share of the college-age population, and that such students need role models on the faculties of the nation's colleges and universities. An yet, the number of such students pursuing academic careers remains far below that required to meet institutional demand. The number of women earning the doctorate has increased sharply in the last decade, but women are still underrepresented in many fields, such as science and engineering. Research in these areas shoud have a high social payoff.

Two other topics seem ripe for further research. The study of academic careers in particular disciplines exemplified by several papers in this volume could valuably be extended across the full array of academic subjects. As more is learned about the peculiarities of each discipline, it may be possible to cluster certain fields together that display common patterns of development. Should that be so, then micro studies could be used for the types of policy generalizations that are sought. We might also learn more about the factors that encourage further intellectual growth and development of faculty, for although retirements will increase in the coming decade, it is still going to be essential to maintain current faculty members at high levels of knowledge and productivity.

The editors hope that this volume has performed a valuable service in drawing together research findings from several disciplines that bear on issues of academic careers and the academic labor market. We believe that the outlook for broader interdisciplinary work in this area is positive, and that such efforts will be intellectually rewarding. Subsequent developements will determine whether our optimism is warranted.

References

Breneman, D.W. (1976) 'The Ph.D. production process' in Fromkim, J.T., Jamison, D.T. and Radner, R. (Eds) *Education as an Industry*, National Bureau of Economic Research, Universities–National Bureau Conference Series No. 28, Cambridge, MA: Ballinger Publishing.

Bowen, H.R. and Schuster, J.H. (1986) *American Professors: A National Resource Imperiled*, New York: Oxford University Press.

Cartter, A. (1965) 'A new look at the supply and demand for college teachers', *Educational Record*, 46, 3, pp. 267-277.

Cartter, A. (1966) 'The supply and demand for college teachers', proceedings of the 1965 annual meeting of the American Statistical Association, reprinted in *The Journal of Human Resources* 1, 1, pp. 23-27.

Cartter, A. (1976) *Ph.D.s and the Academic Labor Market*, New York: McGraw Hill.

Dresch, S.P. (1974) *An Economic Perspective on the Evolution of Graduate Education*, technical report no. 1, The National Board on Graduate Education, National Academy of Sciences, Washington, DC.

Freeman, R. (1971) *The Market for College-Trained Manpower*, Cambridge, MA: Harvard University Press.

Freeman, R. (1976) *The Over-Educated American*, New York: Academic Press.

Freeman, R. and Breneman, D.W. (1971) *Forecasting the Ph.D. Labor Market: Pitfalls for Policy*, technical report No. 2, The National Board on Graduate Education, National Academy of Sciences, Washington, DC.

Garvin, D.A. (1980) *The Economics of University Behavior*, New York: Academic Press.

Notes on Contributors

David W. Breneman, President of Kalamazoo College, is an economist interested in the economics of higher education and academic markets. He is an author of several books, including *Public Policy and Private Higher Education* (edited with Chester E. Finn, Jr.). Previously he served as a Senior Fellow in the Brookings Institution and as Staff Director of the National Board on Graduate Education.

Ted I. K. Youn is an assistant professor at the State University of New York at Albany. He is a sociologist, and his research interests include the sociological analysis of academic organizations and academic careers. He is currently completing a book, *Career Mobility in Academic Hierarchies*.

Robert McGinnis is a professor of sociology at Cornell University and Director of the Cornell Institute of Social and Economic Research. He has published extensively in social stratification in science, particularly career mobility among scientists.

J. Scott Long is a professor of sociology at Washington State University. Long has published several leading papers on social stratification in science and he is also an author of several monographs on sociological methodologies, including *Common Problems/Proper Solutions: Avoiding Errors in Quantitative Research* (forthcoming).

Daniel Zelterman is an assistant professor of mathematics and statistics at the State University of New York at Albany. His research is related to theoretical aspects of discrete multivariate analysis. He also has published several papers on academic career mobility (with Ted I.K. Youn).

Rachel A. Rosenfeld is a professor of sociology at the University of North Carolina at Chapel Hill. Her research interests include social stratification, work and careers, especially of women, social movement and higher education. She recently published *Farm Women: Work, Farm and Family in the United States.*

Jo Ann Jones is a research fellow at the Carolina Population Research Center of the University of North Carolina at Chapel Hill. She is currently a Ph.D. candidate in sociology at the University.

Howard P. Tuckman is a Distinguished Professor in economics at Memphis State University. He is an author of many books in the economics of higher education, including *Subsidies to Higher Education: The Issues* and *Publication, Teaching, and Reward Structure in Academe.*

Karen L. Pickerill is an assistant professor of economics at Memphis State University. She has specialized in the economics of industrial relations, labor and higher education.

W. Lee Hanson is a professor of economics and industrial relations at the University of Wisconsin-Madison. He is an author of a number of leading monographs in the economics of labor markets and higher education, including *Education, Income and Human Capital* (ed.) and *Benefits, Costs, and Finance of Public Higher Education.*

Debra Barbezat is an assistant professor of economics at Amherst College. She has published a number of papers in the economics of discrimination, labor unions and higher education.

Maurice N. Richter, Jr. is an associate professor of sociology at the State University of New York at Albany. He is an author of several books in the sociology of science and technology, including *The Autonomy of Science.*

Michael McPherson is a professor and the chair of the Department of Economics at Williams College. He was formerly a Senior Fellow at the Brookings Institution. His research interest is in the economics of academic markets and higher education. He is one of the authors of *Democracy, Development, and the Art of Trespassing: Essays in Honor of Albert O. Hirschman* (1986). He is also the founding editor of *Economics and Philosophy.*

Gordon C. Winston is a professor of economics at Williams College. His specialty area is economic theory, the economics of higher education and the economics of time. He is the author of *Timing of Economic Activities* (1982). He is now the Provost at Williams College.

Author Index

211

Subject Index

academic ecology 32
academic freedom 174–5
academic institutions *see* organizations
academic rank, hierarchy of 79, 116
affirmative action legislation 6, 139, 159, 203
American Association of University Professors (AAUP), Committee Z, on Economic Status of the Profession 125
American Chemical Society 46
American Council on Education 53, 54
American Men and Women of Science 33
American Occupational Structure (Blau and Duncan) 1
American Professors: A National Resource Imperiled (Bowen and Schuster) 205
American Psychological Association 76, 81
American Psychologist, The 81
Andrew W. Mellon Foundation 204

Berkeley, California, Ph.D. output 202
biochemists, sample of 3, 4, 16–17
   geographic/ecological stratification
      data and measurement 33–8
      results 38–47
      conclusions 47–9
biological sciences 56, 61, 62, 67
Bureau of Labor Statistics, employment definitions 100, 108
business corporations
   job tenure in *see* tenure
   performance monitoring 190
   relationships with academia 165

secrecy requirements 168
wage/promotion structure 178–80

career, academic
   achievement vs. ascription 16–18
   and demand-supply shifts 22–3
   age of individual 61, 82
   entry into *see* entry into academia
   interests 75
   Matthew Effect in 29–8
   multiple markets effect 65–8
   origin of *see* doctoral origin
   overview of 28–31
   part-time *see* part-time employment *and* faculty
   productivity in *see* productivity
   psychological/life-stage analyses of 8
   research limitations 204
   and sponsorship influence 17
   studies/models 1–2, 8–23
      fixed-coefficient 9–11, 20
      human capital *see* human capital theory
      institutional ascription 16–18, 20
      job competition 14–16,20
      market-responsive 9–11
      structural 2, 8, 18–23
      wage-competition 11–13, 15, 20, 21
   and tenure-track 29–8
   tracing over time 204
   see also other career *entries*; labor markets
career outcomes 17, 53, 56–62
   contiguous influences of jobs 64–9

215